DATE DUE			

The **Center for South and Southeast Asia Studies of the University of California** is the unifying organization for faculty members and students interested in South and Southeast Asia Studies, bringing together scholars from numerous disciplines. The Center's major aims are the development and support of research and language study. As part of this program the Center sponsors a publication series of books concerned with South and Southeast Asia. Manuscripts are considered from all campuses of the University of California as well as from any other individuals and institutions doing research in these areas.

RECENT PUBLICATIONS OF
THE CENTER
FOR SOUTH AND SOUTHEAST ASIA STUDIES:

BEYOND PUNJAB

To us there was only the Punjab, the land of 'five
rivers'; beyond it was all Hindustan; and yet beyond,
beyond the frozen Himalayas and the warm seas, it
was all *Walayat*, the unknown world to where some
of our restless men ventured out. And now, suddenly,
it was all beyond Punjab.

*This volume is sponsored by the
Center for South and Southeast Asia Studies,
University of California, Berkeley*

BEYOND PUNJAB

PUNJAB

1937–1960

By

Prakash Tandon

UNIVERSITY OF CALIFORNIA PRESS

Berkeley and Los Angeles

University of California Press
Berkeley and Los Angeles, California

© Gautam Tandon 1971

Library of Congress Catalog Card Number: 73-123620

ISBN: 0-520-01759-5

Printed in Great Britain

To
ANDREW KNOX
and
Unilever

Also to India's new Managers
Her greatest asset

ACKNOWLEDGEMENTS

To many persons this book owes much

Above all to Gärd, to whose support and impeccable sense of the language it owes all. To Maya, Manu and Gautam, for their not always flattering comments.

To Mavis Lely, Phyllis Hoogewerf and Ramakrishnan, who were associated with me at different times as my secretaries, for their many patient hours of deciphering an atrocious handwriting and typing — with always a personal interest; also, to Thiagarajan for retyping many pages; and Jagdish Puri for his help with the proof-reading.

To those who read the manuscript and made many useful suggestions — Roy Hawkins, Bernard Kaye, Warren and Alice Ilchman, and Fred Weaver. To Maurice Zinkin, as before, my deep gratitude.

To a nameless one, whose influence upon the book began towards its closing chapters.

P.T.

CONTENTS

PROLOGUE

THE MOGHUL EMPIRE ended in a sordid chaos that lasted one hundred and fifty years, from Aurangzeb's death in 1707 to the exit of Bahadur Shah from Delhi in 1857. The old poet king, last of a line that stretched back five centuries to Timur Lang, ruled an empire that had shrunk from a thousand miles in each direction to less than a mile in circumference from his throne at the Red Fort.

'Neither the light of someone's eyes am I,
Nor the pride of anyone's heart'.

With these famous lines, long remembered in Delhi, Bahadur Shah allowed himself to be led out of the Fort to start on the long journey to exile in Burma. The British era had begun.

For us who belonged to the Punjab, the British era began promisingly. It ushered in a century of peace such as we had never known. But little did we realise that this era was to close in fractricide and an unprecedented migration. Twelve million people left their homes; thousands never reached the other side. This was euphemistically called the Partition of India. In the quarter century to follow we have taught fate a lesson by further dismembering the Punjab that was left to us.

From 1852, when the British took over the Punjab and consolidated it, till Partition, the pulse of Punjabi life throbbed as never before. Deserts were cultivated, cities founded, roads built. Punjabis spread all over India and across the sea, to California to cultivate, to Nairobi to build the railway, to Flanders to fight, to Hongkong to police and to England to work in factories. Through this period our own family repeated the history of the countless many. My great-grand-uncle after the battle against the British near our home in 1852, went back to his village and persuaded my grandfather to accept the post of a minor revenue official in the new government. My grand-uncle followed the new process and became the first lawyer from our village, and in due course helped my father to go to the new engineering college. Punjabis, especially of our caste, the Khatris, were spreading rapidly into the new professions as engineers, doctors, lawyers, barristers, civil servants, soldiers, but none went into business. That was left to our Vaishyas, the Aroras, whose honoured vocation it had always been. But after the First World War, as the old avenues in services began to be closed to us in the interest of encouraging the minority communities, my father agreed that I should explore a new career. I decided to drop the profession I had been preparing for, engineering, and went to England to study commerce and accountancy.

I spent eight years in England in Manchester, of which three at least were irrelevant to my career. I spent them in literal idleness and in pursuit of whatever appealed to me. Many years later a psychologist, who held a poor opinion of me said that this was my moratorium in life, a withdrawal into readjustments. Put in simple words, a flight it certainly was, but from studies and work, not life. I stopped serving my articles in the accountant's office, put aside some economic research I had begun, and pursued a variety of pleasing occupations.

For nearly two years I wandered aimlessly, playing golf, rambling extensively through the north country and Wales, reading the *New Statesman* and spending hours in the Manchester reference library, attending meetings of all political parties. I heard Radhakrishnan, Oswald Mosley, Winston Churchill, Harold Laski and Harry Pollit. I went to Hallé concerts and the premieres at the Opera House. Most of my friends were like me. Living was cheap and I led a pleasant existence on my allowance of fifteen pounds per month with a small extra amount once a year. Life would have continued as a sluggish stream had Gärd not arrived providentially on the scene. We met at Oxford, at a National Union of Students' conference, and after that I began to spend my summer and Christmas holidays in her Swedish island home in the Baltic, and drifted back to work.

In 1937, with the shadow of war across Europe, I returned home after an unbroken stay abroad of eight years. There were few chartered accountants qualified in India at that time, and, as I soon discovered, the opportunities were equally few. The European firms employed their own kin and the Indians their own kith. The first were not quite ready to Indianize and with the latter it amounted to the same thing; they preferred their own, the family and caste, to strangers. At the very least, you needed an influential recommendation.

At the end of a discouraging week, I walked into the office of the international company of Unilever, and though it was nearly one o'clock on Saturday, the manager called me in and spoke to me understandingly; and asked me to return on Monday morning. When

I asked him, 'around half-past ten?' he grinned. 'We start life much earlier; at nine'.

On Monday morning he spoke to me at length, probing into my reactions to my long stay in England and my return to India. At the end he asked me to go to see the Chief Accountant.

CHAPTER ONE

THE CHIEF ACCOUNTANT was clearly having no experiments in his domain. Accounting to him was the hub of all activity, and he regarded it with a devotion that brooked no interference or innovation. In his own way he was right. The health of his company was the health of its accounts, which depended upon the unchanging sacredness of its system, the unswerving and single-minded pursuit of cash as it flowed through its veins and arteries. Each rupee, anna and pie must be recorded, extracted, translated into 'P & L' and ultimately entered in the holy horoscope, the balance sheet, which, like its astral counterpart, was a picture at a point of time that portrayed past and present and forecast the future.

Indianization, he might have agreed, had begun and he had nothing against it. Into the temples of European commerce Indian acolytes had begun to be accepted, but not into the sacred inner precincts. I had called on many of them: Volkart, Dunlop, Burmah Shell, I.C.I., Bata; the Managing Agency Houses of Bird, Gillander, Andrew Yule; and the practitioners of accounting and auditing, the partnership firms of chartered accountants. In none of these had Indianization yet been accepted as a policy. Some had taken an occasional Oxford or Cambridge Blue, the son of a High Court judge or senior I.C.S., but it was more as an adornment or concession to influence than to fill a genuine want. In the British army, after Indians had fought in it for over two hundred years, there were less than half a dozen Indian majors; British commerce, of even longer connection, had made even less headway. Neither had followed the example of the Government services. Of the thousand I.C.S. officers half were Indian. Indians might be ready to govern, but not to keep books or to sell.

Let others experiment, the Chief Accountant's attitude suggested. His own firm was welcome to make a start; but not in accounts yet. He was logical, for he opposed equally the introduction of British qualified accountants. I don't think he believed in formal professional education. You worked and trained, not read and wrote to be an accountant. The law made an audit compulsory, but he could get on well enough, if not better, without theories and academic notions.

John Rist, on the other hand, whom I was asked to see next, had been told to get an Indian immediately, and I seemed almost the answer to his prayer. They had decided to start market research into their well-known household soaps, Sunlight, Lifebuoy and Lux, and their competitors. For this a man named Thompson Walker was coming out from London in four weeks' time, and he had insisted that the one he would train and leave behind in charge had to be an Indian. Consumer research among Indian housewives could only be done by Indian girls, and an Indian had to organize it and interpret the Indian mind. Rist had been looking round but could not make up his mind. It was the beginning of a new process that led only one way, and he would be the first European manager in Bombay to try it. This seemed to fill him with diffidence, a trait, I was to find later, we shared. It was to become a bond of friendship that matured over the years. Underneath an outward poise we were both essentially diffident in the face of the new. After much covering of ground, near and far from the subject, he eventually offered me probation for six months. What did I think?

Questions surged in my mind. Were they going to put me on the same road of training as their own young Europeans? Would I, as an Indian, get the same terms and opportunities? How far could he see an Indian going—to the ultimate height? I looked over Rist's shoulders at the Bombay harbour framed by the french window at his back. It was a serene morning, washed clear by months of rains. I could see the tops of ships' hulls and their masts against the blue of the sea, and the distant hills of the mainland still green. The scene was interrupted by an occasional country boat in full white sail, its high prow swinging up and down. The rattling of a winch and the hooting of a car were the only sounds that reached us. I loved the view of the Bombay harbour, much as I disliked the bustling town with its look of commercial prosperity, where for the past week I had been an intruder seeking employment, up one lift and down another. And now with an offer in front of me my spirits rose and my feelings towards Bombay softened. I would not mind working here, and in time I might even take to the city.

I never got to asking the question. I think Rist guessed what was on my mind, but he would have been equally unsure about the answer. He knew no more of the future than I did, but he dutifully faced up to it. Was there something I would like to know? I said no. I would gladly accept the job and start as soon as he liked.

There remained the question of salary. He took me into the room of the acting Managing Director, who had originally interviewed me, and had sent me to the accountant. He grinned when I came back in a few minutes looking blank, and asked me to return the next day. It

seemed a pity to let someone like me go, he said. He then asked if I
would forget my qualification and go into their advertising department.
I said I would. I was already wondering if I had not chosen the wrong
profession. I felt sad throwing away the result of many years of
swotting but there seemed no choice.

He offered me Rs. 350 per month, and Rs. 450 on confirmation. I
hesitatingly wondered if it could be improved because Bombay looked
an expensive town. He said that they might make it Rs. 400 for a start,
but could not raise the Rs. 450. I knew from advertisements in London
that English accountants started at Rs. 650 in India, but this was
beyond my hopes. I would have to accept. A week later I joined.

Dougal Building was in Ballard Estate, the European business
quarter, adjoining Ballard Pier where the mail steamers tied. It was
like all other buildings in this area, square, four storied, of grey
stone, with small balconies. They all had English names. The only
apparent exception was Kaiser-i-Hind, in itself of an impeccably
loyal connotation.

I reported for duty on a Monday morning. When Rist was free he
sent for me and briefly explained the advertising department. On
market research he touched very lightly as it was equally new to him.
He then took me into the main office and showed me to a desk with a
heap of the quarterly advertising reports for London, and books full of
specimens of past advertisements. There seemed enough reading for a
week.

The clerks were all men: South Indians, if they were stenographers,
Christians and Parsis, if they did general work. They all seemed
puzzled at my entry, wondering who I was and what I was going to
do. Sitting among them, at an ordinary desk with an armless chair, I
could only be one of them, Had I been a manager I should at least have
sat at the head of the general office, with a large desk and a chair with
arms, a towel to wipe off sweat, and a glass of water with a bakelite
cover. The desk would have had a glass rectangle, writing material,
diary and a blotting pad. But mine was a plain desk like theirs; and
yet if I had been one of them I would have been handed over to a
senior clerk.

I could sense the speculation. Why should I be reading the reports
which the managers wrote and only the managers read? Why did
Mr Rist himself bring me to the office? And my clothes? The younger
Europeans wore all whites, the seniors usually palm beach in light
shades. The clerks wore anything that went as shirt and trousers. I

still wore my English suits, dark and heavy, like the clothes of European visitors straight from the boat who had not yet been to the local tailors.

Guessing continued from a safe distance, but later that morning it came to a head. At eleven the sahibs had their tea. The office boys, who were called sepoys because their forerunners were soldiers who guarded the East India Company's offices, and who still wore some kind of uniform, took tea on trays to the managers. Everyone was anxious to see what would happen to me. I was thirsting for the morning cup of tea that the junior articled clerks used to make in my principal's office in Manchester, and I asked one of the sepoys if I could have tea too. No, tea was only served to the sahibs, and Rist sahib had said nothing about my tea. 'But', he said, 'I will bring you a cup from the Irani shop below. It will cost you one anna for a cup; two annas a day if you want it in the evening too like the sahibs'. I could, of course, go down to the shop and for an anna get a cup of tea, a bun, a cigarette, and a pice back! With all this would also go a glass of iced water, a free look at the daily newspaper, and the fan turned on for the duration.

In the afternoons, whenever he had time to spare, Rist would send for me. He preferred questions to dissertation. My knowledge of advertising had all been from the receiving end, from advertisements in newspapers and on Radio Luxembourg, but in particular from the rows of billboards that disfigured English towns and countryside, proclaiming jams, custards, soup tablets, ales and stout, and ominously, in 1937, air raid precautions. I had often indulged in condemning advertising, little realising that one day I would be earning a living out of it. As I assiduously read through the files and records it appeared to be more exciting than keeping books and building trial balances.

Rist was at that time preparing a new campaign in some fourteen Indian languages and English to create a consciousness of body odour among Indians. 'London office' had agreed to Indianizing 'Body Odour' by translating the name and the concept into these fourteen languages, and then contracting it to initials corresponding to 'B.O.'. India with its hot climate must provide an ideal opportunity for exploiting the idea in local accent.

Poor Rist was to persevere dutifully and vainly at making 'B.O.' a household expression. We do not use initials in our languages, nor are we particularly worried by body odour. If you smell of sweat it is because sweat has a smell and not because you have not washed. Most people have a daily bath; from a bucket, at a well, a pump in the street, or in a river. When water dries, you sweat again, and sweat soon smells. I tried mildly to suggest that the internationalness of the campaign perhaps did not apply here. Rist listened politely, but probably considered this a part of the problem of training an Indian to appreciate modern ideas. If people sweat and smell and do not mind the smell, they can be made to mind. They could be taught to think of it as 'B.O.' and want to buy the only soap that would prevent it. Rist was totally uncynical, and to him this campaign, like all advertising, had a mission and was sacred in belief and concept. Had I expressed all my doubts he might have worked still harder to convert my pagan mind.

Settling in Bombay proved less difficult than I had expected. On arrival I had moved to some relatives in Malabar Hill. They had a large flat in Walkeshwar, an old part of the town. It was a three-storied building in stone and timber, of the kind that was being replaced by reinforced concrete all over the city, but this new development had not yet reached Malabar Hill. Its leafiness and sloping lanes were still unspoilt.

Father had assumed that our only relative in Bombay would welcome me as a guest for ever. Fateh Chand, whose wife was my aunt, was a type of which most of our Punjabi families had a specimen. Thirty years ago he had travelled to England for a perfunctory study of engineering. On his return he had joined father's irrigation department of the Punjab Government, but did little work and spent most of his time talking and eating, both in a monumental style. He was a large man with a booming voice, who at each meal carefully planned the next. He talked easily and interestingly on virtually any subject so long as one did not interrupt him or question what he said, which one was often tempted to do. Thrown out of public service for sheer laziness he had come to Bombay some years ago to make his fortune at speculation. He was convinced that with his education and reading habits he would beat those semi-literates and illiterates who had amassed great fortunes out of speculation in cotton and bullion futures and in the stock market. But he never succeeded, and in fact lost much of his savings. In the evenings his telephone rang continuously, and at first his conversation intrigued me. All he said was 'Right, right'. I discovered later that the calls were from brokers giving the latest quotations from the New York cotton exchange. I do not know when he made his bargains because he never said more than these words.

After rejecting most of his liberally given advice, the little I retained proved useful. Fateh Chand explained to me the diversity of the town, its communities and their ways, its occupations and traditions and its fundamental sense of industry. It was a town in which no one seemed to live his whole life. People came from all over India, and the world, with the sole purpose of work. Some came poor and went back rich, others just made a living, but all sooner or later left to retire wherever they came from. It was not a place where anyone put down roots. Bombay was unique among cities of the world in having the smallest proportion of locally-born population. With the exception of the Parsis and coastal Christians, anomalously known as East Indians, practically everyone had come from somewhere else. But from this transient population grew in time the first truly cosmopolitan city in India.

Fateh Chand would explain all this to me, and he also introduced me to several Punjabi families, which made me feel somewhat at home. At first he found me interesting, largely because I was a good listener, but after a fortnight I think he got tired of me. One evening when I returned from the office he asked me if I proposed looking for some place for myself. I had only vaguely thought about it. Since in about four weeks' time I was going on a long tour all over India with Thompson Walker, the specialist in market research, I had taken for granted that till then he would expect me to stay with them in the customary Indian way. But people might have changed during my eight years abroad, and perhaps it was not the right thing any more. In the past, relatives stayed on for months, and it was never suggested that the stay might come to an end. I felt very upset that my desire for conformity should have been misread as abuse of hospitality. I walked out and began right away to look for a place. After wandering about for some hours I took a room in a hotel a few blocks away from my office. Late in the evening I returned to Walkeshwar and found they were both waiting for me to start dinner. Fateh Chand impatiently asked me why I was late. I told him I had been out to look for accommodation and was moving to the Regent Hotel in Ballard Estate. That was not a bad place, he said, and asked when I was going. 'Tonight, after dinner,' I told him.

My aunt was genuinely shocked, as much at my haste as at his un-Punjabi behaviour but he was not the one to feel embarrassed. With customary bluntness he said he admired anyone who did something promptly. There was very little to pack. He offered me his car and driver. Soon I was speeding down the hill to my first home in Bombay. As the car went past Chowpatty sands and along Marine Drive, my disgust subsided and I began to speculate about the future. Would she come to Bombay, would we have our own home? My thoughts ranged rapidly over Gärd, our life together, children, the firm, and my future in it. I had left her behind in Sweden, and we had agreed to decide about our future after I had settled in India.

At night, as I lay on a wire spring bed in a room with wooden partitions and sparse furniture, I tried to work out the finances of my new life. The hotel, with food and room, cost Rs. 180, the extras would come to about another Rs. 50, leaving Rs. 120 out of my salary. Luckily there would be no deduction for tax or provident fund for a while. In another six weeks I would be on tour for several months, when the expenses would presumably be paid by the firm. I had never before worked on the fruitless task of keeping an account, but in my first half hour of independence I concluded that things looked uncertain. Could I possibly maintain her on this income, even with the additional hundred rupees to come? And I dared not ask father for an allowance, since he had supported me for far too long. He did not even know about my intention to marry. When should I tell him? And when should I tell the firm? I had heard that in British firms one formally went up to the chief to ask permission. How would they take it? The disturbing whirl of thoughts gradually slowed down and I went to sleep.

Next day I went to the office in great anticipation because it was Wednesday, and the boat carrying Thompson Walker was due to arrive. A British business house then had its main contact with head office through the weekly mail steamer, and its whole routine centred round the P. & O. mail days. It rose to a climax from Thursday morning, when the mail came in, till Friday evening when it was posted for the westbound mail boat on Saturday. After that business returned to its ordinary tempo, quickened occasionally by a cable, till the next Thursday rush.

Rist had gone to the boat to meet Thompson Walker, and after helping him through the chaos that is Ballard Pier on boat days he took him to the Taj Mahal Hotel to settle in. After lunch Rist brought him to the office. Both were closeted together for a long time. I was anxious, because meeting Thompson Walker would mean the beginning of my work. I was also curious to know what sort of man he was. We should be spending nearly four months together organizing work that I knew nothing about and visiting places in India that were new to me.

Just as the office was closing, a sepoy came and gave me burra sahib's salaams. I was introduced to Thompson Walker. He was a youngish-looking man in his early forties, slim, with an intelligent cultured face. He spoke pleasantly and looked more like a professor than a businessman. I wanted to make a quick assessment because on how I got on with him and what I learned from him depended the start of my career. The long train journeys, evenings in hotels, places strange to both of us, would bring us together as no other circumstances could. Formal relationship must soon either give way to an easy, well-adjusted comradeship, or else freeze into something unbearable, as it nearly did in the very first town we visited. There was a difference of sixteen years between us, a gap such as I had never experienced in a close relationship before.

Rist had given no signs of anything but a senior-trainee relationship; in fact, I do not think he knew quite where to place me. With his young English assistant, of my age and barely out of training, he appeared entirely at home. They were on first name terms, but with me he was formal. He let me call him sir and I gave him the normal marks of respect, but it would be awkward if I also had to treat Thompson Walker in this formal manner. My first impression however put me at ease. He seemed informal and lively, with a turn of phrase and expression which promised much in common. We talked in a general way, mostly introducing ourselves. He broke off after a while and suggested we begin our work in the morning.

Rist had us move over to a vacant room in Henley House where the head office of the firm was located. When he instructed his secretary to make arrangements for our move it set all speculation about me at rest. Moving to Henley House and sharing an office with Mr Walker could only mean one thing. With formal politeness the secretary offered to arrange about moving my things and, as the final seal on my position, told the sepoy to serve me tea on a tray and hang a separate towel for me in the managers' toilet.

Thompson Walker and I spent most of the next few days finding out from sales managers about sales and markets for their many household products, soaps, cooking fats, cosmetics. Then he explained to me the essentials of market research, sampling techniques, drawing up questionnaires, recruitment of investigators, their training and assignments to work. He drafted an advertisement to the local English dailies, offering young, educated and intelligent woman who could talk easily to housewives temporary work as market research investigators at a daily wage of three rupees plus half a rupee for expenses.

I wondered what type of girl would apply, for I could hardly imagine that educated Indian girls would take on such unusual work. Walking about in the residential areas, calling from house to house, knocking on strange doors and engaging unknown women in conversation was something unheard of. Thompson Walker was equally curious to meet Indian girls.

Middle-class girls in India up till World War II seldom went to work, even in Bombay. The pioneers were the Anglo-Indian and Christian girls, who first took to nursing as a profession; then, in Bombay, came the Parsi girls, more westernized than the average. These girls next turned to secretarial work in European commercial offices, while the first profession the Hindu girls entered was teaching. With the spread of education among girls demand rose for women teachers, and there was no objection to teaching as it did not involve working alongside men. There were no shop girls in those days, and there are few enough even today. The few factories employed hardly any women. The textile mills took some, but only of the illiterate kind, at less than twenty rupees per month.

Our advertisement for girls with an ordinary high school education and no particular qualification or experience, at what was then a good salary, must have looked very attractive. Soon a variety of girls began to turn up, most of them with only the haziest notion of the job. Thompson Walker engaged them in long conversations to find out if they were suitable, but also, I could see, to satisfy his curiosity about their lives and background. And a lot we learned too, for most of them, once they started, were free and uninhibited in their talk. This encouraged us to believe that we need not fear reticence on the part of the housewives; in fact, we were soon to find it the other way round. But many of the girls shied away when we explained that the work meant going from door to door and running the risk of rebuffs, for a rebuff, real or imagined, is something few Indians can take. Of the four we ultimately selected one was an Anglo-Indian, two were Indian Christians and one was a Maharashtrian Hindu. They were a disparate lot, each interesting in her own way.

Nellie Thompson was of medium height, well proportioned and attractive, with a ready laughter that belied her sulky looks. She had come to Bombay from a typical Anglo-Indian colony in an upcountry railway junction. She stayed in a small boarding house for working Anglo-Indian girls in Colaba and managed to live off temporary jobs. A few years later a young English chartered accountant fell in love with her and married her. His firm disapproved of this marriage, and as was the custom in European firms he had to return home. He took Nellie with him. It was an unwritten law in those days that young Europeans in commercial firms, or in any other walk of life, were not to be seen taking out Indian girls. With Hindu and Muslim girls the question usually never arose, and it was not the done thing to be seen with Anglo-Indian or Indian Christian girls. Clandestine relationships were not uncommon, but they seldom matured into marriage. Similar prejudice existed about the community of domiciled Europeans, pure or fairly pure Europeans who had been settled in India for a generation or more.

Ada Rodrigues was a tall, well-built girl of matronly appearance, dressed in a sari wrapped twice round instead of the usual once. She was a Christian from the Mangalore coast and had three children. She had never worked before but the idea of earning some money without a permanent commitment appealed to her. She was shrewd and made the best investigator, and after a few days we made her supervisor of the team.

Miss Coutinho was a small Goan Christian girl who, I think, needed work. She tried her best and was quite lively, but, like Nellie, felt strange with Indian women.

The pride of the team was a young Maharashtrian girl who was delicately beautiful with an equally beautiful name. She was Krishna Gulwadi, Krishna of the valley of flowers. She was slender, graceful and lively in every movement and expression, barely eighteen, but very determined. She had made up her mind to earn a living. We were both anxious to have at least one thoroughly Indian girl in the team. We should have liked to have more as the other girls, like most of their community, were not at ease in Indian speech nor familiar with Indian homes and the ways of our women. Living in their semi-western and un-Indian style they had little in common with the people. Despite all this Thompson Walker was at first not keen to take Krishna because she looked too fragile for hard work, and he also wondered whether she would carry sufficient weight with the housewives. She looked so young and dressed so well that she might find it difficult to establish contact with working-class women. She was really too glamorous to be looking for work. But Krishna was determined to get the job and she got it.

After selecting the girls we decided to spend a couple of days looking closely at the city of Bombay to decide the breakdown of its population for sampling purposes. I found it interesting to examine the social geography of Bombay and later of the many other towns where I conducted research enquiries. We were particularly fortunate in having as our guide an East Indian Christian clerk by name Misquitta, who himself had produced a small book on his community.

Bombay had sizeable communities from most provinces of India, the biggest of course being the Maharashtrians, followed by the Gujerati-speaking people of Gujerat and Saurashtra, Tamils, Malayalees, Mangaloreans, Goans, Mysoreans, Telegus, Punjabis, U. P. Bhayas, Pathans, Bengalis, Nepalis, in fact, groups from everywhere except Bihar, Orissa and Assam, whose people one rarely comes across in Bombay even today. The purely local communities generally lived in the areas their forebears had founded when they first came to Bombay.

The earliest inhabitants of Bombay, when it was still a series of un-connected islands, were the Koli fishermen and the Bhandari toddy-tappers. Many of them had been converted to Christianity by the Portuguese some centuries ago, and they still lived on the coastal fringe of Bombay at Manori, Malad, Andheri, Juhu, Bandra, Mahim, Worli, Colaba and Mazagaon. There is still a fishermen's shed on the Chowpatty sands. When Christians came from Goa, they settled in the areas of the local Christians.

The Parsis came next, with the British from Surat, and settled just outside the original fort, in and around Bazar Gate Street. Later they moved further, but they still congregate in predominantly Parsi localities like Princess Street and Grant Road. The Muslims, Memons, Bohras and Khojas, have their own areas around Mohammadali Road, Zakaria Mosque and Bhendi Bazar. The Gujeratis, who also arrived with the British, settled in Bazar Gate Street and then in Bhuleshwar. The Maharashtrians, interestingly enough, came later, after the Parsis and Gujeratis. They came in numbers as millworkers with the founding of the textile industry, and they naturally con-gregated around the mills in Parel. Their middle class, who entered as clerks and office workers, something which the Gujeratis, whether Hindus or Muslims, eschewed, had their homes in and around Girgaum.

The influx from South India and the Punjab began when the suburbs sprung up, and they congregated in Matunga and Dadar. The cosmo-politan areas of Bombay were Colaba, Malabar Hill, Cumballa Hill and later the reclaimed areas of Churchgate, Backbay and Cuffe Parade. Here lived people of all communities including Europeans. All through this the Christians continued to live in their ancient villages, now suburbs and part of the city.

This was the tapestry of Bombay, variegated and still existing. Its early life abounded in leaders who were Maharashtrians, Gujeratis,

Hindus, Muslims and even Europeans. Starting from the mud flats of the Mahim River, at whose mouth had stood a fort since before 1000 A.D., and ending at the narrow flat island of Colaba, the city slowly spread, through reclamation, and gradually climbed up the hills.

Bombay's stratification for our market research sampling purposes was made easy by the way its communities and social classes were formed. We made little squares on a map of the city and filled in the communities, classes and the sample sizes, till the whole plan for making a thousand calls was ready. By the standards of modern statistical techniques our sample planning was certainly rough and ready.

Thompson Walker next proposed to draw up a questionnaire. It was to be a general investigation of the washing habits, for clothes and body, in Indian homes. The sales people were curious to know the answers to many questions. Since 1888 the firm's products had sold in India, increasing in variety and popularity over the years, but in spite of much empirical knowledge built up by generations of English salesmen there was very little accurately known about why people preferred certain products, what it was they liked or disliked about certain brands, their buying habits, the frequency and the quantity bought at a time, who it was in the family that chose a particular product. You could only guess why some things sold well and others did not. Market research as an aid to sales management was of recent origin in Europe; in India it was unknown and this was the first attempt, and to me fascinating.

Problems were not lacking nor were they devoid of interest. Thompson Walker and I had long talks about the Indian housewife and I would explain to him how different she was from her counterpart in the west. This bothered him, especially the answer to the question about toilet soap in the pilot survey: 'who chooses the soap you use . . . who buys it?' The answer for both was invariably 'the husband'. I explained that a good deal of the daily shopping was done by a man, whose word counted for everything. He decided what was to be bought. Thompson Walker accepted this with reservations. He was not convinced that the women had no say in such matters in the home. I explained that our Indian housewife always deferred to her husband, for she had been brought up traditionally to look to him for decisions. I grew quite eloquent about the classical training of the girls as future wives, the place of the husband as lord of the house, while she is its devi, grihalaxmi, the goddess of the home, demure, submissive and deferential to her master. I even quoted the immortal pair, Shiva and

Parvati, of the celestial abode on the snowy peak of Kailash in the Himalayas. Thompson Walker listened to all this with a wearied look and when I had finished, said, 'Nonsense! What you say about the legendary place of the wife interests me much, but if from that you conclude that she is so submissive as to leave all decisions to the husband, you are mistaken. I bet she not only has much to say, but is the one who decides most things in the home. What she wants, like women anywhere in the world, she gets, including her soap.'

I tried to protest that our society was different. 'Maybe,' he replied, 'but I don't think it makes your women essentially different. Take Krishna, she looks as demure and deferring as the goddess of the home you are talking about, but do you think for a moment that she would do anything she does not want to do? When she marries she will be as determined a wife as you find anywhere. I have done market research in enough countries to find that women are the same all over. They jolly well always decide.'

He decided to probe into the repeated answer 'husband chooses'. He told Ada Rodrigues that next time she came across that answer she should delve deeper. Toilet soaps differ in shape, colour, perfume, emollience; there is something personal about the soap a woman uses. Would she just leave it to a man to choose?

The result was funny and demolished me. At the very first call Ada made, the housewife as usual said 'husband chooses'. Ada began to probe as instructed. Suddenly a light dawned on the woman's face and she said quite simply, 'Oh, I see what you mean. My husband chooses, but of course I tell him what to choose!'

CHAPTER TWO

REGENT HOTEL had a few permanent boarders like me, but most of them were people catching a boat or disembarking at the nearby Ballard Pier. I was the only Indian in the place apart from the manager and his staff. There was a sort of lounge which few ever used, and the usual meeting place was the dining room. People spoke little to each other, but to me hardly ever. Indians could now be seen in purely European surroundings, but they were looked upon only as something that could not be avoided any longer. You could not make rules against it any more. The perimeter was therefore withdrawn to enforceable limits, and in Bombay these were five places, the Bombay Club, the Yacht Club, the Bombay and the Wodehouse Gymkhanas, and the Breach Candy swimming baths. These were to remain inviolable till the end and some even beyond it. Oddly enough, the doors of homes, out of business necessity or sense of duty, were thrown increasingly open, when one would have expected that the initial meeting ground would have been the neutral premises of a club. It was a case of the club rather than his home being the Englishman's castle.

This sacredness of the club was intriguing. On the boat home I had got to know a Norwegian who had lived in Bombay for over twenty years and was his country's Consul General. Sailing was in his blood, and he spent most of his spare time in his boat. He had joined the Yacht Club of Bombay and been elected to its committee, and he told me an interesting story. The Nawab of Bhopal had sent an invitation to this club for a group of its members to sail in the lake of Bhopal. They were treated royally. There was sailing, shooting, parties and hospitality that only Indian princes could offer. Another invitation came from the Nawab which everyone was eager to accept. The Norwegian argued that they should not accept it, as they could not return the hospitality if the Nawab came to Bombay. Their rules would not permit him even to enter their premises. The other members of the committee were a little put out by his logic but, unwilling to miss the treat, they eventually overruled his objection. This club did not permit Indian guests until 1944, when the Indian members of the Bombay Port Trust threatened to terminate the lease, which they in any case did a few years later. Strange, thought the Norwegian, that these Englishmen would have happily invited the Nawab to their homes, and felt honoured by his acceptance. The club, however, was a different matter.

I could understand the desire of a foreign community to have its own club as a centre of its social life, but not the rule that debarred the people of the country from entering, except as servants. When the time came for the change, to me it made it only worse that the rule was relaxed under threat of closure. It was to take me many years to overcome my reluctance to enter the Yacht Club. Some of the British clubs preferred to close down after Independence, others were taken over by Indians, where there were hardly any British members left, and the rest began freely to admit Indians. Somehow I could never bring myself to join such a club, nor understand the anxiety of some Indians to rush in through the newly opened doors.

Entry into the European clubs even for their own people was in those days carefully graded. The Bombay Club took in mostly the civil servants and a few select British businessmen. Next came the Yacht Club which relaxed its rules to admit a little more freely the top managers of British firms. The Bombay Gymkhana took all Europeans so long as they were 'mercantile'. All the rest, the Europeans who sold over the counter in the British department stores or worked with their hands, technicians and foremen, joined the Wodehouse Gymkhana into which also went an occasional domiciled European of sufficient acceptability. The community's life ran in horizontal compartments at these four levels. The Breach Candy swimming baths were however open to all, to visiting soldiers and sailors, to the totally fair domiciled or Anglo-Indians. The only criterion applied, as they passed by the box office, was the colour of the skin. There were amusing instances such as when of two Anglo-Indian sisters, one fair with an acquired tan, and the other a natural brown, only the first could go in. In borderline cases the unerring eye of the clerk at the window, himself an Indian, quickly decided, and crises were practically unknown.

I was beginning to feel bored in the evenings. The routine of hotel and office was becoming monotonous. I spent most of my spare time in my room or walking round the blocks in Ballard Estate, with an occasional Sunday visit to a Punjabi family in Matunga, whom I had got to know through Fateh Chand, and of course to the Fateh Chands themselves. In Manchester life had been full. Stimulating company in the University Union, concerts, theatre, browsing in the Reference Library, occasional golf, week-ends in North Wales had filled the leisure hours richly. In the office in Bombay I seemed to make no friends. The English colleagues were pleasant, but when the office was closed it was all finished there. There were no Indian managers, and this seemed to apply to the whole of Ballard Estate which was almost entirely European, mostly British, with a German, a Swedish and a Swiss house. Thompson Walker, with whom I became increasingly friendly, had his evenings full with invitations from the Englishmen in the firm who would drop into our room and plan his leisure. Their coldness to me made him uncomfortable. I did not expect them to ask me, because one understood that for so long they had been complete in themselves. I therefore made no attempt to find my way in, and looked around elsewhere for company. I suddenly remembered Roshan whom I had met at Oxford five years ago. He had mentioned that he was going to join the Bombay subsidiary of a London company. I looked through the telephone book and tracked him down.

Roshan and I were together at college in Lahore. He was a year senior to me, and although we had rooms close to each other, his great prowess at sports put him on a pedestal and made him socially inaccessible to the undistinguished. From Lahore he had gone to Oxford, where again sports carried him everywhere except in the lecture rooms. Though he never smoked or drank nor talked about women, his clean looks and the Blue which he had acquired in his second term made him well accepted in all but the narrowly academic circles. I met him at Oxford during one Christmas when I stayed with a cousin in the same college. On the strength of this, I rang up to renew our acquaintance. He was a little wary, wondering whether like many others who befriended him I was looking for a job in his firm. I guessed this and explained that I had just joined my firm and wanted to meet him, just for a chat. He seemed to hesitate, but when I suggested that instead of my coming to his office he might have lunch with me he accepted.

Roshan asked me many questions about my job and the firm, my contract, what I thought of our managing director, my designation and the visible marks of my position, whether my English colleagues invited me home. To most questions I gave blank answers. I was on six months probation at four hundred rupees a month, and that was about all I could boast of. I had recently begun to get tea on a tray and had a towel with my name in the managers' toilet. I had no contract, no privileges or perquisites beyond the tea and the towel. I had not met the managing director because he was away on leave. I had not been invited to any home. I mentioned a few of our seniors' names but they did not mean much to him; they were obviously of no special account in the top shelf of Bombay. I mentioned hopefully

that our numbers one and two—I was already learning the jargon—
I believed were members of the Yacht Club, to which Roshan merely
said that that would be so. He thought it all over carefully while I
anxiously looked at his face. He was obviously asking these questions
to make sure that I had started off well, and equally obviously I did
not appear to have done so. Slowly his wide mouth under his long
nose opened in a grin and he laughed.

'I think you have done well enough. It is a matter of getting what
you can. This talk of Indianization to me is meaningless. Why should
they be anxious to have Indians; they have really no need of us and
they can continue to run their businesses just as prosperously without
us; between you and me I think perhaps even better. Look at me, a
pass degree, always barely scraped through; but of course, Oxford
and the Blue make you almost pukka. And having a bright young
Indian in the firm also makes a good conversation piece.' He mimicked:
'No, I don't think Indians are yet fit to hold responsibility in commerce and industry. I concede they can help in Government, and the
start the army has made with them is not unpromising, but industry,
you know, is different. Mind you, they run their own businesses well,
but after a fashion. Our ways are different, they have a different business tradition. I don't say that that will always be so because we have
already made a start. We have a very promising young man: Oxford,
athletics Blue, father in senior government service. But then, such types
are few and far between, and it is up to us to encourage them, though
we must be careful not to hasten it; the process must take its time, it
must not be rushed.'

I too laughed. I told Roshan it reminded me of the French Jew, who
when asked by a hostess in London whether he came across anti-
Semitism in Paris, said, 'No madam, every family likes to know one
Jew who is different. I am that Jew usually.'

I had not expected Roshan to come out with these views; I thought
he would be pompous, and possibly patronizing, but his simple
approach to Indianization amused me. He must have thought that it
shocked me mildly, for he became serious and began to encourage me.
He said that with my professional qualification I had a future, because
in me the firm had seemingly begun Indianization to fill a genuine need.
They might not need a chartered accountant today, but such a qualification was never wasted. It was a skill that could be applied just as
usefully to market research, and that was a field in which Indianization
must have a meaning. If they were going to train me in market research
and hand over to me when the Englishman returned home, it was not

just Indianization but a new development. He himself merely provided a managerial signature and the quite ordinary responsibility that went with it. It had been a tradition in the banks and commercial houses, inherited from the earliest days of the managing agency system, that almost everything had to be signed by Europeans, in whom all authority was vested. A battery of junior Europeans was employed for just that purpose, mainly endorsing the work of Indian clerks.

He had just replaced one of these young Europeans, he explained. He felt he had no right to complain; he received a good salary, a thousand rupees a month and generous perquisites; they called him Rosh and he called them Bill and Harry, which really impressed the Indian staff. The burra sahib invited him home occasionally to parade the bright young Indian, and in the dinner conversation he used to slip in some Indian connection, he added. But what always bothered him was the technique he had had to develop in dealing with the subject of nationalism whenever it turned up, which despite their obvious restraint in his presence it often did.

Like all of us he was a nationalist at heart, but in front of them he found himself either saying nothing, or 'seeing their point', since he lacked the courage to disagree. It was a kind of schizophrenia. They, of course took his agreement for granted. A sensible Indian, educated in England must, they thought, have moderate views and disapprove of the extremists as much as they did. Their value assumption and patronizing restraint hurt, yet Roshan dared not show it.

He must have been bottled up for want of someone he could talk to freely, and admit his weakness in the face of an attitude that he disliked and yet found himself deferring to.

He got up to leave and said that we must soon meet again. His wife, Avi, would be glad to have me spend an evening with them.

With this British mark of approval we became friends. In the years to come I made a point of meeting him wherever he was posted. There was always something to learn. In his earthy way he had the habit of reducing things to their proper, often amusingly improper, size.

Roshan left a lot for me to think over. My mind went back to our fathers' days in Government service and the problems they had come up against. In the early days they were so wrapped up in their careers and so avid to learn that they accepted their position as the natural order of things. In India no one questioned the privileged position of a mentor. When father joined the service he considered the Englishmen who had trained him in the mysteries of engineering entitled to privilege. It was much later, when he was their equal in skills, and more so when the only right of a newcomer to preferential treatment seemed to lie in his belonging to the ruling class, that the injustice of it struck him. With Roshan the problem began differently. Having started off with the equality that his father's generation had strived for, he seemed to derive no satisfaction when he saw a poor justification for it, and despite the equality did not feel a part of the firm. He saw himself not as an experiment, but only an ornament. He would have felt differently had he thought he was meeting a real need.

Thompson Walker's market research survey was now well under way. For the first day or so in each locality the girls created quite a sensation. Some bold housewife would come forward and suggest that this was a foolish way of learning how people washed; if that was what the girls were out to learn, why, she could teach them all about it. Of course, she knew how everyone else washed and she could easily demonstrate it to them, so there was no need for them to walk from home to home asking the same simple questions. The girls became quite clever at dodging such women, and equally at getting the shy ones to talk. Gradually a picture began to piece together. Thompson Walker now began to plan the extension of the enquiry to the rest of India, to Karachi, and after that to Lahore, Calcutta, Madras, Trivandrum, Hyderabad, Nagpur and Allahabad. With the exception of Lahore and a two day job-hunting visit to Calcutta, all these towns were new to me and the anticipation of seeing such distant parts of India thrilled me.

Soon the Bombay enquiry drew to its end and we planned to leave for Karachi by a coastal steamer, a pleasant alternative to the dreary two-day train journey through the Sind desert. A few days before our departure the managing director, who had just returned from England, called me in. At the end he told me that as I would be accompanying Thompson Walker on this long tour they proposed to make no distinction between our travelling facilities. I would be entitled to the same expenses as the European managers. He wished me good luck and hoped that at the end of my tour they would be able to covenant me. This was a custom from the East India Company days when its senior servants were brought to India under a contract, called a covenant. The covenanted officers were a class by themselves, privileged and superior to anyone else, like the I.C.S. of the latter day, who received their contract from the Secretary of State in London.

Thompson Walker thanked the girls warmly. He took stock and felt fully satisfied with the work in Bombay, and confident that despite its difficulties market research could be carried out as successfully here as anywhere else. In fact, in some ways the task was easier. Housewives were not blasé under the impact of heavy advertising. In the lower middle and working classes they seldom went to pictures or other amusements, and apart from fairs and festivals, weddings and funerals, life was unvaried. The arrival of a well dressed, educated girl asking questions about their washing habits was a welcome novelty, and they were willing to talk interminably to her; the problem often was how to get away without giving offence. With the Anglo-Indian and the Christian girls the women felt a little shy, but with Krishna they were quite at home. They felt very sympathetic to her and wondered why she had to work for her living. She was grown up, attractive, educated; why did her parents then not marry her off? She should have her own home instead of immodestly visiting strange homes. How much did she earn, they wondered, and what was she going to do with the money? Was she raising her own dowry, and if so, how much was she aiming at? Krishna gave evasive replies and got on with her work.

I began preparing for the long journey. The first thing one acquired was a bearer with experience of looking after a sahib, especially on journeys. I wrote to ask father if he could trace Shaffi, who had been with one of his English colleagues and was my only notion of a proper bearer. I recalled him from my childhood as someone who always dressed, looked and acted the part of a north country bearer. Father sent for Shaffi from retirement, but both felt that his days of active service were over. Much as Shaffi would like to serve the young sahib he did not feel equal to travelling all over India. He was however not going to let a chance go by. He recommended a relative, and this was Ahmed, who duly arrived in Bombay and reported for duty at the Regent Hotel. From then on, for the next two years, he ruled me.

Ahmed was short and dark, with a beard that he trimmed and dyed black. He wore a white turban in the traditional bearer style, low in front, moderately starched, its fold well pressed, its back-end turned up and tucked between the turban and the cap. It had none of the jauntiness of the Punjabi policemen's, the disciplined severity of the regulation army style, the rakishness of the Khasadars, the Pathan levies, the cockiness of the head office peon, the floppiness of my father's, nor had it the odd liberties that mine took when I was a boy. It was a completely sober turban, becoming a gentleman's gentleman. The rest of his uniform consisted of a long kamiz, cut in the style of the European shirt, and a loose white salwar. He wore black shoes, whose laces were never tied because he always took them off before entering a room. In my presence he always stood slightly bent forward, with his head bowed in attention, lifting it each time he nodded in assent, his hands stretched down with the palms resting flat on his thighs, in the stance of praying. A remarkable feature of his presence was his eyes. He always agreed with whatever you said or instructed him to do, but as he looked back at you to convey his agreement his eyes, though deliberately blank, nonetheless eloquently and deliberately told you what he really thought of it. I never knew how he achieved this contradiction. His voice was equally remarkable. 'Behter huzoor,' ('Very well, sir') would be uttered in a flat, acquiescent way, and I knew at once whether he approved or disapproved. He never once gave me the chance to object to his tone or the look he gave, and yet I soon learned to know what he thought.

Ahmed had been a bearer all his life. In the early years he had served British army officers, one of whom he had accompanied as far as France during the First World War. This was the only bit of information he ever gave about himself. I never knew where he came from, whether he had a family and what he proposed to do when he retired. I don't think Ahmed loved me. For him it was rather a come-down to work for an Indian, and one of unrecognized status at that. After having served 'karnail' sahibs and 'dipity commissioners' he now had to adapt himself to a young commercial, but fortunately the work was light and he was shown the courtesy he had been used to.

I soon discovered that Ahmed had a pride in his position which bordered on snobbery. One evening the hotel manager approached me in great agitation. 'Sir, there has been a big scene. Your bearer has been most rude to a lady on your floor. She complained to me and I spoke to him, but instead of apologizing, he was totally unrepentant.' This struck me as very odd, for whatever his feelings Ahmed was always polite, and when he wanted to be rude, his politeness was icily punctilious. I found him waiting outside the door as usual. He opened the door and followed me into the room, where everything was in order for my arrival. Fresh water in the basin, a jug of hot water on the side, a clean towel unfolded, comb and brush. As I washed, Ahmed stood behind me. After a while he lightly coughed and said,

'Sahib, you may hear this evening about my wrong behaviour, for which I should like to apologize to you.'

'Why to me, Ahmed? You should have apologized to the lady or to the manager.'

'Yes, Sir, perhaps to the manager, but certainly not to the lady. Perhaps if she had been a lady, I would have apologized to her; in fact had she been a lady, I would never have been rude to her.'

Ahmed had no place of his own to stay. The hotel provided no accommodation for servants. He kept his little tin trunk in my room and his bedding rolled up under my bed. In the hot afternoon when there were no visitors about, he used to take off his shirt and lie on his bedding on the floor in front of my door, which he left a little ajar to get a breath of air in the dark and stuffy corridor. The lady in question resented Ahmed's presence altogether; place or no place, he should be seen only when serving. First she only stared at him, but one afternoon when she passed him lying on the floor fanning his bare chest, she told him to get up and get out. He protested that he was lying in front of his master's room and doing her no harm. This incensed her, because she had expected complete submissiveness from a servant. 'Jao, nanga admi. Niklo idhar se!' ('Go, you naked man, get out of here,') she ordered.

If Ahmed had been told the way he was used to, firmly but politely, I think he would have gone. But to think that a woman should speak to him like that, when really the right thing would have been to speak to his sahib! He let her know what he thought of her. He had seen memsahibs like her before, but not among the kind of sahibs he had served. She did not even have a bearer of her own; she wasn't 'pukka'. I think all Ahmed's ire at his changed fortune was vented on her.

I had never talked to the lady, who stared through me too. The smile she gave her own countrymen was the merest flicker. It was obvious that she did not relish her present circumstances; her stern hook-nosed face bore an air of permanent haughty resentment.

There was nothing I could do except gently remonstrate with Ahmed. 'Ahmed, you were rude to her.'

His answer added something lasting to my experience in man-management.

'Sahib, one does not pick on another sahib's servant; one talks to the sahib himself and he takes it up with his servant in his own way'.

More than twenty years later I recognized the lady and learnt who she was. My wife came to know her—times had indeed changed. Daughter of a governor, for whom she claimed descent from Robin Hood, widow of a civil servant, whose forefather had been a great architect of British rule in India, she wanted to stay on in the country. With all the willpower inherited from generations of empire builders, she resisted the attempts of her only son to make her resettle in England. She returned to Bombay with her Pekinese as a stowaway; guest of two kind Parsi sisters, she refused to move from this haven. India had changed and she herself was a piece of Indian history: but India was still familiar ground compared to the England she dreaded, a country she had only seen in her youth. There she sat, eighty-four years old, small and stocky, but straight as a rod, meticulously dressed and rouged, happy still to have a servant waiting at table. To her circle of friends she was quite an attraction, for she could speak interestingly of old times, to her hosts the attraction gradually wore off and no doubt they felt relieved when her son at last managed to put her on the boat. I used to wonder what she would have thought had she recognized me.

I was always learning from Ahmed. When I asked him to do something he froze if I reminded him about it before it was due to be done. He would tell me with quiet dignity that 'he had already been ordered'. He taught me the pleasure of complete dependability. Whenever I went on a train journey I would hand over the tickets to him the day before. He would find out the station from where we left, the train time and all about the journey. Progressively, on the day of the journey, he would begin the packing. At lunch, when I returned from the office, there were still my comb and brush, the newspaper and the slippers; in the evening I would go straight from the office to the railway station and find Ahmed waiting outside my compartment. Inside, my bunk and the table beside it and the bathroom adjoining were exactly as I had left my small hotel room, complete with the book I happened to be reading on the table, open at the page where I had left it the previous night. Tea and shaving water would arrive the next morning at the halt closest to the time I usually woke up. He would order my breakfast, lunch, tea and dinner, all to be brought to my compartment at appropriate stations. But he was a tyrant. For life to function smoothly I had to be the slave of a system which he had culled from a study of my habits; where I might have taken liberties, Ahmed would permit none, and I cheerlessly suffered it.

These upcountry bearers were an institution that disappeared with the British in 1947. You saw them no more in district towns or military stations after the British civilian and military officers left. In some humble house would still hang, tattered and rusting, the head bands that went over the turban and the cummerbunds they wore round the waist, in regimental colours with metal insignia of the regiment, or the school or university colours and monograms. Most are dead, though some must live on in a village, nursing memories of the Raj which threw a small part of its glory on those who literally also served as they stood and waited. Under the shade of a tree in the summer, or warming their old bones in the benign sun of the cold weather, these retired

37

bearers will tell their tales to the young, home from work in towns and
factories, about Smith Sahib and Williams Sahib, their parties and
shikars, and of the power they themselves wielded when Indians of
rank and wealth depended upon them for an interview with the Commissioner Sahib, which when obtained meant a reward in silver
rupees.

We never had bearers, we just had servants. There was a subtle
difference between a bearer and a servant which Indian masters did
not usually understand. It was not the pay nor the uniform, it was the
power of the class to which their masters belonged, and something more
as well. It was the respect they received in the domain that was theirs
which even the memsahib never transgressed; in the way they were
consulted and trusted in matters delegated to them.

After acquiring Ahmed, or Ahmed's acquiring me, I went on a buying spree to equip myself with travelling kit that on the morning of
my departure made a minor mountain on the pavement outside the
Regent Hotel. In India travelling is a national pastime, undertaken on
any pretext, and travelling light was never a virtue unless born of
poverty. A message from another village that some relation is ill sets
the whole family on the move; similarly a wedding. To visit a holy
place a villager in the old days would walk across the whole of India,
to return after months, years, perhaps never. With the arrival of railways the travelling passion could be more easily satisfied. Whole
neighbourhoods would arrive at the station with mounds of baggage,
beddings, pots and pans and provisions—even a half-burnt log from
the hearth—and sleep on the platform to catch the morning train, to
bathe in a holy stream on a special full-moon day. The most unhesitat-
ing travellers are those whom paucity of worldly goods enables to
carry the bulk of their possessions with them wherever they go.

My baggage was more diverse than that of the average traveller
as it also contained modern impedimenta designed by generations of
British. There was a large cabin trunkful of clothes for such different
seasons as the frosty winter of Lahore and the perpetual summer in
Trivandrum; a boxful of books and gramophone records and a player
to liven evenings in dak bungalows and small hotels; an ice-box with a
capacity of nearly a half hundredweight of ice, and containers for beer
bottles, food and fruit; a bed-roll with pillows, sheets, counterpane,
quilt and blankets. Then there were minor containers for shoes, sun-
topees, an enamel basin and jug, and of course bundles of market
research questionnaires and forms; more than enough to make a home
out of the bare room of a rest-house.

Around the heap of luggage there stood an equally impressive array of hotel servants, many of whom I had never seen before. Everyone was most anxious to help, with a degree of specialization and care that was fascinating to watch. One carefully balanced on his head a small bundle of forms weighing perhaps ten pounds, another carried just my thin leather brief case, the third seemed to be staggering under the weight of the empty twelve-inch basin in its leather cover. I made a mental calculation of what was going to be the cost to me of this specialization. Apart from the table bearer I hardly recognized anyone. Ahmed had sheltered me from their none too anxious service, but now he surveyed the scene with an air that made me wonder whether he had not spread the word of departure to savour the importance of his patronage and make me pay for the minor facilities he himself had been receiving from the hotel staff.

While the bags and boxes were being fastened on the luggage carrier, at the back, on the running boards and between the bonnet and mudguards of an old Chevrolet open taxi, a stray walker on the pavement across the road stopped and watched. I happened to notice him. As the great moment came and I dipped into my wallet, which I had wisely filled with a supply of change, this man crossed the road. When everybody had been tipped he also stretched out his hand.

'But I saw you standing on the other side; you don't belong to the hotel, nor have you helped.'

He was quite unabashed. It was his bad luck that I had spotted him. He grinned and walked away.

CHAPTER THREE

As we travelled to Karachi in the coastal steamer, my memories were still vivid of the last trip over nine years earlier when I came from Karachi to Bombay to catch the mail boat to England. At the height of the monsoon the three thousand ton steamer, never far from the coast, had tossed and pitched in my first miserable introduction to the sea, and I had longed for the solid land of the Punjab. In the intervening years my acquaintance with the sea had grown. Numerous crossings of the North Sea and the Baltic, and trips in Gärd's family yawl had at last given me sea legs. Atlantic rollers and equinoctial storms had broken my Punjabi resistance and turned it into a kind of love. If Viking blood were going to mingle with the peasant Punjabi there should be some concession to the sea, which at least had the merit of a distant horizon in common with our interminable plain.

On the first day of 1938, when I stood on the deck of the Karachi boat, watching the calm blue of the Arabian sea fringed by the palm-lined coast north of Bombay, the sea was like a new friend. In its sight I was to live for the next thirty years of my life, to gaze at it through my office window or from the terrace at home, sometimes for an answer to a problem, sometimes to share my joys and sorrows. The sea was like the dumb love out of a Tagore story who listened intently with features unruffled by words and sounds. Like her it reflected your own mood till it softened and drew peace and calmness from the vacant depths. From the brown heaving monsoon mass, when I first saw it at Karachi, to the Persian pottery blue of this fresh January morning, I had acquired a love of the sea, which was to become a part of me so that I could not bear to live away from it.

Karachi in January was pleasant. The air was cool and dry, the sun benign; its winter weather a perfect mixture of the sea and the desert, as was indeed Karachi itself. Ships, donkeys and camels made the harbour scene quite unlike Bombay's, where the West permeated Ballard Pier and the commercial area of Ballard Estate. In Karachi, the Sind desert came right up to the quayside. The stalwart turbaned Sindhis and Baluchis, aquiline and lean, struck a familiar note from the years I had lived in Bahawalpur and travelled in its desert districts bordering on Sind. From the harbour we drove along a wide boulevard through the commercial part of the town into the spacious suburbs with their low ochre-washed and green-latticed brick bungalows covered in cascades of purple and red bougainvillias. The boulevard ended at Clarke's Hotel, an old British upcountry hotel of the type you came across in all provincial capitals and hill stations. Clarke's, Percy's Faletti's, Spencer's, Maiden's, Barnet's, were names familiar to generations of European travellers and those like me who succeeded them. Most of them were founded at the end of the last century, usually by a European couple, as a cross between an Indian dak bungalow and a British boarding house. While some rose to the stature of a provincial hotel in England, others remained glorified rest-houses. But they all inherited from their Indian prototype the luxury of an attached bathroom, though this luxury lay entirely in its privacy, for the bathroom possessed only the simplest of fittings—a zinc tub, an enamel basin and jug, water buckets and that great invention for which the Romans in Britain might well have envied the Britons in India, the thunder-box. Alongside, on a wooden stool, rested a china receptacle with a lid.

The rooms everywhere looked alike. They had standard furnishings, an iron spring bed with a cotton or coir mattress in the more sophisticated ones and a cotton tape bed in others; a chair with two protruding flat arms on which you stretched your legs, with a swivelling contraption under the right arm for placing your drink; dressing table, writing desk with chair, and a massive cupboard with old newspapers spread on the shelves. On the walls there were usually one or two old prints like the 'Highland Monarch', the 'Tempting Bait' or the 'Master's Seat'. The floors were covered with cotton carpets, durries, that harboured the dust of ages. Every morning the durrie was violently swept and the dust blew up in clouds to settle on the furniture from where it was again forcibly unsettled by a small duster tied to the end of a stick, and returned to the carpet. Some of it did escape through doors and windows but came back with interest during the day, and so this process of dust conservation went on.

The couples who ran these hotels always seemed to be relics from the past. They did not appear to know how to run a hotel, they had just strayed into it. It was a pleasant servantful life to which the only alternative was running a pub or a tea shop back home—no servants, no sun, and more demanding customers.

Once again I was the only Indian in Clarke's hotel, which was otherwise full of various Europeans, mostly British commercial travellers. There were, just before the war, some Nazi spies, observers and contact men, travelling as representatives of German firms. You could tell them by their stiffness, sometimes their duelling scars, and faraway look of rendezvous with fate. The thought occurred to one

that, should things go in their favour, we might get their selfconscious
haughtiness in exchange for the assured aloofness of the British.
Superficially, there was perhaps little to choose, but after even a second hand contact with Nazism the thought of having to live under this
race of supermen sent a shiver down my spine. The British were on
their way out, with the first elected Congress governments already in
power in the provinces. Even my father had seen it coming ten years
ago and a lot had happened since then; but to get the Germans instead
after a World War was a depressing thought that looked not far from
reality when one saw these determined men taking a close look at their
future estate.

Clarke's in Karachi, my first up-country English hotel, felt strange –
a strangeness that took me some time to get over. I often wondered
why I, who had lived in England for eight years and become integrated
in their life and society, should feel strange in their hotels in India. Yet
if the place had been full of Continentals, I would not have been
embarrassed. The Englishmen made me feel a stranger. It was indeed
curious how the British managed to make one feel positively ill at ease
in the familiar surroundings of one's own country.

To my English colleagues in Karachi I posed the familiar problems.
Customarily they would have invited Thompson Walker to their
homes from the very first evening. It was a hospitality natural to
expatriates, spontaneous and generous, to take care of a visiting compatriot who would otherwise have had little to do with his evenings.
One after the other they would have asked him home, invited him to
the club, taken him to the pictures, and to see the crocodiles being fed
a goat at a shrine some miles out of town. But as we were staying
together at the hotel, they did not know how to do it without including me, and that they could not bring themselves to do. I did not look
the type who could be ignored and must have looked as if I minded
being ignored.

Thompson Walker must have sensed the problems and I think he
was amused. A few days later he decided to break the ice and himself
threw a party. He further embarrassed his compatriots by inviting an
Indian couple from the firm, Parsis, who although well connected
must have been on the social fringe so far—one of those one-way
traffic lanes of Parsi hospitality, cheerfully given, guiltily accepted and
seldom returned.

I think Tom's invitation was attributed to his lack of understanding
of their problems in the country. It was not unusual, they would argue,
to see an Englishman out for the first time behaving like that. In his

ignorance or insensitivity he was apt to do the wrong thing out of a fresh enthusiasm. He soon learned, if he stayed on, the wisdom of his predecessors' aloofness. The odd one who did not learn was usually sent back. But Thompson Walker was only here for a few months and therefore his idiosyncracies had to be tolerated.

Tom was charming with women, and at the party he delighted in asking them naive questions about their social life. Did they like living in the country? Presumably they had learned the language and made local friends. They might have put him wise but for my presence. The Parsi lady was the one most appreciative of their difficulties and interjected to explain that it was not possible for European ladies to mix with orthodox and backward women who had not acquired the modern ways as the Parsis had. They often did not even know how to shake hands with men. The women of her own community, she went on, were of course different. They spoke English, used make-up, many played the piano, some even danced, and most of them knew how to eat with knife and fork. She felt much encouraged by Thompson Walker's interest and the Englishwomen's approval, but suddenly became conscious of my presence and hastily added that there were exceptions, and she felt sure that my mother was not the type she had described. I assured her that mother was in fact exactly what she was describing; she was a very simple Indian woman.

Thompson Walker roared with laughter to everybody's chagrin, and I felt almost bad for not having agreed with this well-meaning lady.

When they were leaving, one of the guests asked him if he would care to come to dinner at their club. It was a rather pleasant place and he might like to see what an up-country club looked like. Tom agreed readily, which surprised me, because I would have thought that not having been invited to any homes he would have politely declined an invitation to a club. I decided to look up some old friends of the family who had helped me eight years ago when I left for Europe. I rang them up and was asked to dinner. I had not intended to see them, though it would have meant lame excuses later, because I did not want to desert Tom since he was not asked out because of me. Now I felt let down when he so readily accepted the first opportunity to go out, without me. It peeved me, and I showed it.

Tom, though he guessed the cause of my altered behaviour, bore with me for a couple of days, hoping that it would pass off. But on the third day he thought I was going too far over too little and decided to tackle it. As we were going to be together for many weeks it would never work if small incidents like this were going to create misunder-standings. He had gone to the club because he was curious to know what an English club in India was like. One had read and heard so much about them. But if it consoled me to know, I had only missed an evening in which the conversation seldom rose above the level of the weather, dust storms and Home. 'We did not even discuss what was wrong with Indians. I noticed your impish humour with the Parsi lady. You would have had no such perverse satisfaction last night. Stop being sorry for yourself, Prakash! I know how you feel; perhaps I don't, but I do know what you think.'

It cleared the air. It hurt, but it also put the first guide post on the long path of a relationship that I had to build for myself. There would be no one as candid as Tom to help. It was a situation of loneliness at work in one's own country, and from it developed a side of my charac-ter that I can still recognize. It was hard to bear at first, but I soon adjusted myself, and accepted the imposed aloofness as part of me.

The three weeks in Karachi went by quickly. Our experience in Bombay gave us confidence. The office had advertised for girls, but the choice was limited mostly to Christians and Anglo-Indians. Muslim girls were out of the question, and the Hindu girls as yet not ready to work. After recruiting the best we could get, I began to look into the communal life of Karachi as a background to an understanding of the market.

The Muslims of Sind were an orthodox lot and among the middle and upper classes purdah was strictly observed. Few women went to school, hardly any to college. Some studied a little at home, usually Koranic reading and scriptures. Muslims from outside—Punjabis, Khojas and Kutchis—were a little more forward, especially the Punjabis, but even their women would not dream of going out to work, except the few who taught in girls' schools.

The Hindu Sindhis were of two castes, Bhaibands and Amils, two of the most remarkable communities of India. Denied the right to farm or serve as soldiers under Muslim rule, the nimble-minded Bhaibands turned to banking and business at which they got their own back by mulcting the Muslim peasantry and landlords, while the Amils with their sharp intellects served the rulers as minor officials and thus exercised considerable power. With the coming of the British, new avenues were opened to them all. The Bhaibands spread as far afield as Gibraltar, Lagos, Kuwait, Aden, Hongkong, Singapore and Hawaii, where they opened stores dealing in general merchandise, mostly luxury goods. They prospered remarkably, always returning to their home towns, where the mansions they built were evidence of the fortunes they had earned abroad. They also came back to marry and to die. Wherever they settled, the Bhaibands earned a reputation as shrewd store owners, hardworking and peaceable, but quick at making a profit. One who made a fortune in Hawaii and the West Coast of America left large sums in trust for education and scholarships. The Amils spread into professions and government service all over India, and like all good Indians they too came home, to Hyderabad, Sind, to marry, to build and to die. The Amils also liked to show their prosperity and developed overtones in dress, manner and speech—though overtones were never lacking in Sind, whether among Hindus or Muslims. Some of the most flamboyant characters in religion and politics came from among the Sind Muslims.

Karachi had also a small Parsi community of six hundred, the most advanced and prosperous of all. They were in business, stores, professions and government service, and equally—always a strong point of the community—active in civic affairs. Their leader was the agent of our firm, a venerable old gentleman, as loyal to the British as anyone the Parsis ever produced. His great ambition to receive a knighthood was never fulfilled and he had to be content with the local title of Khan Bahadur, but this did not deter his philanthropy. To mark his long career of public service, he finally endowed the Corporation with a statue of himself, which was placed in a commanding position. Since he also happened to be the mayor that year, he himself unveiled it.

At eighty-six he was still going strong and had just been on a trip around the world, the high spot of which was a pilgrimage to England when he called on Lord Leverhulme and the King. I was presented to him during my first visit but I don't think I made much impression. Probably he saw no need for Indian managers. What was wrong with the Englishmen? They knew their job, didn't they? His son who was also ambitious and civic-minded looked after the agency. He too later became mayor, but his great interest was the boy scout movement, which he took very seriously, distinguishing himself as its chief commissioner. He prized both the honour and the uniform, and wore the boy scout regalia at every opportunity.

The Parsi community led a cohesive life, only regretting that they were too few to support a Tower of Silence. Instead, they had to be content with a shady little cemetery in the desert.

There was also a small group of Goan Christians, working in the railways, Port Trust, post and telegraphs, in the foreign firms, and running liquor stores. They lived a life entirely their own, went to their own schools, run by nuns and priests, and stayed in a tight cluster around the Roman Catholic Church in an area named Cincinatus Town after one of their leaders, who, unlike most Goans, had a flair for business. He had built a prosperous insurance company with branches in Bombay and Calcutta. But he came up against the inevitable problem of an Indian business: he soon ran out of relations, and Goan Christians with talent for business. He then had to make up his mind whether to go forward and engage men from other communities, or restrain the pace of his growth, and he chose the latter. In many Indian firms upon whom I had called in search of a job I had sensed the same dilemma. Well qualified though I may have seemed I did not belong to the right community. Indianization in business had not even begun amongst ourselves.

Not far removed from the Goans were the Anglo-Indian families, who, however, felt superior with their British names, a speech larded with British working-class expressions and with a sing-song Welsh intonation. On my first journey from Bombay to Lahore I had shared the compartment with a very fair Anglo-Indian, and never having met one before I mistook him for a Welshman. He was visibly pleased.

Meeting the different Indian communities, as I went about with our market research girls, was a new and interesting experience. I had only seen Indian Christians and Anglo-Indians from a distance in Lahore. There had been one or two Christians at school, but they were of the indigenous kind, wearing our clothes and speaking Punjabi, though their names were biblical – but the Anglo-Indians intrigued me. Speaking only English and living with an outward semblance of English ways, they were yet not English. Nor were they Indian. They seemed creatures of a twilight world into which neither India nor England had clearly penetrated, though both had mingled furtively. Their girls were usually physically attractive, cheerful and hard working; their men often desiccated in appearance and energy. There was something sad about them. Their sadness was summed up by one of the Anglo-Indian leaders in the opening words of a book written as the time for the British going drew near: 'Who are they, Oh England, but thy sons!' It was a piteous appeal to parents leaving the nest.

Saddest of all was the small community of so-called domiciled Europeans, often pure in blood, whose parents had not been able to send them to England for education and thus lost them their birthright. Sometimes England was only a generation or two back, but through lack of contact, the family gradually became Anglo-Indian. The word 'home' had to the domiciled European a bitter sweetness. Cast away as they were by their own, they yet clung to their heritage and asked no more than to be sustained on the periphery, to avoid being swallowed by the mass.

Our work was smoothly completed in Karachi, and at the end of January we started for Lahore. As we settled in our compartment in the Lahore Mail, we were advised to pull down gauze blinds, glazed windows and Venetian shutters, and properly barricade the room. I protested that I wanted to look out and see the Sind desert, but I was told not to worry; the Sind desert would come to see me. And it did. When I woke up the next morning the whole compartment, floors, walls, furniture and beds were a uniform grey with a layer of fine sand. Our faces and hair too were powdered. All night the Mail had been rushing through the desert blowing up a miniature sand storm which kept it company till we entered the Punjab, where the sand changed to fine dust.

During the day, at the meal halts, we walked down the platform to the dining car while our compartment was dusted and tidied. The catering service on the Indian Railways for the upper class passengers was a remarkable organization with monotonous results. At hundreds of station restaurants and in scores of dining cars, from Peshawar to Chittagong, four course English meals were served whose English boarding-house standards were hard to beat. Thick or clear soup, fried fish or minced mutton cutlets with a bone stuck in, roast chicken or mutton, custard pudding or soufflé, were the two standard menus for dinner. For lunch there was a choice of curry and rice or last night's tepid roast, euphemistically called cold meat, with thin slices of tomato and beetroot called salad. This menu was drawn up at the end of the last century when the British catering firms began their railway service, and served faithfully till 1947 when something worse took over. Thompson Walker, who was fond of good food and reviewed London restaurants for an evening paper, was greatly touched when on his last meal in the Madras-Bombay Express he read 'Roast Foul' on the menu. He felt rewarded for all the indifferently cooked but correctly spelt fowl he had consumed on India's railway system.

Train travel in India was then a complex affair, divided into eleven layers. The Europeans travelled first class and usually did not let Indians in even if there were vacant seats. Though by this time things had changed somewhat, an average Indian would still look hard elsewhere before he had the courage to enter a compartment occupied by Europeans, and never if they were army officers. The better-placed the Indian the less he dared, for fear of a snub or the remote but possible chance of being physically thrown out. As late as at the end of the last war one read of occasional incidents at railway stations. The leader of the Anglo-Indians, a Viceroy's special nominee on the assembly in New Delhi, was thrown out along with his bags at his own home town when an English army officer returning from the station restaurant discovered this unwelcome intrusion. By now the Indian railway staff had begun to feel indignant on such occasions and made common cause with an Indian. The station master would not let the train start and the officer did not care. Eventually the leader had to content himself with a long hurt telegram to the Viceroy. I don't think the British officer much cared about England's unrecognized sons.

Indians travelling first class were mostly senior government officials. The business kind and others felt more at home in second. The difference in amenities was negligible, consisting in a single cane arm chair and reading lamps above the bunks. The real difference lay in the exclusiveness and twice the fare.

After the second came the class called intermediate which catered for the lower middle-class Indian. This was more crowded, less comfortable, without fans and special lights, with hard mattresses, and you were not entitled to the full length of the bunk at night nor could you reserve a seat during the day.

Then came the fourth class called third. It was little better than cattle cars, with long wooden benches and accommodation for fifty or more, but often crowded to twice the capacity and bereft of any refinements except for one or two dim lights. At each station there was a determined invasion by those wanting to get in, equally stoutly resisted by those already in, with those who wanted to get out pressed in the middle. Men, women and children poured in through doors and windows with a diversity of baggage, and once installed they praised God. The hostility of the vanquished never lasted long but welded into a common cause as the train reached the next station.

The fifth class was the strangest. It was specially reserved for the intermediates who were neither Europeans nor Indians, the 'sons' and the professed ones. For the impecunious domiciled European, Anglo-Indian and Indian Christian of the anglicized kind, a separate compartment was provided of the intermediate grade. When you reached the Christian end of the colour scale it was difficult for the average railway staff to distinguish them from Indians though to anyone who knew the difference was obvious. But how was a minor official of the railways to know? To him they were all Sahibs. A rule had therefore been inserted in the official guide, laying down an overall qualification that the passengers travelling in this class must be dressed in European clothes. This rule created its own complications, and the story was told of a somewhat dark Christian gentleman who went to the European guard invoking his aid to remove a native who had got into the privileged compartment. The guard promised to look into it at the next station, where he found one very dark man and a fair Kashmiri, both in European clothes. He had forgotten the complainant, and without further ado he proceeded to do his duty. He picked up the bags of the protesting dark passenger and told him to get out of there and not to bother the fine gentleman. Earlier these compartments were marked Eurasian; and as that word went out of coinage they were marked Anglo-Indian. They often went temptingly empty.

For all these classes, except the Eurasian, there were feminine equivalents, but again with a subtle difference. The first and second were called 'ladies'; the intermediate, 'women'; and the third was marked 'females'. The same went for the station lavatories.

The tenth kind was a third class for troops, British in preference. The eleventh was a small wire coop protruding out of the back of the dining car right at the end of the train. In this were kept live chickens. Through a sliding shutter the cook brought out the birds to convert them into the standard dinner. The leg of goat for the lunch was, however, picked up at a wayside station.

I wonder what Mark Twain would have said had he travelled in India a century later, when travelling had become more complicated. His quip on Indian railway travel was however as true now as then: 'The first class passengers look down on the railway staff, the railway staff look down on the third class, while the second class passengers look down on each other.'

CHAPTER FOUR

After twenty-four hours of steadily hauling itself up the gently sloping desert and plain that rose seven hundred and fifty feet in seven hundred and fifty miles from the sea, the train from Karachi reached Lahore. Lahore station had a character entirely its own. Its bustle and chaos beat that of any other. Upon the train red shirted porters swarmed like birds of prey and in a few moments emptied its innards of anything that looked like baggage, while the bewildered passengers extricated themselves from the mêlée. Hastily pointing out the number on their metal badges the coolies disappeared with the baggage and the passengers found their way out. In the porch both parties met with a swarm of tongawallas who dragged passengers and bags to their carts. How the luggage was sorted out, the coolies satisfied and the passengers got into the tongas was a miracle that characteristically introduced the Punjab. Like everything else in this vital land things somehow got done, but through what vigorous chaos!

It was my first long visit to Lahore since I left it as a college student, ten years earlier. On the first evening I went on a tour of rediscovery. There was little change in the city itself but it had developed many new suburbs, some haphazardly built slums but others well planned. I wandered through the Victorian Gothic building of my old college, through the hostel in which as a freshman I had had the misfortune to be squeezed into a room with three brothers, who all stammered. Their frequent quarrels, when all three stammered with excitement, always ended up in a joint front against me. From my old room I looked down on the spot where in 1928 two Punjabi students fired the first terrorist shot, killing a young English police officer. It made a deep wound in the pride of the British, and the loyal Punjab was never the same again. Something had snapped. From the other side of the room I looked upon the Round Garden, where we sat on the grass in the winter preparing for our examinations. I walked through the gardens till I came to the massive gun, Kim's Zam Zama, that the British had captured from one of the Sikh clans. It faced the wide avenue of sophisticated shops and restaurants, the Mall Road. As students it was beyond our pockets, though once some of us did sum up enough courage to have tea at the Standard, where for one rupee you had a large spread. There I saw for the first time the strange sight of men and women in embrace gliding about to music. From the Mall

I strolled to the famed shopping centre of the Punjab, Anarkali, past the shops selling fruit and spicy tidbits, and entered the city. Old Lahore inside the wall was as narrow, congested and noisome as ever. It had lost none of its fascination. I walked through the sunless lanes to the quarter of the girls, euphemistically called the Diamond Market, where painted, kohled and lightly dressed they specialised in the ancient arts of singing, dancing and love. Through the intricate maze of lanes and passages I returned to the spacious lawns of Faletti's Hotel.

During the month at Lahore, I went home to stay with my mother and father over week-ends. They had now settled in a new suburb. I thought of my student days, how good it was then to return home for holidays, never long enough to wear out the welcome. This time I ran into complications. News had travelled that I was now in a job in a large foreign firm in Bombay, and this at once made me the quarry of two kinds of aspirants, those with daughters looking out for a son-in-law, and those with sons looking out for a job. My parents felt embarrassed, though mother certainly thought that it was time for me to think of matrimony. They could not turn away friends and friends of friends who came with proposals, and yet they did not want to spoil my visit. I was even more embarrassed, for about matrimony I had made up my mind but dared not say so yet to my parents, and as for the jobs I could not convince anyone that I myself was only an unconfirmed probationer and my power of patronage did not even extend to the appointment of an office boy.

Matchmaking had changed, I found. In our circles it was no longer a deal between the parents arranged through the good offices of the family barber, in which the views of all except those most concerned were sought. The hereditary barber to the family was always asked to take a proposition to the other side and broach the subject discreetly, to save the two families the embarrassment of a refusal. It would then have been considered positively indecent to consult the boy and the girl. Modesty anyway would have prevented them from doing more than bowing their heads before their parents and mumbling 'just as you wish'. But now it was a quarter way to courtship. The family barber out, friends or relations would suggest a likely match. Often married brothers and sisters suggested someone they or their spouses knew at school or college. After discussions with the parents, some mutual friend was found to broach the matter with the opposite parents. If the response was favourable the parents would sound the children, giving details of the other family, the boy's or the girl's qualifications, his salary and prospects. If both evinced interest, the next stage was to bring them together. As yet this meeting was a mere formality, for all they could do was to look at each other shyly and make sure that there was no actual dislike at first sight. No words were exchanged, nor were they left alone. If both agreed straight away, or with due persuasion, an engagement ceremony was arranged and in due course the wedding. Independent choice was still rare.

This was quite an advance on the time when my uncle and my aunt saw each other for the first time after they were man and wife. In those days they had to be content with coloured descriptions from their parents, and mothers in particular were adept at glorifying their choice.

In 1938 we were still at the stage of the silent interview, but as I had been abroad a point might have been stretched to let me talk to the girl. But the girl I wanted to marry I had talked to in plenty over the six years I had known her. It would have been termed by the expression that was just entering the Punjabi vocabulary, 'a 'lav match'. But I did not know how to mention it to my parents. Had I not promised my father when leaving for England that I wouldn't marry an English girl? In a way I had kept the promise, for she was not English, but Swedish. It was a bit embarrassing when people dropped in to look at me and both they and I had to go through the conventional motions, when only I knew that I was not available.

Those who wanted jobs were worse. Usually it was the father who came to see me to extol the virtues and qualifications of his son, insisting that there was no need for me to see him. They refused to accept my protestations that I was quite powerless. Nobody would believe that I had no influence. All I had to do was to 'speak to the Sahib' and he would immediately send for the boy and give him a job. Sahibs, they would add, used to be like that in the Punjab until competitive entrance and communal ratios came in, by which only the Madrasis, for their ability, and the minorities, Muslims, Sikhs, Christians, Harijans, for their birth, seemed to qualify. But surely it was not like that in the companies; the Sahibs would take in anyone I recommended. I ought to do something for my province which had few commercial and industrial opportunities. And then there was a long appeal to my duty to my community, my caste and my neighbours. That was the way of our biradaris—the strong and the successful helped the weak and the needy. Who else would?

And so the arguments and entreaties would go on till I almost began to see some sense in the nepotism so deeply ingrained in us. Once your loyalties to region, caste, relations and friends are accepted this becomes inescapable. Having started the admirable innovation of recruitment on merit, the British government had gradually begun to slip. Considerations of region, caste and patronage for loyalty became supreme till all the good of fifty years was undone. Agriculturists received special preference, but the most favoured treatment was shown to those whose families had rendered loyal service to the crown. People carried wrapped in white handkerchiefs general letters of recommendation from generations of high English officials. To us this system was most debasing; a sad reflection on the Raj which had to resort to such means to shore itself up.

Gradually the impression spread that long education abroad had alienated me from my own people. Whether they came for marriage or for a job, they went away disappointed.

My father was as usual very helpful. Always ahead of his time, he believed in fair opportunity and the rest left to merit. He could not understand the complex rules that seemed to favour the mediocre and protect the inefficient. In his day only merit took you further, and plenty of it could take you far. Having risen without help he did not see why he should recommend his friends' sons to me. It went against the grain.

In the dining room at Faletti's Hotel, I looked forward at meals to seeing a slight pale-faced girl who sat alone. She had features uncommon to these parts and yet not unfamiliar. They were finely chiselled and surrounded by smooth black hair, parted in the middle and pulled severely over the ears. But quite unforgettable were her dark eyes of unnatural lustre, hauntingly enlarged by the deep pallor of her skin which contrasted with her brightly painted lips. She sat and stared as if into eternity, uninterested in anything around her, looking deeply into what others could not see or suspect. Occasionally she lifted the fork and held it poised in air but put it down again, and then one saw her exquisitely modelled hands, small with the grace of a waterbird in flight, but tired and transparent.

One evening I took a wrong turning in the corridor and saw a board announcing an exhibition by a painter whose name meant nothing to me. Curious, I walked in to have a look. In the centre of the room, surrounded by paintings on the walls, sat the girl from the dining-room with her usual far-away expression. Apparently few came to see the paintings. In my confusion I apologized and said I was merely going to look around for a few moments.

Like her face I remember her pictures. Their colours were bold and joyous, quite different from the popular schools of painting then reviving Indian art, which looked back to the Ajanta frescoes in poor imitation. Here was a vividness that belied her frailty. The subjects were folk Punjabi, mostly grave and demure women. Particularly beautiful was 'The Mourners'—a group of women with bowed heads covered with mantles, surrounding a pathetic figure, a bundle of a girl deep in her bereavement. No faces were visible, only the covered heads and shoulders convulsed in silent sobs.

Five years later when I was once travelling through the U.P. north of the Ganges—it was a long and tedious journey with the interminable delays of the war years—the only other passenger was a Sikh, reminiscent in dress and bearing of a Sardar of the early nineteenth century. We only exchanged some desultory conversation. Late in the afternoon the following day as we neared his station he asked me if I would like to break the journey and spend the night at his house. Without hesitation I accepted his courtesy.

As I walked into his room in the evening I looked at the walls in surprise. Between exquisite Persian carpets hung paintings by the girl from Faletti's. There they all were, with their sharp colours and all their sadness and joy. 'I have seen them all before' was all I could say. 'Yes,' he answered, 'they are my niece's paintings. This is all we have left of her. She died not so long ago of consumption. She was too young to die, but she really never seemed to belong to us.'

She was Amrita Shergill, our first outstanding modern painter. She painted for only a few years, but in that short space she left behind some immortal pictures of the Punjab, to which she added something of the Hungarian heritage of her mother. She showed the way to a new birth of Indian art which seemed to coincide with the coming of freedom, though not actually motivated by the freedom struggle. Too long had Indian art lived on tradition—freedom opened the door for new impulses from the West that led to a new flowering and made India part of today's art world.

On the way to Calcutta we broke the journey at Delhi to do some sight-seeing. I had never before been to Delhi, and the first sight of the new capital left me with mixed feelings. It was a great concept, but a conqueror's, of the heart of an empire. No rulers before them had been more alien at the end of their rule than in the beginning. When next day I saw the Taj Mahal this thought stood out more clearly, for here was buried a ruler who, though his ancestor had come as a conqueror, was himself, through his mother and grandmother, of the country, and had assimilated his heritage with that of the land. But the

founders of New Delhi after two centuries of connection were still
alien and had come to regard any influence of the people a taint. Born
of such racial aloofness, the new capital could not be expected to stir
the feelings of the subjects. Yet, ironically, the architect had realized
that their own contemporary architecture was too unimaginative to
create a monument to their power. He therefore boldly used the
materials and style of the country, a style which itself was a fusion of
the indigenous and that of earlier invaders.

As I walked down the Kingsway, the widest avenue in the world,
past King George's statue and the triumphal arch that commemorated
the wars Indians had fought for Britain and her empire, I saw the
heart of the Empire, the Viceroy's palace flanked, by the massive
blocks of the two secretariats like sentinels. Built on a rise, the Viceroy's
residence, known, in a colossal understatement, as the Viceregal Lodge,
was suitably elevated above the city of New Delhi. On the flat land
below stood the hall of the representatives of the nation, who were at
the time either nominated by the Viceroy or elected by a fraction of
the people. It struck me as cynical to relegate this symbol of democracy,
however limited, to such an obsequious place below the throne.

The red and yellow sandstone buildings with rows of columns and
Moghul arches were conceived in a grand style as indeed was the whole
of New Delhi. Grudgingly I liked it all. I wondered in what style we
would have built our own inevitable New Delhi, had we not inherited
one. Perhaps not very differently. In fact, forty years later we added to
this central complex new secretariat buildings of a similar style. As in
many other fields, once our turn came we often did through choice
what we before had hated the British for doing.

Calcutta was an implausible town even before the war. The cream
and green architecture of its spacious suburbs, so well suited to the
climate, the well planned squares in the city, the wide sweep of
Chowringhee facing one of the largest parks that a city could boast of,
made Calcutta very pleasant, and gave it, unlike other large towns in
India, a metropolitan character. But there its grandeur ended and
neglect and shabbiness took over. Roads unmended, footpaths with
stone flags dug up years ago and lying in heaps, streets with garbage
which brahmini bulls and pi-dogs scattered over the pavements,
houses with plaster and paint peeling off, were a common sight everywhere. The city had an air of a past more affluent than the present,
typified in the handsome square mansions of the old landowning
families. Once these houses and their gardens must have been well

maintained, but now the yellow ochred walls were mildewed by many monsoons, the green shutters cracked and warped, the gates rusty and the gardens overgrown. The houses built by the big merchants of the East India Company along the river also stood deserted in their wilderness that was once magnificent park. And yet with all its decay, the city throbbed with life. In its covered markets or in Clive Street one felt the animation and vitality. There was great activity too in the docks and the industrial suburbs, where around the workshops and factories, with magnificent managers' bungalows, there had sprung up some of the blackest slums anywhere.

Calcutta's total impression was of vitality and apathy, wealth and poverty, life and decay; here was a town without a social conscience. Its civic life had once made a great name for the city, its politicians were men of all-India stature; but they appeared to have left no legacy of running the day to day affairs. In fact one wondered whether the vision of her great men of today was ever clouded by such minor things as a clean and efficient administration. It seemed that some fifty years ago a break took place in the affairs of the city. The Scots, who had founded and ruled the town, began to mind their own business, as long as their own interests were protected, and those of the land who took over were so ready to be appalled at the injustices around them that they had continued to be just appalled ever since. The city began to go its own way and no one seemed to mind.

Perhaps Calcutta's cosmopolitanism added to its neglect. Big business, once dominated by the Scots, was gradually taken over by the Marwaris; the Punjabis seemed to be everywhere—in small business, shopkeeping and plying taxis; Parsis filled minor positions of trust; a growing number of South Indians manned the ledgers and typing machines; the Biharis pulled rickshaws, served in the police and guarded houses; and of course the Bengalis were everywhere, men of learning and culture who had delegated admirably to others the task of running their town. In Bombay cosmopolitanism seemed to work, but not so in Calcutta.

The curious thing was that everybody complained that Calcutta was not what it had been: it was becoming crowded, ill-kept, dilapidated, its slums ubiquitous, and yet nothing ever happened. There was an acceptance of the deterioration. People blamed Government and Government could well have complained that the people did not cooperate; everyone pronounced judgement but no one acted. One new governor pronounced the bastis, the shanty slums, a blot on Calcutta that must be removed. The press gave this much prominence, and everyone agreed and hoped that a call from the highest quarter would generate the much-needed action, but once again nothing happened, and so the deterioration went on.

Calcutta filled me with depression. It was to grip me each time I visited it in the years to come. Alighting from the train at Howrah station and crossing the Hooghly over the pontoon bridge, which sometimes delayed one for hours when it was opened to let through the river traffic, driving through the streets where cows roamed and nuzzled at the litter for possible sustenance, while graceful kites poised overhead, waiting to swoop down on some remnant of food; men in the streets bathing in the muddy water from the fire hydrants; the emaciated, panting rickshaw pullers threading their way through the stream of traffic, often hauling a whole family—rotund husband, wife and children plus luggage; skeletons sprawling on the pavements with empty cans in their outstretched hands in the hope that someone might drop a copper coin; a homeless family eating a scanty meal out of a leaf—boiled rice flavoured with a few spoonfuls of spiced liquid. Through this depressing scene the taxi honked its way. Before the panorama of Calcutta's life my spirits always sank. Yet slowly, through numerous visits, I began to like the town. Though no one did anything for its people, they themselves got much happiness out of their festivals, when whole streets went gay for a week in cooperative celebrations of a deity. They were a sensitive but helpless people, ready to laugh and willing to suffer; wrongly maligned for their sensitiveness, but rightly accused for their apathy. I never got to know them well for they are proud and shy of strangers and prefer to stick together, but once convinced of your genuine liking, the curtain of pride will drop or at least become translucent, and charm and affection will emerge, but rarely a friendship.

It was a long journey of over forty hours from Calcutta to Madras in which a whole vista of Indian life slid past the carriage windows. Through west Bengal, south Bihar, coastal Orissa, Andhra and Tamil Nadu, the train rushed through two nights and a day, carrying with it a ribbon of excitement through a quiet countryside quickened to life by its progress. In the silent night sleepy wayside stations would suddenly waken at the distant sound of the train, and as it ground to a halt the confusion of passengers rushing up and down the platform mingled with the cries of hawkers selling tea, cold drinks, sweetmeats, food and fruit. In the day the same scene repeated itself under a blinding glare, and with it all there was to me the excitement of country and people I had never seen before. The fascination of Indian rail travel has never palled for me.

Madras was as remote to us in the Punjab as 'Walayat'. The world to us Punjabis had consisted of our homeland, beyond which began Hindustan soon after our fifth river, the Sutlej. Distantly, somewhere to the South, lay Madras, which to us represented the unknown. Beyond that was the black water and then Walayat—all the lands beyond.

The people of Madras, their language, food and dress, had only a distant heritage in common with us. Between a Punjabi from beyond the Jhelum river and a Tamil from the Cauvery the links were few and not easily recognizable. Erudite Brahmins had their Sanskrit learning like the priests in mediaeval Europe had their Latin, but two ordinary men found little in common. Madrasis to us meant anyone born south of 'Poona—Satara', north of which was the land the Marathas came from.

Madras was like its people, simple, clean, orderly and well balanced. There were not the Calcutta contrasts of mansions and shanties, gilt-mirrored restaurants and beggars outside. Everyone took the air at the Marina and sucked his coffee in the ubiquitous cafes. But there were differences of a different kind, and very deep ones; not of wealth but of caste. There was Brahmin and non-Brahmin areas, Brahmin and non-Brahmin coffee houses; temples for the Brahmins and for the low-born the roadside, from where they could look in through the temple door and say a distant prayer.

It was a joy to work in Madras. A single advertisement brought a score of pleasant looking, intelligent graduate girls, free in speech, and dressed in saris, who were willing to do any work, willing to work permanently and to travel anywhere in India. We chose four, three of them sisters, two of those twins. And then I discovered that all the girls who had applied were Christians, mostly Syrian Christian—a community I had never heard of before. None of them was a Brahmin. As elsewhere, only Christian girls came forward to work, and our only exception so far had been Krishna in Bombay and a married lady, Savitri Devi, in Lahore, who must have been almost the first among middle-class Hindus in the Punjab to leave home and work out of doors. Savitri Devi was quite remarkable. She had found herself in circumstances in which, had she followed tradition, she would have accepted parental help, but instead she went to work, despite the handicap of a scanty education that did not include English. Her husband did not work but trailed happily behind her. Later when her market research work stopped on account of the war, I felt compelled to engage him instead.

The three sisters were gems and took to work with great enthusiasm. They suggested that they would travel to Trivandrum, where my next market investigation was to be held, for they belonged to Travancore. My only problem was the twins' shyness. They were a talkative pair, but mostly talked only to each other. In a low voice they carried on an interminable conversation about seemingly nothing at all. Whenever I asked one of them a question both faces, chubby and to me indistinguishable, with huge dark eyes, would light up in comprehension, yet neither would speak first. I would repeat the question and then one would bend her head near the other's neck and both would giggle almost silently. That I could never tell one from the other did not matter because they were really one, not two. Not only did they look alike and think alike, they thought themselves one. I learned that the only way to make them talk was to let them talk together. Though they called separately on the housewives, I soon found they took every opportunity to discuss their work in such detail that when I asked a question I had to let them both answer. Nature had put them into separate moulds, but as long as they were treated as one entity there were no problems. The third and older sister was different. She had a keen mind and was an interesting talker. During our long conversations at work and afterwards she told me a lot about South India, of which so far I had been totally ignorant.

From Madras Thompson Walker decided to return to Bombay and then leave for England. He felt the work we had done in the five towns had gone well, and from now on I could manage alone. I returned with him to Bombay, and saw him off with a heavy heart. For four months we had worked and travelled together, discussing much that was as new to me as it was to him, and both of us shared a keen sense of curiosity. This constant companionship had helped me to feel my way in the organization and also in the general order of things.

Free as he was from prejudices and conventions he was able to laugh and make me laugh at things that might otherwise have hurt me and left scars. When, for instance, an office sepoy brought back a small cash requisition of mine that would have been within the competence of a very junior manager to approve, with a message from the accounts department that it needed a 'European signature', I was hurt but Tom was amused, and eventually I saw the humour of it too. 'They simply have not caught up with your existence, and I bet you it is not the chief accountant but one of his Indian clerks who returned the slip, and he will take longer to accept your position than will the Sahib.'

With his sharp perception Tom saw the foibles of both sides, and as he interpreted them I began to learn the viewpoint of the British and develop a tolerance that became essential in my later responsibility. There were barriers, and some were hard to take, even though I was not particularly inclined by nature to challenge or even question them. But Tom sensed it and often encouraged me to bring my hurts to light. At first it was painful even to face them, but in a sensitive way he could be ruthless. What helped most was that he was not interested in defending anything. 'I believe you will rise in this firm,' he once said, 'and you will have twice your share of problems. It will be a great strain which you will have to take well, and as the first you will have to find your own solutions. I hope that you will let only the big things worry you and not the numerous small ones; those I would leave to small men on both sides.'

It was not easy in those days to find much in common with an Englishman in India, and neither side could be blamed. They were now convinced that they were going to go sooner or later; hopefully they felt it would be later. In the meantime, whether in industry or government, much was being done to train, to share, ultimately to hand over. They were therefore resentful of our impatience and our flat denial that anything at all was being done. There were wrongs for which they felt that they alone were not always responsible; while we were blissfully convinced that, once they left, all wrongs would overnight be put right, whether they were ours or theirs. They felt that some credit must surely be due to them; we conceded none. Few of us appreciated what it must feel like to be so misunderstood at a time when their supremacy was challenged; a supremacy that not so long ago had seemed part of their destiny and therefore unshakeable. It was a barrier of misunderstanding with a no-man's-land on either side where exploration was considered transgression.

Many young Indians returning from British universities, in their working contact with the British in India, bruised themselves on this wall of misunderstanding, sometimes suspecting insult where none was intended, and however far they progressed, the bruises usually re-mained. I was fortunate to have as my mentor a man untouched by the climate in India, with whom I could discuss my problems and mis-givings without restraint. This must have helped give my ideas a healthy orientation and acted as a corrective, which was to be of great benefit to me in the far more delicate years to come.

BEYOND PUNJAB

I did not see Thompson Walker again, till 1949, when at the early age of fifty-three he was nearing his end. His nerves had always been in a bad condition, and much as he loved life he was convinced of his imminent end. In Lahore, he had had one of his attacks which made his legs numb and brought the fear of a creeping paralysis. Fortunately a bad influenza created a diversion, and I put him in a hospital where with rest and the care of some lively Anglo-Indian nurses he soon recovered. But back in England, his nerves gave away altogether and in a few years he retired from work. In the summer of 1949 I visited him in Yorkshire, where he lived on the edge of the moors. We spent three happy days driving through the country he loved. He took me to York Minster, to Fountains Abbey, and to an old derelict woollen mill tucked away in a hollow by the stream from which it once drew its power. For reminiscence's sake I went across the border over the Ribble River, up Pendle Hill. It was as windswept and sun-drenched as I remembered it, and there were the lone seagulls sailing in the sky. Pendle Hill had been a favourite spot during my student days, hallowed by the walks together with my Swedish wife in the summer of 1932 when we first met.

I never saw Tom again. Soon afterwards he died.

CHAPTER FIVE

AFTER THOMPSON WALKER'S departure I returned to South India to start work at Trivandrum where the three sisters were waiting, with a fourth girl recruited and ready to start. This made the beginning easy for me. I appointed Sarama, the elder sister, supervisor of the team, in which capacity she worked with me for many years. She looked after the team so well that I always had plenty of opportunity to indulge my passion for learning about the people and the country wherever we went.

Sarama and I became good friends and in our free time she showed me around the countryside, explained the people, their life and their customs. She had been to school in Travancore and to Women's Christian College in Madras, which was the earliest institution for advanced education for women in India. From there she joined the Y.W.C.A. as the superintendent of a hostel, but this she found restricting. While conscientious and devoted to work she was not religious by nature and found it difficult to conform even to the light discipline of this institution. She was restless and too independent for an arranged marriage, but in those days for restless and independent women politics and social work were the only outlets. She was the first girl I met from this new class where education and independence were leading to a rejection of the past without a corresponding future.

Years later Sarama did accept an arranged marriage, for she was now unhappy at work and wanted to settle back in her village, and matrimony offered a prospect. It turned out to be a failure from the very start and she soon came back to work, but eventually she left again and disappeared altogether. Perhaps it was too early then for women to go to work in industry; and yet twenty-five years later I was to learn that women at work still did not achieve much more than Sarama did.

Trivandrum, and all Kerala, was as different from anything in the North as it was far away. The city stood on undulating ground, its residential areas scattered among groves, so that from the Observatory Hill you saw below almost nothing but tree-tops and hills. Everything had a tropical lushness and an air of perpetual summer. There was water everywhere, in ponds, canals and rivers, always densely fringed by palms.

Instead of the familiar chaos there was space and order. Small houses, well built and airy, with red-tiled roofs, each standing in its own small plot cultivated with coconut, pepper vine, jackfruit, tapioca, drumstick, hibiscus and flowering frangipani, formed a kind of urban development totally new to me. Very different too to look at were the people, so well washed and dressed always, both men and women, in clean, simple white. Even the bright red earth was different. You had to be a Punjabi to appreciate the difference. For one used to purdah, it was a new experience to see women walking the roads alone after dark, some still bare-breasted in the old way, with only the loose mantle thrown across.

Travancore was in great turmoil at the time. Here the struggle was between the people and a government that was Indian, headed by the Maharaja, though it was his highly able Diwan and the dowager Maharani who in fact ran the state. Both were of great ability and determination, with deep understanding and supposed affection for the other. In this progressive state the conflict between people and government took an almost parallel course to the struggle going on in British India. With the struggle in Travancore the British had nothing to do, and it gave me a shock to see a political phenomenon that was quite contrary to the popular belief that there could be differences only between us and an alien government, never among ourselves.

Every evening processions came out shouting 'Gandhi ki jai'. The slogans and invectives were familiar, the difference lay only in the target of the attack—curiously, always the Diwan and never the ruling family, even though they were known to support him. There were mass demonstrations, picketing and even police firing. I asked Sarama about it. She was totally opposed to the Diwan, though loyal to the Maharaja, and painted him in lurid colours as responsible for all the ills of the state. The highest literacy rate in India, the level of higher education, the best-developed public health and communications, even the growing industrialization; for all this she gave him and his government no credit, but all that was wrong was ascribed to his evil machinations. She considered her own community of Syrian Christians the particular target of his designs, because they were the most progressive and relatively better off than the rest. He was out to break whatever economic power they possessed. One symbol of their progress, a bank, was alleged to have been brought into liquidation by his manipulations. Even the police fire seemed to single them out.

Through a natural sense of justice that sought to compensate for this headlong attack, and also to gauge the depth of her feelings, I suggested that perhaps the Diwan was not such an unqualified tyrant as he was made out to be. No, she was adamant, he was bad through and through.

Even the state transport service that he had organized so well was a
tool in his hands designed to favour one section. Only when he went
would things improve, and everything immediately change for the
better, for had they not the resources, the will and the best human
material? Look at the way they had spread so successfully all over
India in services and professions.

The Hindus, the Nairs and the Ezhavas, all felt the same way about
the Diwan though in each case there were particular factors; only the
Muslims, largely in business, held nothing against him. The Nairs
owned land and were a higher caste, with more education and wealth.
The Ezhavas were poor, landless and not high-born. The Nairs felt
he favoured the Syrians, and the Syrians that he favoured the Nairs,
and the Ezhavas felt he favoured all except them, the dispossessed and
unprivileged. And yet whatever the suspicions and fears, they all
combined in a wholehearted hatred of the regime, and such pure hatred
I had never seen before. Here was a people, I thought, among the most
gifted in India, to whom nature was kind to a fault, a land where food
grew around your house in sufficient quantities, a long coastline
yielding much fish, a climate that varied from the tropical luxuriance
of the coast to the cool but equally luxuriant mountains, where rubber,
tea and coffee grew. What miracles, they tried to convince me, would
they not perform once they were rid of the hated regime, once they
could manage things their own way?

At work the girls came up against considerable resistance from the
housewives, which, considering their general level of advancement,
surprised me. Rumours went around that these girls from Bombay,
who curiously enough spoke Malayalam fluently, were spies of the
Diwan, paid to find out things under the garb of innocuous questions
about washing habits. But the work progressed smoothly even so,
and I asked Sarama to help me with a small survey of rural conditions
and habits. We would motor out to some part of the country and go
from one village home to another, without a set questionnaire, just
talking to the peasants and their wives, or whoever happened to be at
home. This was long before this simple technique became known as an
open-ended interview. To me there was the added fascination of
learning about a country and people that I found very attractive.

Before we finished in Trivandrum I drove down to Cape Comorin.
There may have been little in common between us in the Punjab and
the people of Travancore, yet when I stood at the promontory where
India literally ends, and thought of the land that stretched behind me
to the frozen cave of Amarnath and beyond, I realized the common

bond of shared beliefs. Two thousand miles north, in the Himalayas, I had seen thinly clad men and women from the South panting their way up the snow slopes to see the miracle of the milky ice lingam in the Amarnath cave, just as I now saw pilgrims from the North sunk in devotion here at Cape Comorin—to us Kanya Kumari, the virgin whose feet are washed by a confluence of three seas. She and the ice lingam are joined together into the unity of India.

It was worth the dusty train journey of two long days and nights in the heat of May from the state of Travancore to the state of Hyderabad, to see two such extremes of Indian India. Travancore was mountainous, wet, green, clean, and its people well educated. Like anyone else, the Maharaja went to the temple every evening wearing a simple unstitched garment. Hyderabad was flat, stony, parched and illiterate. Its ruler went to the mosque every afternoon, but then all the traffic was stopped and the roads cleared of human beings. The women were heavily veiled and guarded behind high blank walls. All you saw of them was their hennaed toes. Travancore had mostly small landowners, earning at most a few thousand rupees a year; Hyderabad had enormous estates owned by landlords whose income ran into lakhs of rupees. Travancore was seething with unrest while Hyderabad lay in a mediaeval torpor, its many noblemen living in an isolated splendour hard to imagine. Their eccentricities were not without their humour and seemed to increase with rank. The road was cleared for the Nizam's First Lady while policemen stood stiffly to attention. The car with windows curtained would sometimes stop suddenly and begin to reverse. It rolled several hundred yards, stopped again and began to move forward; for no seeming reason. I was told that one of her favourite pastimes was to make the car go backward and forward. The First Gentleman equally sported his eccentricities, the most notable being caution in money matters. Stories went that he carried his thrift to such lengths as serving exactly six cakes on a plate to a party of seven, and therefore nobody dared to touch the plate and all six pastries were saved for another day.

I got to know a young Punjabi staying in my hotel. I had known his elder brother in Manchester, so we became quite friendly. I noticed that he did not seem to have any work to do and yet was absent for most part of the day. This made me curious, and one day he explained what he was doing in Hyderabad.

A Punjabi Khatri family had come to the state some generations ago. Of sturdier stock than the locals, through hard work they rose rapidly and were ennobled. One even rose to become the first nobleman of the court and was given the title of Maharaja and a large estate and even a knighthood by the British. Though the family was by now entirely mulki, a term used for the nationals of the state, the Maharaja Sahib stuck to one custom. He would not marry his daughters into the local nobility, because they were not infrequently an extravagant lot whose pride in life seemed to be piling up debts and mistresses; the two habits usually going together in a spiral. He therefore arranged their marriages with carefully chosen young Khatri men from the Punjab, of good stock and education and professional training. This particular young man was a prospective son-in-law. He was handsome, healthy, had finished his education abroad, was of the right height for the girl, and altogether made to specifications. Visible qualifications, however, were not enough. He had to be tested for temperament and manners, and trained to receive the title of Raja from the court, and he was therefore brought over, and spent most of the day at the palace as a member of the family, on trial.

One Sunday he asked me to accompany him. I might see the girl and give him my opinion on the whole set-up. He held out the temptation of a moghlai feast, a change from the eternal roast mutton and Anglo-Indian curry at the hotel, varied occasionally by a muddy-tasting fish caught from a pool in the garden. We arrived at the palace just before mid-day. No one seemed to take any notice of us, and as we sat on the verandah he kept pointing out the figures of the family as they flitted past, impatient to show me his future wife, whom modesty perhaps kept out of the way though no doubt she was furtively peering at us. The house was large and built in many sections, furnished in a mixture of tastes, both western and oriental. In the interior quarters there was an informal chaos of family, furniture, servants and animals, and as everybody went his own way I soon felt perfectly at home.

At one o'clock when the May heat was getting unbearable with the shade temperature nearing one hundred and fifteen, there was great commotion, Servants ran here and there, dogs barked and family members came out to meet the young Raja Sahib, the only son of the Maharaja Sahib. He rushed in and sat down in a state of collapse, wiping his face which was streaming with perspiration. When he recovered a bit I was presented to him. I sympathized with him for having been out in such heat. To my surprise he said he had been out for his daily exercise and however hot he had held out for a full half hour.

It seemed incredible for anyone to take exercise at this hour, and what kind of exercise? Even mad dogs would be indoors. And the

Raja Sahib's figure did not make you think of exercise, but he seemed to assume that I of course knew all about it. His future brother-in-law took me aside and whispered that the Raja Sahib had been told by his doctor that he was putting on too much weight and needed a little exercise. This seemed a fantastic suggestion to the young nobleman who had always been helped by a horde of retainers to perform even the natural functions of life. Eventually he hit upon a bright idea in consonance with his dignity. Now, every day between twelve-thirty and one o'clock, he went out to drive his car. The driver and a servant sat at the back while he took the wheel and the car madly careered along deserted roads. He pulled the steering wheel hard from side to side and the servants clung to the straps for their precious lives. All the time he blew the rubber bulb horn and jumped up and down in his seat. At the end of the appointed time they all three returned, near-wrecks.

Soon afterwards lunch was announced, something I had been keenly looking forward to. There was a promisingly large table at which the Raja Sahib and other male members of the family sat down, waited on by a number of servants stretching in a line to the kitchens. To my astonishment the meal began with a watery soup and followed its course through indifferently prepared English dishes—mince chops with bones stuck in, fried fish, roast mutton and a steamed pudding. Instead of the famed Hyderabad moghlai cooking I faced a meal as dull as my daily hotel fare. I accepted my fate, but noticed that the family only picked at the food, which I attributed to their noble blaséness. My friend managed to whisper that the English meal was a touch of modern formality of which one took no notice; the real meal was yet to follow, and it did. As soon as the pudding was removed, there began to arrive an unbelievable succession of dishes served in beautiful Persian style utensils: pullaos and biryanis, nans and farmaishes, rogan joshes and qormas, chickens, quails and partridges, upon which the family, led by the well exercised Raja Sahib, fell to. Indifference gave way to healthy and vocal appetites, and I followed suit with my second lunch.

After an hour's relish we relaxed back in our chairs, when the Raja Sahib suddenly announced the second half of his exercise. In the somnolent air, when all I wanted was a siesta, he called for a game of bridge, and for the next two hours we went through a slap-happy session of cards at which he displayed the gusto of his driving, with cheerful disregard for rules and conventions. At bridge I committed another indiscretion. The sun was pouring through a window and I got up to lower the blind. The horrified Raja Sahib literally shouted me back into my chair. He clapped his hands and asked a retainer to have the blind lowered. The retainer walked importantly a few paces to the window, leaned out and clapped his hands and passed on the order. It must have been relayed down the line of service hierarchy to the outhouses because quite some time later a ragged looking servant appeared, and under the direction of the senior retainer he loosened the cord to lower the blind.

In the evening I was introduced to the Maharaja Sahib, a fine old courtly figure, unaffected by time and pleasure. My friend told me that, after his fashion, and within his limitation, he still had gay evenings. His own quarters were magnificently furnished, with a delicate touch of luxuriousness, I thought, in the red velvet cushioned seat of the privy, which in the absence of modern plumbing had fresh straw placed underneath each time.

Here was a state, feudal, poor, ignorant, where progress ended with its capital city. Hyderabad itself was a relatively prosperous looking town with handsome public buildings, a variety of institutions, palatial homes and wide cement concrete roads that ended abruptly outside the city, where uneven metalled roads took over and the general ostentation gave place to poverty and squalor. And yet Hyderabad was peaceful while Travancore was seething. The great contrast in wealth seemed to excite no one's envy or protest. The noblemen of the court ruled with unchallenged absoluteness, afraid of no one except mildly of the Marwari moneylender, whom to keep quiet they also made a nobleman, at least in title. He was never sure of his money, but like the tailor and the jeweller he charged so much that even small and irregular payments were ample reward, and of course there were always the hard-pressed upon whose properties he foreclosed.

While the young noblemen were often an unattractive lot, either frail or obese, extravagant, with manners whose charm was a thin veneer over deep selfishness, their young women were different. They were attractive and sensible, and combined demureness with innate self-confidence. Their education was also superior. In a special high school these girls received training in homecraft, in manners, in poise and grace. If one of them through marriage outside the state came out of purdah, it was remarkable how she would take to her new life with an assurance that showed no trace of her secluded upbringing. An English colleague, Maurice Zinkin, once invited such a couple to dinner. The young, attractive wife had just the right mixture of vivacity and poise. When they left she got into the car, took the wheel and with great ease drove away. My friend looked admiringly after her and said 'Do you know, less than three years ago that girl was still in purdah.'

Hyderabad had character, but not so my next stop, Nagpur, a nondescript town, except in the miracle of the monsoon when practically overnight its dusty heat gave way to cool freshness, and the burnt greyness to a luxuriant green. Here I had my first experience of a proper monsoon. After the searing heat, the monsoon came with a swift metamorphosis. I had not at first believed when someone told me that once the rains began the grass would grow knee high in less than a week.

I spent one interesting month in Nagpur, living at the railway station. There was no hotel, only a gloomy dak bungalow, but at the station I got a retiring room that was well furnished and possessed the luxury, rare for Nagpur, of modern sanitation. Through a kindly Anglo-Indian matron I managed to prolong my stay for a whole month by the simple device of buying a new ticket every morning for the next station, costing a rupee or so, and an occasional packet of cigarettes for her. The railway restaurant completed my needs and I led a self-contained life. In the restaurant I observed a custom, presumably new. I noticed in the evenings that the verandah beyond the main dining room was kept dark, as also the end of the dining room, through which some strange looking persons shuffled. They were not the type who ordinarily patronized western-style railway restaurants, but most of them were dhoti-clad, vegetarian-looking small business men. I decided to investigate and found that they came to indulge in secret vices. Some drank beer and whisky but most came to eat savoury omelettes with potato wafers, or even mutton chops. The darkened verandah of the station restaurant provided a safe place for indulging these newly acquired tastes that would have horrified their women at home.

Living in a large Indian railway station had its own fascination. Gradually I fell into a pattern of activity. I would lean out of the window every morning, as I shaved, to watch a cloud of steam and then the metre gauge train pulling out from the platform below. The same train, its day's work done, returned to its platform as I was brushing my teeth before going to bed. In the evenings I walked about the deserted platforms and talked to idle porters or groups of villagers waiting for their trains hours hence. One interesting visitor who dropped in to my room for an occasional bottle of beer was the Anglo-Indian station master. His great worry was how to deal with the new class of politicians who frequently passed through Nagpur, because of its proximity to Wardha where Gandhiji had set up his ashram. The station master had done well under the British, whom he understood, but the coming rulers, already in power in the provinces, were hard for this simple man to understand. They wore the clothes of the peasant, but well laundered and starched. They travelled third class, but wanted the attentions and facilities of the first. If a few important ones travelled together a whole compartment had to be put at their disposal. All this they did with a show of humility, as a pointed reminder that unlike the British they did not want privileges. One did not realize it then that when power came, this expensive humility was to lead to many of our problems.

The station master poured out his doubts and misgivings because he felt that I understood his problems, which I think consisted mainly of his inability or reluctance to adapt himself to the coming order. He had to be courteous to those people but found it difficult to like them, and perhaps they did little to put him at ease. He found it natural to be civil and even deferential to an Indian like me who had stepped into the Englishman's shoes. With me he felt at home. I could sit down with him and offer him a beer and listen to his troubles. While the Englishmen kept him at a working distance, the new set left him bewildered. Pathetically he told me that he envied me, my ease with both sides, my English education and my Indian origin and ways. His was not an isolated problem; it was going to be the problem of many more than this simple station master.

For the first and last time in my life I lived in a state of expenselessness. The two rupees a day for the retiring room and the few rupees needed for food and drinks were allowed by the company, and Nagpur was the kind of town where there was nowhere to go and nowhere to spend. There were some pleasant walks during the rains along a ridge but they cost nothing. The usual clubs, the well appointed Central India Club, mainly British, and the Indian Club offered no temporary membership to an itinerant businessman like me. One evening I felt I had to spend some money, so I went to the one decent general store which also sold books. I looked at liquors, imported tinned provisions, stationery and cheap novels, and eventually walked out with a bottle of Rose's lime juice and the *Concise Oxford Dictionary*. I have since often pitied the lot of many in business in India who live in perpetual expenselessness, with every wish gratified.

In the next town, Allahabad, I caught up again with my friend

Roshan from Bombay who had been transferred here. After five years
he was only now being tried out in an assistantship in a sub-branch
office. I often visited his home and saw the life of the new Indian business executive in a provincial town where, in 1938, he still was a type
unknown. In the average provincial town, apart from the mass of
workmen, artisans, craftsmen, small and big shopkeepers and government clerks, there was a thin layer of perhaps a quarter to a half per cent
of the professional class comprising lawyers, doctors, teachers and
government officers. The few British stuck together, admitting into
their company only the senior Indian government officers. The Indian
professionals formed another group which even the well-to-do businessmen seldom entered, not due to prejudice but because the two were
yet not miscible. It was rather a question of the influence of western
education and its permeation through manners and living habits.
Schooling and university education in the English language had
so moulded the outlook of the professional Indian that he found little
in common with the businessmen, who usually also belonged to a
lower social caste. Some marked external differences also set them
apart. The businessman as a rule preferred to live inside the city, he
built his house in the old grandiose but uncomfortable style; he
squatted comfortably on the floor and wore loose and airy Indian
clothes; he spoke in his mother tongue. The professional preferred to
live outside the city in a bungalow furnished with chairs and tables;
his language was riddled with English; his clothes were usually a
patchwork of both styles, often ill-fitting and uncomfortable besides.

Their values too had become different. One wanted money for
further investments in gold, property and business—his one fling in
life, when to outdo his neighbour he sometimes came close to ruin,
was the wedding of a daughter or building a house, when his modesty
and thrift scattered before the desire to be praised by his community.
The professional had begun to regard such expenditure as wasteful,
though his wife would not always agree with him. He saved for his
children's education and to build a modest but modern house; and if
he spent unwisely at a daughter's wedding it was only to attract a
well placed professional son-in-law by offering a dowry beyond his
means. In his single-minded pursuit of money, through means undisturbed by social judgement, salved by occasional prudent but
conspicuous charity, willing to corrupt and to self-efface, the businessman had a secret contempt for the new professional class with their
hollow pretensions, their standard of living unbacked by solid worth,
their subservience in dropping the ways of their forefathers and

adopting those of the rulers only to seek favour and acceptance. But underneath it all there was also a streak of envy.

The two classes were thus apart, with hardly any social intercourse or inter-marriage. A wealthy businessman might, through a dazzling dowry, get his daughter married to the son of a highly placed professional, but in their search for a son-in-law it was unthinkable for a professional family to give their daughter away to a young businessman.

The late thirties saw the first specimens of this third class, the commercial and industrial executives. They were always sons of professionals who had not been able to get into the now saturated government services. In Bombay and Calcutta this class was becoming noticeable, but in the provinces it was still new, and its position in the social hierarchy of the district still undetermined. Through careful selection and privileges analogous with those of the I.C.S., Roshan's oil firm managed to obtain for their executives acceptance into the senior levels of the district hierarchy. Oxford education and the Blue in his case helped to give him the proper status in the eyes of British officials. Yet there was a kind of rootlessness about him and his wife. Roshan, who was basically Indian and simple, as was also his wife Avi, found it a strain to live the part of a sahib. While his Indian opposite numbers in government had through fifty years of Indianization acquired a permanence of status and could afford to be themselves in their private lives, these two felt obliged to conform to the pattern of the British, which his firm demanded. The British in his firm were themselves trying to conform to a pattern set by their predecessors in order to gain acceptance among the British officials; a pattern that lifted them out of the category labelled 'boxwallahs'. These commercial British perhaps outdid the official British just as, Roshan told me, some of his Indian colleagues in the firm tried to outdo the British.

Avi with her cynical humour told me that Roshan was often mistaken for a senior government official when he was travelling in the districts. She added with affectionate malice, 'He plays the sahib and enjoys it since he has come to Allahabad. In Bombay no one cared.'

Their living pattern seemed to have been laid down by the firm. Avi had to have an ayah, a cook, a butler, a bearer, a sweeper, a chowkidar and a driver to look after the two of them and a small child. She had to learn mahjong, acquire a taste for English food and for small talk. She made me laugh with her descriptions of their life in Allahabad, which seemed to consist of little work for Roshan and none for her except looking after this battery of servants, themselves with very little to do. Roshan's main function was to inspect the ramifications of a well organized monopoly and hers to play a role new for an Indian housewife.

To this otherwise unprepossessing town, the confluence of the rivers Ganga, Jumna and the mythical Saraswati gave some character. The rivers ran high in the month of rains. The surrounding country was a lush green with bamboo clumps and copses of stately mangoes and mowha trees. I walked about the country, talking to villagers, asking questions about their ways. The land looked rich but the people very poor. They had a drabness I had not seen elsewhere. Men and women wore white cotton that was seldom white, just a muddy grey, and their villages were mud hovels devoid of all colour. The only beauty lay in the rich crops of the flat country. This was the epic country of the Ramayana, and it was now the home of the Nehrus and many other leaders of the country.

Congress was very active in this area. One day as I stood under a tree talking to some villagers, a man on a bicycle, dressed in clean khadi clothes, stopped to see what was going on. Since he showed immoderate interest I tried to find out what he did himself. He lived among the villagers and taught them their rights, their rights against the zamindars, the Government and against their own society when it was oppressive. I asked him how far he succeeded. More often than not, he said, the villagers did not succeed in asserting their rights, but still it was gratifying to him because at least they had learned what was theirs, when for centuries nothing but their life had belonged to them. He did not mind the many failures; the surprised chagrin alone of authority at being questioned was to him enough reward. His real disappointment, however, was the little headway he made against the excesses of the society itself, for here he was up against a blank wall and a resistance on which the appeal of nationalism made no dent, nor did society, convinced by long usage, feel any remorse. In dissuading a father from flagrantly defying the Child Marriage Act, a Brahmin from refusing to let a Harijan draw water from the well, a community from forcing a poor member to go bankrupt by giving a ritual feast, he made no impression whatever. While it was encouraging to see the way in which, once they had learnt their rights, they were willing to stand up to the police or the hirelings of a landlord, it was equally disappointing to see the way they would bow abjectly before the most unjust social dictates, he said sadly.

I wonder where that village worker is today. I don't imagine that either he or his successors pedal about on a bicycle in the selfless pursuit of teaching people to understand what is theirs. If he visits these villages again it is probably in a large car flying a flag, to ask for their votes, or to open a school. In his starched white clothes he will step forward with his head instinctively bowed to receive the garlands, with hands joined in smug humility. But maybe it happened otherwise. Maybe this one fell by the wayside in the later struggles, one of the nameless heroes who was not there when the rewards came.

On my last day in Allahabad I went by boat across the river to one of our holiest spots, where Ganga and Jumna meet. In the monsoon their muddy red waters swirled into a swift embrace and soon the two flowed together as if they had never flowed apart. As before at Cape Comorin, it struck me how moved I was by these unfamiliar manifestations of our religion, of whose practice and conscious belief I knew so little. I began to discover that rivers, mountains, trees and stones were really the centre around which our ritual revolved.

Across the river stood the large jail of Naini behind whose blank walls stayed off and on India's leaders. As I returned to the hotel through dingy and crowded streets, avoiding the roaming cows and still more carefully the frequent heaps of their droppings, I thought of what Thompson Walker had said of the Indian cities, especially those in the north: they had the appearance of the aftermath of an earthquake. A shanty standing next to a tall modern building; next door an occupied but unfinished house with girders and reinforcing steel rods sticking out; another half broken down but patched up and lived in; cattle in the streets with an air of ownerlessness; everything working in the chaos of an order newly broken. I continued my favourite walk through the railway station, over its long bridge, and descended into the green, trim oasis of the civil station with its low lime-washed bungalows and well kept gardens. The avenues of neem and hedges of myrtle washed by the rain added a clean acrid smell to the fragrance of flowering bushes. I returned to the hotel and sat on the lawn, sipping a beer. Allahabad, Naini and Barnett's Hotel, where I was staying, seemed worlds apart.

On my last day in Allahabad Avi had invited me to dinner. Roshan had asked an old friend who had been the first Indian president of a British university union. He had settled in Allahabad in a perfunctory sort of legal practice but was mostly understudying for Nehru in odd jobs, learning to be a politician, though eventually he rose to be a judge, an ambassador and a governor. There was also a civil servant.

I think Avi found life usually dull and seized upon an opportunity for a lively discussion which she lost no time in provoking. I sensed too that she was beginning to take a delight in chivvying me.

'Prakash, what did you think of Naini? Do you feel that this is where you ought to be, or are you too comfortably installed at Barnetts and would rather let those behind Naini's high walls do the job for you?'

I asked her what Roshan had said to this, for she must have put the same question to him. Avi grinned unabashed. Here was an interesting group of four young Indians, all with similar background and education both in India and in England, and each with an uncomfortable feeling of guilt. Ought he in these times to be doing something more than building a comfortable career? Even the young barrister, who was the closest to making some kind of sacrifice, was not sure whether he ought not to take the full plunge instead of skirting gingerly around. The civil servant was probably the unhappiest of the lot because he was an instrument of the authority that some Indians defied but all Indians disliked, defiance being only a matter of the degree of risk you were willing to take. Everybody, except he, could at least talk against authority; he being part of it could not even lightly indulge in that simple luxury.

Avi had us arguing in circles that widened and narrowed as the discussion became general or particular—but always around her as the provoking centre. The main theme was whether we were doing the right thing by standing aloof; did we make any contribution at all to the freedom process; did it need us all or would the country's interests be better served in the long run by having a class of us ready to take over when the time came?

My mind wandered off the discussion and I watched Avi's handsome face with its well-cut features and smooth, dark skin. Her face had the purer cut more often found in villages than in towns of the Punjab, but she had a sophistication that was uncommon and new to me. She had left Lahore and its conventional upper middle class convent education to go to an experimental school in Bengal, where she walked barefooted in its wooded estate and learned to sing and dance, and to dress in handwoven and block-printed sarees. Her figure had a sturdy Punjabi fullness. She had a better, less conventional mind than Roshan. I said to Avi:

'Why don't you join the Movement yourself? Your heart is obviously in it.'

'I would do it if Roshan was also interested. There is the inevitable jail-going if you once join, and I am not sure that that would appeal to

me. If only one could do something useful without becoming a full-
time worker attending meetings, joining civil disobedience marches
and courting arrest. Besides, we might have to live in an ashram and
"God give me chastity, but not yet"! I would find it hard to live without Roshan for long; I have not had enough of him yet.'

We all laughed at her practicalness and said we envied Roshan for
her frank appetite for him. I told her that I could understand where
she drew the line. She might think of it later when she mellowed down
a little, though if the Movement could now draw only some of her
fire it would gain quite something. She too laughed and thought we
were denigrating the Movement and the part played by the many
dynamic women who had thrown themselves wholeheartedly into its
turbulence. When I asked whether its turbulence gave them some
vicarious satisfaction, she gave me a long, penetrating look.

I went back to the hotel disturbed by Avi and what she said. If only
the leaders of the Movement had not insisted upon an all-or-nothing
attitude, or the Government on one of 'those-who-are-not-with-us-
are-against-us'. The days of the sophisticated opposition had gone,
when professional men in frock coats and hard collars could be in the
Congress, and call their thinking progressive and liberal. The only
real role left to their kind was taking messages between the Viceregal
Lodge and some British jail in the name of negotiation and formulae.
These men had neither popular following nor, since they could not
deliver the goods, any influence on the government. The people
now followed only those who gave their all. It could be argued that
this might be a pity, as it deprived many of the chance of any personal
identification, but equally it could be argued that all-outness was
necessary if opposition were to be anything more than an armchair
resistance.

The path of graduation from a limited self-government to Dominion
Status was closed with the departure of the Simon Commission in
1930. Congress was now committed to complete freedom. Many
argued that Churchill was right when he said that it was meaningless
to talk of Dominion Status; it could hardly be applied to India.
Australia and Canada were dominions, but with all their autonomy
their peoples were more British in their love of the sovereign than the
British themselves, and this to them was the ultimate, the indissoluble
bond. Who wanted the King in India or who cared? What did he
mean, except to the kindred souls of maharajas and nawabs? And they
also would have preferred to be independent rulers, could they only
be sure of their independence.

Ultimately I decided to shelve the question. I could not solve it in a hurry. Politics did not interest me at all, and short of entering politics there was little I could do. I was interested in my work, which in no way furthered the interests of the government, though equally it did not even remotely further the cause. The civil servant could sort out his worries and the barrister decide for himself. I consoled myself with the thought that Roshan and I were learning something new in commerce, something that would surely be valuable in time. The country did not need all its 350 millions. Roshan and I could very well leave it to the leaders, and, whatever Avi's feelings, I don't think either of us rated our possible contribution highly. On this unsatisfying note I left the matter, with the feeling that what I in fact lacked was the courage. That, I was sure, was what Avi thought.

Next day I returned to Bombay, exactly seven months to the day since I left on the first of January 1938. It was my longest single tour, of absorbing interest and a new education. For the first time I realized that there was an India. I savoured fully every moment of the long months.

Before my return I received a letter from the chief, the 'number one' or 'burra sahib' as they were called, saying that as he was leaving for England on his annual visit and would not be there when I returned he would like me to know that he was satisfied with my progress. He had confirmed me in the company's covenanted service – the magic word, but now with a difference. My company was covenanting its first Indian, whereas the old John Company of hallowed fame never covenanted even the British born in India. My covenant was a pale blue document containing innumerable clauses about secret processes and patents that I could put to no other use than the company's. Drawn up by some legal adviser in Liverpool at the turn of the century the contract gave away precisely nothing, but couched it all in incomprehensible but important sounding language. The one thing it did make abundantly clear was that I could be out of a job at three months' notice. Here too there were some suitable exceptions and safeguards. Had I only read it through, it made sure that I could be made to leave at once.

CHAPTER SIX

ACK IN BOMBAY I was told to organize another market research job of major proportions that would take me over much the same ground as before. It was to begin after the monsoon, and would last for five months.

In my spare time I decided to find a flat and make some kind of a home. Before my return from the next long tour I would also have to think of getting married, and acquiring a flat seemed a good starting point. Bombay in those days was a pleasant uncongested town, but even so I decided to live in the suburbs, and my choice eventually settled on the end of a road, on the slope of a hill, facing the sea. It was a modern flat of good design and ample space, in which every room had a view of the sea. I loved particularly the view from the verandah where a clump of palms screened the sea with their waving fronds, at its best in early dawn when sometimes a whole fleet of fishing boats, forty or fifty of them, would set sail on the morning tide. The sea, she wooden hulls of the boats and their sails were all a rose pink, gradually turning to mauve, and as the sun rose, to silvery blue. It was beautiful too on the nights of the moon when the light shimmered on the water and on the palm fronds. On full moon nights the light was sometimes so bright that you could see the blue of the sea and the green of the leaves. It reminded me of another sea far north where also the moon shone brightly on late summer nights. I was feeling restless.

My suburb stretched along the sea for two miles from a sloping headland over a valley to another hill. On the crest of my hill stood a Neo-Gothic church of no architectural beauty but with an interesting legend. On its site had once stood a Hindu temple to which people came to ask for boons. The Portuguese razed it to the ground and built a church to the Virgin Mary, but the Hindus continued to come for worship and wish. The image of the Lady was considered a sister of the local goddesses Mumbadevi and Mahalakshmi to be propitiated with a candle instead of flowers. Once a year, when the monsoon slackens its grip over the coast, an itinerant fair comes to this church. Except for the months of rains this fair keeps moving from one temple or mosque to another. In September it comes to the Mount of the Lady. The church has improved on the legend of wish fulfilment by offering wax objects to illustrate your wish. There are on sale arms, legs, feet, hands, hearts, chests, babies, anything to give form to a prayer. Poor

Christians buy these from a small factory run by the church at the back and sell them to the visitors in front.

The whole suburb was dotted with small villages which in time had formed a township but in 1938 were still distinguishable and known by their old names, with some kind of separate entity. It was a charming combination of the old Maharashtrian and the old Portuguese, and equally interesting were the customs of the Christians interwoven with influence from their Maratha ancestors, then from the Portuguese, and last from the British. One day I saw a small Christian wedding procession with little dark girls in white frocks holding the train of a bride who stood beside the groom in a thick black suit. Everyone looked sweaty standing in the street under the broiling sun and I wondered what they were waiting for till I saw the local bus draw up and the procession board it, the girls still holding the train. It was very charming.

I loved my first home and the suburb. Gärd was to join me here, and here our three children were born. Ten years later we built our own small house on the other hill.

In the office I now found greater acceptance. The covenanting removed all doubts among the clerks and I was now regarded a proper manager. I realized what a difference status made in our society. Whether high or low it had to be defined and named. While I was away another young Indian had been taken on, and he turned out to be someone I had got to know well on the boat. He had studied at Cambridge and was returning home with his wife. I felt happy to meet him again and have someone I could talk to freely, and I became part of their home where I spent most of my free time. We used to talk much around the topic of interest to both of us, our future in the firm and in industry in general, for we both came from the same background of professional families of whom we were the first to go into business. Arvind took a more limited view. Belonging to Bombay, he argued that here industry was largely Indian and developing fast, so that the few British firms would feel no need to Indianize, and of course the other foreign firms would take no notice. In Calcutta it was different; there industry was so predominantly British that some concession might be necessary and politic. I asked him why he had not joined an Indian firm. His father knew most of the Indian industrialists, whereas in this firm he was unknown and the future and scope for an Indian uncertain.

His family had unconcealed nationalist sympathies. His father was in the I.C.S. and had twice been made a high court judge, each time to be reverted to a less senior post in the district because in the cases he tried during one of the disobedience spells he had stuck to the spirit of the law while Government were anxious to mete out exemplary punishments; in addition, he openly had Congress friends who were sometimes in jail and sometimes out. Arvind's only sister had joined Gandhiji's ashram at Wardha with her father's blessings. I wondered therefore why Arvind had joined a British firm. He explained to me that most Indian firms were family businesses or belonged to a particular community, and it was the accepted thing that all control and privileges went to the family members; an outsider, however useful, could not normally expect to rise high, and certainly not to a top position. After the family came caste, then community and then region. When a father ran out of sons he turned to nephews and other relations. The logic of nepotism was to them impeccable: 'Whom can I trust more: my sons and those who are related and known to me, or strangers?' In a Parsi firm no one contested that the top position had to go to the family and the next senior to other Parsis. In Gujerati firms there were Gujeratis at all levels, and so on.

His wife, Aruna, was the first Indian girl I had met who had married outside her community and province, and there were not then many like her. She came from one of those rare Punjabi middle-class families that had turned Christian. In the Punjab, as all over the north, Christianity did not make much headway beyond converting an occasional poor family, but in Lahore, a few well-to-do Hindu and Muslim families had gone over. Unlike the poorer converts elsewhere they had stuck to their original names. In fact it was a mark of conversion through conviction rather than social and material improvement to have retained your Indian name instead of changing it to Daniel, Martin or D'Souza. They formed an *élite* of Lahore on account of their education and professional advancement. She came from one of the Muslim Christian families and it seemed a far cry to marry a Gujerati Hindu.

She was so unlike him. He was easy-going and good natured and nothing ever seemed to worry him. She was like the late monsoon weather—totally unpredictable; out of a clear sky would come a squall that made you think the monsoon was back, only to be followed by a sky so innocently blue as if nothing had happened. You never knew what made her happy or unhappy, but it could not go deep for she had no permanent moods. The only permanence lay in the alternation of sun and cloud; she had no middle temper. She must have been beautiful not long ago, for she was still young, but she seemed to have stopped caring. She had a round laughing face with roguish eyes, but what amused me most about her was the demureness she could suddenly switch on if one of Arvind's elderly relations arrived. She would pull her sari over her head, half covering her face; laughter went out of her voice and she talked in earnest tones. As soon as they left she returned to her normal self, angry or happy as the mood took her.

No two women could be more different, Avi and she, in looks or temperament; yet both were so different from the Punjabi girls I had been used to before I left home ten years ago. Products of convent schools, one had come under the influence of cosmopolitan Bombay, while the other was influenced by the new Bengali culture, but both had acquired a kind of restlessness. They were both always goading their men. I wondered if this restlessness did not come from a change that had led them nowhere. Their men had studied abroad and started on careers that were a natural corollary of their education; those girls had also prepared themselves and yet, just when they should have been putting their education to some use, they had married and started a life no different from that of the girls who had stepped straight out of home. It would have done them good to have worked for a few years instead of plunging straight into domesticity after an education that promised a life of equality and purposefulness, and yet led nowhere. They took a great deal of vicarious interest in their husbands' work, and the cynical thought came to me that either of them would have been better at the jobs their husbands did, for they were unusually bright and strong-willed. It was their like that found an outlet in politics and social service; they had stepped out into public life because it was the only career then open to them.

I began my next tour anti-clockwise round India. I started at Trivandrum where I was greeted at the station by Sarama and, hiding behind her, the twins who had lost none of their shyness. They went to work with great enthusiasm because I had promised to take them to Madras, Calcutta, Allahabad and Lahore. They were thrilled at the idea of seeing these cities, though frightened by the thought of winter in Lahore. I spent long hours giving them a working knowledge of Hindi. In Calcutta our Punjabi lady would join us to make a permanent team, trained and experienced. With the work of this tour well planned I relaxed into pleasant anticipation of renewing contacts with the towns and the country and people I had got to know. But soon the clouds gathering over Europe began to worry me in a personal way.

F

Gärd lived on a small island in the Baltic between Sweden, Russia and North Germany. We had been writing regularly to each other, and more than a year's separation did not seem to have altered things. We had settled on letting time decide, and it did. Her letters were acquiring an urgency which the proximity of Hitler made understandable, but then she had all through been cheerfully optimistic, which I was later to find stemmed from the confidence of an infinite capacity to adapt rather than ignorance, as I then thought. Marriages between Indians and Europeans were not rare in those days, but few worked out totally well. Most were between Indian students in England and English girls. Few Indians studied on the continent or in the United States. In England, for a variety of reasons – strangeness, social awkwardness, diffidence, and straightforward colour prejudice – young Indians mostly stuck together. They lived in a society where social contacts among the sexes were normal and easy, but denied such contacts among their natural equals they found them lower down, not at the college socials but at the local palais de dance. They went out with shop girls who were impressed by their superior education and liberal pocket money, and many of the boys laid it on thick about back home, the large houses and hordes of servants. There were exceptions, but it was generally from this class of girls that our boys married. When the time came for returning home, faced with the prospect of finding a job and of giving their wives even an elementary standard of living, some lingered on, but it was then virtually impossible for an Indian to get more than a lowly job in England. The best off were the doctors who could always set up their own practice, usually in a poor locality, and do well. There was great belief in the healing powers of a dark man, which in reality was just their basically sympathetic nature and willingness to take trouble.

Those who returned home with English wives ran into many problems. In the search for a job they had to stay with the parents, who were often simple, unwesternized people. Their habits, food and way of living were so different that the unsophisticated girl found the going hard. When he got a job it was at a salary inadequate to lead an English way of life. Oddly enough, you could live as cheaply as you liked as an Indian, but to live like the poorest Englishman cost a great deal more. Even to maintain the working class English standard of two pounds a week cost many times more in India. But at least when he got a job the girl had her home and independence and the certain comfort of cheap servants and when her husband's income went up she could live in relative ease, though by then another set of problems bothered her –

the social ones. She had little or no social life: the Indians she found unfamiliar, and her own kind cut her dead. Sometimes the marriages failed at an early stage and the girl was glad to return home but if it endured the early shocks she was usually happy enough in a cut-off way, showing much courage and grit. Her home was a little England, the children got English names even though they were not christened, and her intimate friends were other English girls like her. This was the familiar pattern of such marriages, and I found it difficult to convey it to Gärd. The problems were all so small in themselves that I would have appeared to be evading the main issue. I think I misjudged her quite unique adaptability. A factor that deterred me—more than the traditional attitude of the European community to such marriages—was the likelihood, not to be ruled out, of the spread of Hitler and his ideals. The irony of it was that a union between one from his favourite Aryans and a true Aryan would be taboo in his race theory.

As the news from Europe became still gloomier and war seemed only a matter of time, I decided to go ahead. My elder brother had visited me in Bombay and I had casually sounded him. With his usual generosity he promised to speak for me at home. I now wrote to the chief, who I felt should know, just in case any views or feelings stood in the way. He could be lukewarm and point to difficulties. It was also painful to write to him because not so long before I had written at his wife's death. He replied promptly with an encouraging letter. Later, when I reached Lahore, my parents took everything for granted. My mother would sometimes come into my room, sit on my bed and ask me little questions about Gärd.

CHAPTER SEVEN

GÄRD, AT THE other end, spent the year and a half of waiting teaching in her old school, on terms of uneasy equality with old masters she had been wont to curtsy to. In the summer of 1938 she went on holiday to Germany, and returned home wondering if the war would catch up with her. School had hardly settled down to its term, and it was September. That fateful month would always in her memory be linked with the awesomeness of a blood-red Aurora Borealis, on a latitude where the northern lights are hardly ever seen. In Visby people ran out of their houses to stare at the wondrous sky covered with red shafts of light, and said the red aurora was a sign of war. It was an omen no one doubted.

When the Munich crisis was over and church bells all over Sweden rang in thanksgiving for peace, no one felt more deeply thankful than Gärd. The dearly-bought peace might be only a postponement of war, but it would give her time to join me in India. The longest separation we had ever had had been hard for both of us, but in those September days we felt our own fate hung in the balance with the wider destinies. Our letters crossed each other on the way. She wrote that she was afraid of waiting any longer. I wrote 'Come as soon as you can.'

She gave notice for the end of the term. Autumn darkened into winter and the school closed for Christmas. Gärd sent in notice of her engagement to the press, bought herself a plain gold ring, Swedish fashion, and went up to Stockholm to settle her visa for India and book her passage. Getting the visa at the British consulate proved no mere formality as she had thought. Asked why she wanted to go to India, she said 'to get married there' and, requested for proof, she picked up the morning paper from the desk in front of her and pointed to the engagement column. The man's face fell. 'But it is an Indian! You cannot get a visa without permission from the Government of India'. He explained that a visa could only be granted after the authorities in India had satisfied themselves that the man concerned earned enough to support a European wife. It sounded strange to her that a marriage anywhere could be the subject of such a test, and would the British authorities in India view it unprejudiced? She worried how high the income limit might be fixed in order to exclude most cases. So, in spite of the promise of a reply at the earliest by cable, she felt thoroughly miserable and unable to enjoy her last Swedish Christmas, wondering what she would possibly do if the visa was refused, and to whom one could appeal.

She bitterly regretted that we had not got married before I left Sweden. This was something I had been against, though I had not been very clear about it. In the face of so much uncertainty back in India, determination alone was not enough, and I had left her with a future painted in doubtful colours to protect her from the shock of a possible non-fulfilment. Now when fulfilment seemed near came the maddening frustration of a bureaucratic barrier suddenly thrown up which might not be removed quickly enough before the flames of war leapt. She had no eyes for the loveliness of Stockholm deep in snow and was glad to get back to Visby where she was called back to school to substitute for somebody who was ill. This made the days pass until one morning the cable arrived. The visa was through. I had been out of Bombay on tour, and during my absence a European police sergeant had arrived at the office and asked to see the chief about the enquiry from the British Legation in Stockholm. It was fortunate that I had already asked him for permission, and though my salary was meagre by their own standards he blandly told the sergeant that I would be able to support a wife.

With this hurdle cleared Gärd booked her passage by P. & O. from Marseilles. In Sweden it is the custom for a bride-to-be to go to church on the three consecutive Sundays when the banns are read from the pulpit, and afterwards be at home to her friends who then present her with the wedding gifts. I had filled in a form declaring myself willing to marry her, but for the banns it appeared that she would also have to produce my non-existent birth certificate. So she had to forego the banns, but not the party. Her mother and the maid got busy baking all the traditional cakes and on her last Sunday at home there was a grand coffee table and another table for exhibiting the presents. For the last time she saw the old house filled with a gay crowd, everybody asking her when did she think she would come home to visit.

Gärd used to say that being bred on an island makes you prepared to go far abroad, for all through childhood and growing up you have been possessed by the feeling of being hemmed in by the sea, and a longing to get away. In the long warm summer the island was open to the world; it was a holiday resort where people from many countries came and huge steamers anchored—she once saw off Visby the black hull of the *Viceroy of India*. The children found it great fun to test their schoolbook English and German on the tourists. When the evenings again got dark the visitors left, the music in the garden cafés stopped, the promenades along the shore lay deserted and the only sound left was the murmur of the waves. Life was once again enclosed inside the city wall. The only link with the outside world was the daily steamer to the 'mainland'.

At last came the night she was leaving Visby for good, wondering if she would ever again see the towers of the city wall, the ruined churches, the red-tiled roofs of the mediaeval Hanseatic merchant houses, and the home where she was born. The Swedes believed at the time that in the coming war Germany and Russia would fight for the strategic possession of the island of Gotland, and feared the destruction of the city. This did not come to pass and she was to see the city again, but never her home and never again her mother. Mamma was very brave; she had never cried at the thought of her only daughter going so far away, and even at the quayside she kept her tears back, though as far as she was concerned Gärd was going to another world.

The friends who saw her off had filled her cabin with flowers. For a newly-wed daughter of the city, the steamship company would have put up coloured lights between the masts, but as it was she missed both that and the fireworks from the jetty. The bell rang the first warning, starting the long farewells of a parting by sea. The third bell went and she stood alone on the deck, the few other passengers having already retired. She saw well-known faces growing dimmer until the steamer rapidly swung round the pier. As winter darkness hid the coastline, it also seemed to engulf all that had been part of herself.

On the train journey through Sweden she stopped here and there to say goodbye. It was the most desolate of seasons, bare winter with frozen grey fields. She visited her old uncle just in time for his eightieth birthday, and when he drove her himself to the station in the dark of an early morning, ten miles through heavy slush, she knew it was unlikely she would ever meet him again. Similarly all through her journey across Europe, with the large shadow looming, the thought was always in her mind, 'Shall I ever see it the same?'

In the train to Marseilles from Malmö there were two men in her compartment. One, a retired banker, was a true globe-trotter who entertained the others with yarns about his travels till he dropped out at Hamburg. He had never been to India, because, he said, it was the most expensive country in the world for a tourist. The other traveller was a young violinist from the Stockholm Symphony Orchestra on his way to Paris on a stipend. With a couple of hours to wait at Hamburg they went out together to have supper. He was adamant that with his musician's reverence for the Jewish race he would not go into any place which bore the legend, 'Jews not wanted'. As Gärd knew before, all eating places had the same sorry tale, and eventually hunger drove them into a café where a band of faded blondes caused him acute agony.

Early next morning they got off the train at Cologne where she was spending a day. She suggested to the violinist that before his train left for Paris she might show him another Germany to take away the taste of last night. They stood in front of the cathedral and saw its immense structure gradually revealing itself in the dawn. Then they walked through the Altstadt, the old Gothic city where one of the winding alleys still bore the name Judengasse, till she had to tear him away from the sculptural abandon of the council house and rush him back to the station. In the evening she went with a German friend to the opera which had still been open to all the previous summer but now also bore the detestable legend. The young German said, 'I am sorry you should have to see this. The opera was the last place of freedom in Cologne.'

Her last glimpse of Europe was a quayside at Marseilles on a grey drizzling morning, with a grey-looking, huddled sort of crowd from which odd words in German could be heard, waiting dejectedly to be allowed over the gangway to the steamer next to hers, destination Australia. Like her, they were escaping at perhaps the eleventh hour — they to a country where they hoped to be able to live in dignity; she to a country of her choice with very vague ideas what the future would be like, but sure she would never regret.

There were very few passengers for India in the first class—married couples, some with daughters; a few single men — all of them English. In the second class there were plenty of Indian students and some European girls, perhaps travelling for the same purpose. One evening the second class passengers were invited to a dance in the first class lounge, and some turned up but very soon left. For the next invitation nobody came; the atmosphere was too chilling. The first class passengers had probably found out about Gärd by discreetly asking her table companion and decided to ignore her. It was a peculiar situation to find herself in. It is one thing to be alone in a big crowd, and it can be amusing to wander about all on your own in a foreign city. But to be absolutely alone in a small crowd, in a confined space, day after day, she found trying. She spent all her evenings in the cabin and read most that was readable in the ship's library.

Of course she was not unprepared for such a situation. She knew

England well in a way, having spent two years there, if she added up all her visits to me. But most of her contacts had belonged to the student world, a world which in most countries is outside the pale of ordinary society, detached from the individual's social background; nevertheless she had heard and read of a different England east of Suez. In Sweden of course racial considerations did not exist. Marrying an Indian was more adventurous, and certainly more interesting than marrying a German or an Englishman. No one she knew had ever been to India and most Swedish people had only vague ideas about it. Indians and Europeans originally came of the same stock; there was Tagore who had got the Nobel Prize; and Gandhi: that was the sum total of their knowledge of India. She used to tell me she was often relieved that my lack of fluency in Swedish saved me from revealing my ignorance of Indian philosophy. The fact that she was marrying a Hindu and that our children would be Hindus did not seem to upset even the truly religious-minded old people, but they would certainly have pitied her if she had had to become a Catholic — a religious hangover! It was very reassuring that her father-in-law to-be was something as modern as an engineer and I with a company whose products were well known in Sweden.

When I had moved to my flat I had sent Gärd some snaps of the house, the garden, and even my secondhand two-seater Ford. These pictures, she told me, were a great blessing, as they saved her answering so many questions. A grand-aunt, who was always something of a joke in the family, had exclaimed, 'I am so glad, my dear, that you live in a house. I read somewhere that all Indians live in mud huts!' What she had heard from me to the adverse she had never confided to anyone, or the misgivings she had felt about our future.

Whiling away time on the P. & O. *Strathmore*, she was cynically amused to imagine what her kind friends would have thought if they could have seen her in her splendid isolation. The ship's library had its limitations, and Gärd thought the ten days between Port Said and Bombay were the longest she had ever known. It was a great relief to see at last the coast of India rising out of the sea.

CHAPTER EIGHT

THE RUMBLES OF war came nearer, and they now came from both sides, while Gärd and I settled into the life for which we had been waiting for seven long years. The Germans had declared the Japanese 'not non-Aryans', and there appeared a growing understanding between the true and the honorary Aryans, for whom India seemed a likely meeting place. There were many in India who, despite his derogatory reference to us in *Mein Kampf* as people only fit to be ruled, dreamt of Hitler as a saviour. India and Indians had always been popular in Germany. Gärd had seen for herself how Indian students were treated and fussed over there. It did not surprise her that people in India knew little of what Nazism really stood for, when she had seen how in democratic Europe people could still disbelieve its excesses and look upon Germany as a bulwark against Communism. Hitler's pact with Russia changed this, but in India thinking was confused; our own struggle blinded us to the bigger issues, and very few clearly understood that Britain's defeat might mean the defeat of all freedom.

We argued something like this. It would be good to see the Germans and the Japanese teach the British and the other colonial powers a lesson; we would rub our hands with glee, and what came afterwards could take care of itself. It would not be our war, and we did not possess the freedom that in Europe Hitler was out to destroy. The expression, used by the British, of the choice between the known and the unknown devil made no impression. We felt instead that the unknown might hold in it a chance for the better. Besides, among all Europeans, had not the Germans come closest to understanding India? It was they who had discovered the kinship of languages and racial relationship, and we shared the emblem of the sun wheel, the swastika.

Gärd well understood our frustrations, in fact straight from Sweden she felt perhaps even more strongly the indignity of being a second class citizen in one's own country. But the idea that Nazi Germany might help us to freedom and dignity seemed to her utterly fantastic. She found equally baffling the assumed complacency of the British, who joked about Hitler being welcome to India so long as the Germans left the Breach Candy swimming pool in Bombay alone. At that time Germans, both Jews and non-Jews, were much in evidence at this treasured European preserve. The foremost topic was prohibition, just introduced by the first shortlived Congress Government, with absolution to anyone born in Europe.

When I returned home, fresh from an English university, full of the dangers to democracy and intellectual freedom, I had tried to interest an occasional Englishman I met in the subject of Nazism and Fascism. It was always received with a cold shrug, because, I think, of an uncomfortable feeling that this was not the sort of subject to discuss with an Indian. There was the stiff upper lip 'Oh we shall manage somehow,' and sometimes was added the infuriating patronage 'You Indians don't have to worry, it will be our headache. It might of course teach these Congresswallas something, but I don't suppose you agree with that crowd either. Take prohibition; you drink like one of us. Mind you, I am not against giving them power, for they have to learn; I would rather that chaps like you took it. Anyway, you don't have to bother your head about Hitler and all that, you had better think of your own problems; I mean these white topiwallas.'

One or two such conversations cooled my ardour, but I found talking to Indians no less trying. 'You are worried about the British losing and a thousand years of darkness descending? It might be a thousand years of efficient rule instead of the decay that has set in where only maharajas, zamindars and a few millowners thrive. We have got used too much to the yoke. Let us not shed tears for Britain, the Mother of Parliaments and all that she stands for; she certainly doesn't stand for any of those things here.' The rancour against the British was deep and few sympathized with them in their attempt to stem the tide.

I think it was the attitude of our leaders that put the issue in this light. The rank and file were ignorant of the implications, but even to leaders like Nehru who felt very strongly and emotionally about the dangers of Nazism, Fascism and Japanese imperialism, India's first task was to clear the British out. They did not want to compromise with one evil in order to defeat a greater evil. The common man had no idea how much greater was that other evil, and his leaders seemed unconcerned. He would have been surprised that to a refugee German Jew in India the life of the conquered seemed rather enviable. But on the whole, while we criticized the British and almost hoped there would be a war, we did not want them altogether to lose it. A close shave, close enough to humiliate them, to weaken them enough to grant India self-government was what we would prefer. So we argued while time ran out.

The outbreak of war came rather tamely. The crisis that kept rising and subsiding for once just went too far and it became impossible to satisfy Hitler's appetite any longer. There was some praise in India when Britain at last took the plunge, particularly as she was so unprepared against an enemy whose sole energy had been bent to this one purpose, and unsupported by France, who was equally unprepared and did not even possess the will to resist. We might have let ourselves be persuaded to support Britain in her ultimate stand against Hitler, had the Viceroy Lord Linlithgow not been such an insensitive person. There were at the time the first elected governments in the provinces and a central assembly of sorts; but more important, there was now a public opinion and strong leadership. Some consultation and show of confidence in our leaders therefore might have carried them along with him. But he made no attempt. Perhaps he was afraid that with the casuistry of the Congress, and the Muslim League always willing to profit by any difference between Congress and Government, he might get bogged down into arguments, clarification, terms and conditions. And sure of the control over resources, with an army whose expansion would present no problem, and backed by the ready pledges of fealty by the princes, landlords and the other honoured ones, he went ahead and committed India to war, and took a chance on the Congress Governments walking out of office. That might even suit him as he could then run the provincial governments with a more single-minded pursuit of the war effort. This is what happened and I don't think the Viceroy or his British services shed any tears over it, but a great opportunity was nevertheless missed.

For the first one year and a half the war had no visible effect on India and work went on as usual, though I was personally affected. Thompson Walker had got the firm in London to agree that I might extend my market research activities to the associate companies in Ceylon, Burma, Thailand and Malaya. This splendid opportunity was however knocked out by the war. In fact, market research in India too was soon to be wound up.

I think it is only now we Indians have begun to take an interest in the countries to the east of India. Earlier, nothing took us there. And yet to east and west, Indian communities have gone to trade and settle: in a big way in East Africa; in smaller knots in Iran, Afghanistan and the Persian Gulf. They practically invaded Ceylon, Burma and Singapore, and settled in groups of varying sizes from Dakar to California, Hawaii and Fiji. But after generations, they still regarded India as their home. Some have returned periodically to build a house, marry off a daughter, or perform some important ritual as a sign of affluence and also of sentiment. In a small town north of Bombay there is a street of vacant mansions belonging to a particular Muslim community whose affluence abroad is reflected in the size of the houses and the freshness of their blue paint. But what we lacked, and are only slowly acquiring is the understanding that comes through visits at a different level, students, tourists, businessmen looking for new venues. Similarly, all these countries know us mainly through the settlers, and that not always favourably.

The effect of this ignorance of each other did not matter as long as we were all dominated by a European power which provided us with blinkers that left only their own country in the field of our vision and maybe a tiny bit of other European countries on the periphery. It became evident later when all of us gained independence that for too long, instead of developing the natural ties of trade and culture with our neighbours, we perforce continued our dependence upon the distant European powers, regardless of whether they needed us.

With market research closing down, Rist put me into the press section of the advertising department, which had now prospered into a full scale agency with account executives, art director, press media and all other ramifications of an agency set-up. The press section dealt with nearly 450 newspapers all over India in thirteen languages, including English. The Indian press comprised then, and still does, an amazing variety of newspapers ranging from the sophisticated English language dailies that came off the rotary machines to those written by hand on waxed paper, whose copies were pulled off stones prepared for each edition and afterwards scrubbed with pumice stone and washed clean for the following day. There were dailies, weeklies, fortnightlies, monthlies, quarterlies, annuals, and some that appeared with intervals determined by the financial position of the proprietor. In the lead were a few British owned dailies from the major towns, followed by one or two Indian owned dailies, also in English, from the provincial capitals. The entire lot of between two and three thousand publications amounted to no more than two million in circulation, and a good three-quarters must have been represented by a handful.

The British dailies mostly originated from the middle of the last century, and many had had distinguished editors who had been bold, and sometimes downright scurrilous in their criticism of Government and personalities, especially the Governor Generals, but by the thirties of this century British editors had become staid and pompous. Even in England poking fun and lampooning had gone out of fashion, but instead of developing a lively reportage and variety of interests our

English papers had become dull, subservient supporters of the government reporting their news like the movements of royalty. They piously praised anyone who supported the government and preached homilies to Congress.

The Indian papers were poorly financed, but what they lacked in resources they made up in verve. All nationalist, they attacked the government on principle. Its every motive was suspect and all its actions injurious to the country's interests. The reporting was entirely political, and, as in the English language press, things that had purely human interest were firmly eschewed. Between the two there was little to choose for readability; they kept you informed of basic news at home and abroad, their one grace being a complete lack of interest in crime and scandal. For nearly two years I had not subscribed to a newspaper and only occasionally glanced at the headlines, and now they suddenly became my job.

The new work consisted in acquainting myself with the several hundred newspapers that approached us for advertising, evaluating them by studying their circulation claims. As they all needed advertising and we were the biggest advertisers in the country, all but the British papers converged on us for support, and I spent endless hours interviewing their representatives, usually the proprietors. This was the most interesting part of all. I met men from every corner of India, personalities as diverse as one could imagine, all on the same errand but each using a different technique. It took most of them some time to accept me as they had been used to dealing with Englishmen and were not sure of this new devolution of responsibility. The British newspapers' advertising managers were sure of their position and went straight to Rist, nodding to me in passing; the leading Indian papers were also fairly certain of receiving advertising and were content with an annual visit to Mr. Rist. The less important ones who came to see me optimistically gave inflated circulation figures, fully expecting a radical cut. The few straight ones usually asked for incommensurately high rates. The most tiresome were the unctuous lot who always worked for a cause. They were struggling to help the country or the society at a personal sacrifice and therefore expected, nay demanded our support, especially now that there was an Indian press media manager. A few of them were indeed genuinely selfless, and then they were modest. The aggressive lot who used their paper for political influence considered that we as a foreign firm who had no right to be in the country owed them a living. They insisted that I should support their paper by advertising all the firm's products, in large spaces and with the greatest of frequency, otherwise how were they going to serve the nation, boycott British goods and buy only swadeshi.

I learned from Rist not to take them too seriously and keep our advertising free from political bias. A paper could be as anti-British as it liked as long as it had an honest circulation. This consideration many considered unfair, since our insistence on value deprived them of support for the cause. They used to harangue me about my duty to the country when I suggested that their circulation claims were dubious. At times they almost convinced me; only I was never certain whether they, any more than I, were serving the cause or just themselves. It was my first introduction to the self-seekers who had jumped on to the band-wagon, which some of them would be steering some years hence, when they would be in a position to command instead of ask.

But the type I dreaded most was the dynamic woman social worker of Bombay. Some came quietly for help in the shape of advertising space in an annual report or brochure for a little institution among the slums of Bombay. They were interesting to talk to, modest and much moved by the misery they were trying to relieve. The ones I was genuinely afraid of, however, were the high-powered socialites who never touched a cause unless it was first blessed by Government House, where at a tea meeting called by the Governor's lady they would organize a grand fête on its gracious lawns sloping down to the sea, or an expensive dinner-dance at the Taj Mahal Hotel. With thunderous energy these women would fan out through the business houses for advertisements. A large Parsi lady, the doyen of the corps of fund raisers, one day swept into our office with protesting sepoys following her. She had the looks and ways of a dowager duchess, and when one of the sepoys pointed to me, she brushed me aside. She wanted to see someone senior, obviously a European, and before I could stop her she stormed into Rist's room. In two minutes she was out triumphantly waving a printed form and demanding that I fill it in and send it with an advertisement block to her office the same morning. She was in a class by herself, and dominated the Bombay social charities scene for a quarter of a century. Many needy institutions owe a debt to her tireless energy.

Even to the many genuine newspaper managers it was difficult to convey that we bought advertising space like a commodity or service; that there had to be some criteria of value. The thought that they might run their publications on sound business lines, with proper investment and decent profitability, and thus offer more value to their readers, seemed irrelevant. It must always be service, however poor and inadequate. The suggestion that they might give more value to the readers seemed to make the adverse impression that I was suggesting to make the service mercenary; an idea that seems to run right through our thinking. Anything that produces a profit is bad, even though it might widen the scope of service; poverty and inefficiency are virtues because they are untainted by profit. I did not realize then that we were developing a way of thinking that was to recoil upon us later.

There was a lighter side to press work. I had to scan through all specimen copies that came to our office, and my favourites were the Hindi and Urdu magazines of the north for their vivid articles and advertisements. The stories were usually sexy, more so the pictures, but it was the medicinal advertisements that I particularly enjoyed, because they are untainted by profit. I did not realize then that we preposterous that it took your breath away, couched in a language so intimately reassuring that it made you feel almost cured as you read. They poured scorn over modern science, because western medicine could only cure one thing at a time, while they could with one and the same medicine induce diametrically opposite results. As for the mysteries of sex and birth their knowledge was boundless. There was for instance a medicine that claimed to act both as contraceptive and preventive provided you followed some simple instructions. So long as the wife took a daily tablet 'you can enjoy vigour that will leave your partner amazed, and all this without any fear of nature intervening.' But one day you decide to have a child. From then, for fourteen days, you leave the tablets and the lady alone. 'On the fourteenth day, she takes a tablet, you both bathe and anoint yourselves with emollient perfumed oils, and after following suitable instructions, exactly nine months from the day she will bear a child with the luminous face of a full moon. The whole thing is guaranteed and in the unlikely event of failure you can ask for your money back.' There were the hair oils that sharpened your memory, gave you good sleep, cooled the brain and generally toned up the system, including an aphrodisiac effect. The whole medicinal lore seemed to centre around sex, skin diseases and stomach ailments.

CHAPTER NINE

RIST CALLED ME in one afternoon and asked if Gärd and I would attend their son Tony's christening at the English church on Malabar Hill, and after the ceremony join them at a party at their new flat. It was to be both a christening and a housewarming. I thanked him with the social formula I had heard the British use: 'May I check with my wife and let you know?' Later, in a busier, more senior life, it made sense, and if on occasions I ignored it I often found myself in trouble. But now our evenings were usually free except over the weekends when friends dropped in, often uninvited.

Driving home that evening I felt uneasy. I knew I had really used the formula to gain time. I had found it difficult to say yes, as I would have liked to do, or no, as I did not want to. Had Rist invited me in Manchester I would have accepted with enthusiasm; in Bombay I hesitated and felt unhappy doing so. I had been to Rist's home once before, the evening before Thompson Walker sailed for England. I had accompanied him to Bombay to see him off, and we were going to spend the last evening together musing over our journeys. Now that the time for leaving had come he was looking forward to it less than he had expected. When Rist asked him to dinner in my presence Tom looked unhappy, and plainly asked if I could be invited too. Rist readily said, 'Yes, of course.' It just had not occurred to him to ask me.

Equally genuine though Rist's invitation was this time, to me it was not within the normal dimensions of his social world. In the two years that I had worked with him, in a society both his and mine, in which custom threw homes open to friends, friends' friends and strangers alike, Rist had not asked me home, nor had I asked him. We invited freely our Indian colleagues, most of them educated in England, but we had not thought of asking any of the English in the office. Even between Indians who had been abroad and were used to their ways, and were in fact leading an increasingly westernised life, and English who had lived in India a lifetime, there were rarely social contacts of any significant kind; only an occasional formal party, very occasional and very formal.

My introduction into mixed society at the only mixed club of Bombay, the Willingdon, founded by the well-meaning aristocrat of that name to bring Indians and English of the right kind together, was indeed an experience. Roshan had taken me to see the club and

offered to put me up for membership. You walked down its terraced
lawns through two worlds, each on its own side, one affluent, the other
holding the power. Occasionally someone crossed over for a brief
chat, but you rarely saw mixed tables. I found that as a young manager,
unknown and without family influence, I would be entirely lost.
Roshan was popularly sought as a partner on the tennis courts, but I
had no assets of any kind to qualify me for a place in either society, so I
instead joined a purely Indian club.

In this strange social equation I found Rist's invitation uncomfortable. After Gärd had joined me I had made some attempts at
throwing bridges. I took the initiative, thinking that it needed one
side to break the ice, and invited the managing director to dinner;
later his deputy, the man who had engaged me, and some others.
The parties were unsuccessful for an obvious reason, with no one to
blame. The subjects uppermost in our minds and theirs at that time
ranged us on opposite sides, and the relationship between the ruler and
the ruled precluded free discussion, anything more than a passing
reference. War to them was the war in Europe; they felt embarrassed
discussing it with us because they knew we saw it in our own light, and
so they avoided the topic altogether. To us politics, the formation and
resignation of the first Congress governments in the states, was an
unavoidable subject of conversation; but by them it was strictly avoided.
There was left only the weather, which in Bombay hardly changed for
eight months of the year. Social small talk at which the English ex-
celled was also out for lack of common familiar topics, and in impersonal subjects like art, literature and philosophy few of them were
interested. We thus ploughed politely through these evenings, groping
for conversation and even avoiding the only subject of common
interest, shop, for I was far too junior to venture on an intelligent
discussion at their level.

If conversation was one problem, food was another. We would
naturally have served Indian food of a festive kind, but their casual
comment had made it clear that this was part of a self-imposed social
taboo. The food of the country, like dress and customs, sensible
products of climate and environment, they firmly eschewed. Light
woollen suits, collar and tie, shirts tucked inside the trousers, heavy
shoes and woollen socks throughout the year for the men; though
their women, more practical had at least taken to bare legs and airy
sandals. On food they were firm: 'We do enjoy our curry and rice
lunch on Sundays when one can sleep it off afterwards. Our Goan
cook of course does not make it quite your way, but we like it, though

we wouldn't care for it more often.' Under such clearly expressed preferences arranging a menu was not easy, so we compromised on Swedish meals. The evenings were sufficiently unsuccessful to prevent repetition, and we were never asked back. This lack of response soon stifled my good intentions, but left me a little sad.

Interestingly enough there was freer mixing at the pure level of duty. Most English managers were at one time or another invited home by our senior agents and in course of time the invitations were returned with equal ceremony. To their mediaeval houses in the narrow lanes of Lahore and Amritsar, the simple agents invited the sahib and his wife with less self-consciousness and more poise than did the westernized type, and the sahibs also went there with greater ease. It was an equation that worked rather well.

Old Lala Ramchand, our agent for twenty-five years, played host with a gusto that I envied. He invited us and them with equally admirable unconcern though in my particular case, as I was a Punjabi, there was an intimacy of language, custom and convention that brought me closer, particularly to the women who spoke no English. The English were charmed and amused, and the parties ended hilariously with Lala Ramchand and the sahib drinking scotch in large measures while the wives in sign language or broken Hindi talked of children, clothes and their people back home. Both sides began with a formality bordering on the ludicrous; yet less of a strain than that of our party.

The special room upstairs, where Lalaji usually retreated, was refurnished with the upright wooden chairs from the shop, placed in a circle with a table in the middle. Cushions and tablecloths that the new generation of school-going girls had embroidered in designs of English cottages and gardens with 'Welcome' chased diagonally across, were brought for decor together with the permanent bouquets of paper flowers. Indian sweetmeats flavoured with synthetic essences, pungent savouries followed each other; bubbling red and green drinks with flavours of rose, banana and lemon were kept poured in glasses to prevent a break in the continuity of service; tea boiled with milk, sugar and spices was served in the flowered Japanese tea set, brought out of the glass-windowed cupboard for the occasion. There was a welcome frankness in all this; no self-effacing concession to the guests' tastes, but robust hospitality like at the tentative visit of a future son-in-law. It was pressed with cheerful unconcern for the gastronomic capabilities of the unprotesting sahib, who politely insisted that he loved all Indian food and drink in any quantity, with secret visions of lifelong dysentery. The sahib's wife was less bothered because she was soon drawn into a circle of women and could always excuse herself from eating on some mysterious grounds.

Eventually Lalaji brought out the bottle of scotch bought specially for the visit. Each past occasion had been a further education in how to keep the guest company in order to make him drink more, till he had himself acquired a taste for it, growing into a habit, and eventually quite a capacity that in my young days I learned to respect. The sahib turned with relish to the scotch after the cups of tea laced with fizz, and the evening soon lost its restraints and barriers till they parted company having well cemented the business relationship. The mem-sahib, who by now had exhausted all available topics of conversation, was glad to go home to her own gimlet or scotch, which Indian custom forbade her to accept at Lalaji's house.

Lala Ramchand felt equally free when he and his family visited Bombay and were invited back. He arrived accompanied by his wife, his married and unmarried daughters, sons, sons-in-law and daughters-in-law, and a few nephews who had not seen Bombay, encouraging them all to feel at home in the unfamiliar atmosphere of a Bombay flat where they sank down in low chairs with their feet out of shoes resting uncomfortably on the floor; with servants formally dressed, speaking a language of formal deference. Lalaji urged his family to try the tasteless sandwiches and weak tea. Often the hostess had specially provided Indian sweets, but Lalaji wanted his family to taste all the English delicacies, till his turn came for the scotch. After that it was as much of a job to bring the evening to a close in Bombay as it was in Amritsar. Before leaving, Lalaji would walk up to the refrigerator and open it to display to his family the type of food and drinks their hosts consumed.

The ritual of these visits was always carefully explained to a newly arrived European couple before they set out on their first trip. It gave them something to talk to their friends and to write to their parents about. But where Lala Ramchand succeeded with simple ease we made a complex failure, missing the essential point that the English were trying to avoid relationships in which they felt out of their depth. At work they felt at ease with us because they were sure of themselves. They had much to teach, little to learn, less to fear—at least not yet. At leisure they wanted to be by themselves, to take it their own way, with their own kind, with conversation familiar and of their own choosing, without the strain of topics unfamiliar or unwelcome, or of trying to impress and being impressed.

When I conveyed Rist's invitation to Gärd she was pleased. She was curious to go inside an English church, to watch a christening, to meet people, to attend a real party with cocktails and supper and see how it differed from Swedish celebrations with their mixture of strict formality to begin with and increasing gaiety as the evening went on. What should she wear for the occasion? I went back next morning and thanked Rist and told him we would be happy to come.

As the day drew near I became increasingly apprehensive. It was my first experience of attending a large English party in India starting in the unfamiliar precincts of a church. I even asked Rist quite earnestly if it mattered if Gärd wore a sari in church. Rist looked puzzled and said he did not see anything untoward in that. On the day I contrived to arrive late, and we tiptoed into the church and took seats at the back. While the guests surrounded the parents and the baby to felicitate, I led a protesting Gärd away and drove to the club on some pretext of making an urgent telephone call, and thus managed to slip in late and unnoticed as the party was in full swing. Poor Gärd was utterly nonplussed by my behaviour; but if she understood my confusion she never acknowledged it nor conveyed any disapproval. There were areas of my behaviour we left unrecognized and unexplored. She knew that the barest recognition would hurt me; so she looked away, with a naturalness that I can now only admire.

The disaster came sure and complete and in a manner I least expected. As the party progressed I began to move around, feeling freer with each drink. At the level of light conversation about the changing Bombay, its growing traffic now that there were well over seven thousand cars on the roads, its emerging skyline from the sea, the gradual change in its weather as evidenced by the lateness of the monsoon each year, its superiority over Calcutta, I began to feel relaxed. My feeling knowledge of England's North Country and people, rather purer accent and a choice of word and phrase that came from years of a well cultivated university life of leisure rather than work, brought out a side of me that had lain fallow for years. Its resurgence pleased me too, for having acquired and moulded it over eight years of an impressionable youth, I think I treasured it almost as much as my Punjabiness; I do believe in some ways more.

The easy fluency of the evening was a salve to my feelings. Rist looked genuinely pleased, and his Australian wife happier still, for their experiment seemed to be working well. I think Rist was always inwardly proud of his pioneering choice, but this evening I was to let them both down, though quite heroically and humourously.

There were present at the party an Australian couple, James and Sally, both artists and highly temperamental, with a full measure of characteristic Australian warmth. They had lived in Paris and in London for some years and acquired a new way of life, a kind of grafting of Chelsea and Montmartre on Sydney. When an advertising agency offered him an assignment in Bombay they took it with an innocent alacrity they were to rue bitterly, for it altered their whole life and virtually ruined it. Strangely, as it ruined theirs, it helped to shape mine.

On the day of their arrival, according to custom, their English boss threw a party to introduce them to the colleagues and their wives. Sally warmed to this thoughtful welcome and responded with a spontaneity which failed to judge the underlying staidness. The lavish mixture of scotch and pink gins before dinner, and brandy and cold beer afterwards made her feel happy with Bombay and these friendly, though rather formal people. She wanted to draw them into her warm informality and give the group a cheerful togetherness. She clapped her hands and in her rolling accent exhorted everyone to relax. Then she performed cartwheels, giving each turn her favourite variation of a dextrous pause as her legs rose vertically above her head and her blue skirt fell back like a newly opened morning glory. But instead of the whoops of delight into which the parties in London and Paris used to break here was silence, broken by 'Well, Sir, a lovely party, we must be getting along,' and before she had collected herself she stood and faced her hosts alone in an empty room – the guests had gone, the party was over!

The news soon spread, and when the welcoming round of invitation was over and there was no overlap, they realized their isolation. Genuinely interested in the country and with no inherited restraints, they turned to the Indians who were glad to accept them because though generically European they were so different and uninhibited. Some mutual friends brought them over. We found them very likeable, and before I realized it they were in and out of our house like Indian relations; but I found Sally edgy. She was sufficiently at ease with us, but the hurt of the rejection by her own people would come out in forms that concerned me. I did the wrong thing; I tried to console her.

We ran straight into James and Sally at the party, and feeling nervous myself to begin with I stayed on with them for a while. Later, as I moved about and felt increasingly at home, Sally kept fortifying herself with drinks and felt progressively worse. Once or twice she made an attempt to come close to me for support and comfort, but I was now too busy shedding my own diffidence to be sensitive to her problem. Towards nine o'clock, as the party was beginning to thin, I noticed Sally sticking close to the bar, and walked up to her. Characteristically, instead of conveying understanding, I made some facetious remark about her cartwheels. All Sally's pent up feelings rose to anger, and the anger was all directed at me and Gärd. I have never been any good at coping with women who are upset; I somehow always make them feel worse, and often push them over the edge. Sally picked up a drink, poured it down in one long gulp, and Rist's wife acted quickly. Gärd and I, James and Sally were the next moment being shown out with a we-do-understand-you-have-to-go-but-so-glad-you-came! They soon left India.

CHAPTER TEN

IN 1940 THE war came nearer, both from the west and the east, and at one stage threatened to enter India. At the darkest hour our leaders decided on a complete breakaway and launched the 'Quit India' movement which burnt our boats behind us, and also the bridges in front. From then non-cooperation turned to active obstruction which gave the Government no quarter and left our class with divided opinions. Those working against the regime had now the satisfaction of action; those working for it felt there was duty of another kind which in the long run would bring its own reward and satisfaction; and those like me were left just nowhere.

Earlier, in 1940, when the debacle in Europe began, I had gone on a long tour and sent Gärd to my brother in north Bihar. On my return there was a letter from her to say that she believed she was expecting a baby, and would I come and join her for a few days. She had lost one the year before and was feeling unsure. I asked Rist for a week's leave and travelled up. On the way I felt a growing determination to join up. With a secure job in an expanding firm, where my chances were getting brighter as the war progressed and took away the young Englishmen one by one, my family would consider my volunteering meaningless. Of those in India who joined the army I wondered how many did so out of a feeling of duty, and duty to whom? It did not seem to make sense to anyone that an Indian might join the British Army out of conviction. Even the British nationals usually waited till they were called up because they felt they were doing an equally important job of work holding fort in India. I therefore did not think it was worth sharing my thinking with anyone on either side, and in her present state not even with Gärd.

On the long journey back I brooded over the problem, trying to isolate my desire to join from the unsympathetic influences of the environment. Had I stayed on in Manchester there would have been no second thought; I would have joined instead of returning home, as over there I would have felt the purity of my conviction, uninfluenced by the deterring factors of what was happening in India. During the three days in the train, through the rainwashed land, I thought of Gärd, her coming baby; the war that so far had only distantly rumbled in Western Europe, the growing shadows of the two hands, rising one over the eastern horizon and the other from the west, closing in a vice-like grip over India's throat. Yet thousands were being herded into jails, many of whom would have wanted to fight the war, had they been able to fight their own way, with the pride of decision theirs.

On reaching the office I asked to see the managing director. He was a little puzzled at the request and asked if I had spoken to Rist. I said, no, this was about a personal matter. I explained to him how I felt about the war; how I had felt about it ever since the war seemed inevitable. In England there had been the one side to it, but in India there were two. My problem had been to reduce what I saw in clear terms in England back to its simple one-sidedness in India, and I believed I had managed it. I had decided to leave the firm and join up. If they gave me a lien on the job I would be glad to return, but I would not insist on it. Having at last spelled out my decision, I looked closely at his face for a reaction. He laughed and said 'Good God, I don't think the war has reached the stage that it needs your joining. I think you are doing well enough in your job and we will take care of the fight.' I agreed and left the room.

In the 'Quit India' movement, two years later, I found myself uncertain and isolated again. Late one evening Chitre rang up. He was a Maharashtrian barrister, married to an English girl who had got to know Gärd. We lived not far from each other, and as petrol rationing became severer we were thrown into company in our suburb, and we met often. He was interesting till he reached the first third of a bottle, from when on he became engrossed solely in finishing the rest. She was a pleasant Cockney, full of fun and friendliness, and a wonderful cook of Indian food, which she taught me in her kitchen on Saturday evenings while Chitre drank and Gärd played with their children.

Chitre wanted me to come right over because an old friend had dropped in for the night and wanted to see me before he left early next morning. It sounded very mysterious, more so when I walked into his house which on a hot October night was all closed. Chitre opened the door slightly before he let me in, and under the dim light of a shaded bulb I saw two half finished drinks. After all precautions were observed he brought out of the bedroom a sheepish looking Purshottam Trikumdas with a beard that looked as if he had just put it on. Purshottam explained that after the first outburst of violence, when he had organized sabotage in the Nasik-Poona area, he had gone underground. A close friend of ours was in charge of an important sector of power communications in the region, and Purshottam had taken a wrecking party one night to disrupt them. The police had got wind of it, and in a monsoon storm on the Western Ghats had opened fire on them. He himself had escaped and turned up at our friend's house, and was now lying under cover to take stock of the situation.

All the Congress leaders and most of the militant socialists had been caught by the police and put in prison. The communists, who could have provided some organized resistance, did not see eye to eye with the Congress. They saw the war, from the time Hitler attacked Russia, in a different light, and considered the extermination of Germany a first priority, even if it meant cooperating with the British in India; and there was some uneasy cooperation between the two, which in fairness could hardly be held against either and which both preferred to forget later.

We talked till late at night, and before leaving I asked Purshottam if the struggle needed someone like me. He looked at me kindly and said 'No. You can get up and go to jail tomorrow as a protest, but I don't think that would be any particular contribution now, if you have not been in the movement so far. No, stay where you are, we may need all kinds when we are free.' I had heard the same answer before, in an opposite context.

On the promontory, at the foot of the hill where we lived, a lot of military activity began one morning, and we discovered that a transit camp for British soldiers was going to be opened. I was dismayed at the prospect of a thousand idle and transient soldiers in a suburb that offered no amenities to occupy their spare time. At a time when newspapers were full of Indian hostility to the war effort, I wondered what the effect would be upon the simple minds of those young men freshly arrived in India, when they read that people who were officially their allies openly opposed the war that they were so strenuously fighting. But our suburb was mainly Roman Catholic and Parsi. Both these communities had, through religion and culture, an affinity with the British, and the soldiers gradually began to find their way into their homes. It was interesting to watch the interaction between two cultures, of which one was a prototype to the other. Our East Indian Christian homes, rich and poor, had a distinctly Victorian or Edwardian touch. Furniture and pictures, except the religious ones, were very lower middle and working class of Britain two generations ago. But for the Indian features, the grandparents' enlarged portraits could have hung in many an English living room. Patriarchs with starched collars, drooping moustaches, sideburns and hair carefully parted and plastered, pince-nez glasses with chain over the side; stern matrons with puffed up hair, lace collars and gold chains with crosses on their ample fronts. The young soldiers gaped at these familiar but unexpected sights.

The Parsi homes had a similar flavour, but their contact with the rulers since the time of the British arrival at Surat, and their own culture overlaid with Hindu influence, further enriched by their trading contacts with China in the last century, made an interesting mixture. The Victorian fourposter beds and heavy carved rosewood furniture; the portraits of the grandparents, men in Parsi hats and closed collar coats and the women in lace blouses with saris draped over the head; prints of the British royal family, particularly one that showed three generations, Victoria, Edward and George, from three angles as you walked across the room; another happy British touch, the aspidistra on a tiled-top table; these were proud possessions of middle-class Parsi homes. Invited by kind ladies anxious to take care of the brave boys away from home, the soldiers sat stiffly sipping tea brewed with lemongrass. These ladies worked assiduously for the war effort, shoulder to shoulder with their British sisters. Out of their enthusiasm shone a deep sincerity born of thirteen centuries of loyalty to every dynasty in power, whose language, food and way of living they accepted layer upon layer in till it congealed into the most strikingly diverse culture in the country. Though an inbred community of just over a hundred thousand, they showed nevertheless amazing vitality in whatever they took to, arts, science, technology, business, politics or philanthropy. All this was of course not understood by the soldiers, but they were glad of the natural warmth of the welcome, the mere contact with a home, women and children.

Otherwise the soldiers had little to occupy them except the single cinema or the Irani teashops. The highlight was an occasional dance at the local club. Generally well behaved they walked along the sea and up the hill past our house. One day our little daughter Maya returned from her outing carried by a soldier. She had begun to talk to him and they had made friends. Between her questions in Hindi and his answers in English they understood each other, aided by the little Goan girl, Maya's ayah and playmate, who tried to interrupt in broken English. Every evening the man used to wait for Maya on the shore and see her home. He politely said a few words to us, delivered Maya and went away. We hardly knew him. At such an uncomplicated level of contact communication had no problems. Every evening he gave her some sweets from the canteen, which were not available in the shops, though Maya hardly appreciated the difference. They expected nothing from each other, not even understanding in words. One day he came to say goodbye, as his unit was moving on.

Late one Saturday night a Punjabi neighbour and a cousin of his went with me for a short stroll along the shore. As we were walking up the slope two soldiers came down arm in arm, staggering with drink. We were not particularly in their way, though in their state and on the narrow road it was not easy to avoid them altogether. One of them shouted 'Get out of the way you bloody Indians.' I protested that this was not a nice thing to say, which seemed to incense them to more abuse and aimless hitting at us. It was not much of a fight as they were too drunk and we were anxious to avoid trouble, but suddenly one of the soldiers came lurching up to the young cousin with a particularly unsavoury abuse about his Indian origin, and hit him over the eye. The abuse and a warm trickle down his cheek made him lose his head, and he bent down and picked up whatever came into his hand, a small piece of stone, and holding it in the hollow of his hand with fingers stretched out he smashed it on the soldier's forehead. There was a deep roar as stunned and bleeding profusely the soldier slumped on the ground. His friend ran, and he got up and followed him bellowing with pain, while we walked back to the house a few yards away. Windows opened, lights went on and off, heads peered out in the dark, whispers were heard, but soon darkness and silence reigned again.

Silently I walked into my bedroom and lay next to Gärd who woke up and asked me what the shouting was about, but went back to sleep. Soon there were sounds of heavy military boots up and down the slope, and I sat up in bed and put my head stealthily to the window sill, trying to avoid the beams of powerful torches flashing in all directions. There were soldiers all over, swearing, cursing and looking for murderers at the top of their voices. By now Gärd was up, but I pushed her back on the bed and whispered to her to keep quiet. Slowly the voices died, I heard the boots clattering down the stony slope, and all was still again. I wondered if they would return; I wondered if they would run amok and start a rampage. Their officers had separate quarters some distance away from the camp, and I wondered if the guard at the camp gate would hold the men back. But the silence continued and I went to sleep.

Next morning the news spread and gathered the usual momentum of exaggeration. A soldier had been killed last night; two soldiers had been robbed and murdered; some underground 'Quit India' terrorists had attacked the camp and in a skirmish with a patrol late at night they had all been killed; the camp was sealed because their authorities were afraid that the soldiers might wreak their vengeance on the population. It was a Sunday, when normally on a clear day in the monsoon the place was thronged with cars and people, but today no one came, and the deserted shore added to the sense of fear. Several times in the morning groups of soldiers came to search the road and the neighbouring compounds and went away. As the tension mounted, I became worried and wondered what I should do. It might pass off; yet if the soldier's skull had been crushed and he died his thousand idle friends might cut loose, already agitated by the hostile environment where the single repetitive slogan 'Quit India', chalked and painted on walls everywhere, was a constant reminder of their unwantedness. Disciplined as they generally were, even the regular British soldiers had on occasions wrought their ire on a village near a camp because one of their mates had been beaten up for molesting a woman. And these were volunteers who were heartily sick of India and of the war that had taken them further and further away from home, from Europe to Africa, to the Middle East, to India and on to the hell of the Burma jungles. A little defiance of discipline would give an understandable vent to frustration. I decided to walk down to the camp.

I asked the guard if I could see the duty officer. He looked at me curiously because, apart from servants and suppliers, no Indian ever came to the camp. He motioned me to a wooden hut in which I found a freshfaced young lieutenant who looked barely out of school. I introduced myself and explained that I had come to see someone about last night's incident.

'What has that to do with you?'

'I was involved in it.'

'Do you know what you are talking about? This is a serious business.'

'Yes, Lieutenant.'

He pulled out a sheet of paper and began to take down notes. I explained how I was returning home from a walk and met the two men. They were drunk and shouted at me 'Get out of the way, you bloody Indian.' I mildly protested, at which one of them charged at me and used some particularly unpleasant language. I had lost my temper and picked up whatever I could lay my hand on, and with a piece of stone hit him on the forehead.

'You are sure it was not a knife or a sharp instrument?'

'No, Officer, I was carrying nothing.'

'We sent out search parties to look for a weapon, though we did not find any.'

'You wouldn't, as it was only a flat piece of stone.'

'Well, now that I have recorded your statement, you will have to come with me to the officers' mess to meet the major.'

He drove me in his jeep to the sanitorium, and I was taken into a small room before a middle-aged Englishman of simple bearing. He dismissed the lieutenant, looked very grave and told me how perturbed he was at the incident. He had served in India for many years and knew little incidents like this could happen, particularly on a Saturday night, but conditions were different today. There was a war on, and the young officers and men who had not known India before did not understand the problems. They were sensitive about the unfriendliness of the press and the people, and hated being here. He was always glad to see them move on before they became impatient. He talked on about the India he knew and the India today he did not understand at all.

'I shudder to think of what would have happened if this had been a camp of Germans or Japs,' he said. He asked me who I was, where I worked and questioned me further about last night. In the end he seemed convinced that there was no more to this incident than what I had told him; but he must hold a proper enquiry.

'I am glad you came forward. That and the announcement of holding the enquiry will soothe the camp, where feelings, I must say, have run high. This will put the incident in its simple perspective. And would you please leave your address and telephone number. I think we will handle it all ourselves and not bring the civil authorities in.'

I felt relieved and thought that keeping the civil authorities and the police out was a better idea than he realized. In the present conditions when civil authorities were jittery the local authority might almost want to run the whole 'Quit India' movement to earth in me. And if they found that I had met a bearded underground friend, my joining the cause, that I had so long debated, would have been assumed.

Next day as I was coming out of the office I met the chief and mentioned to him about the military enquiry that was going to be held. I thought I would tell him just in case the whole thing took an unexpected turn. His comment was characteristic and amusing.

'I see you are starting a "Quit India movement" of your own.'

The enquiry did take a different turn! The major was at his desk with a captain and the young lieutenant on either side. In front stood the two soldiers, one of them heavily bandaged and looking pale and weak. Neither the soldiers nor I recognized each other, but there was no attempt at denying the incident. The major asked questions in a simple, brisk way, till he came to a point which made him suddenly look hard.

'If the soldiers, who were obviously a little high, asked you to get out of the way, what was your objection?'

'Major, it was not just that. I was not concerned with their drunkenness, nor particularly their asking me to get out of their way. I might not even have objected to drunken language; what I resent is being abused in India for being an Indian.'

'But they did not say anything like that. They merely said "Get out of the way", peremptory, I admit, but hardly abusive.'

'But, Major, they said "Get out of the way, you bloody Indian".'

'I am sorry, but this is not what your statement to the lieutenant says. I will read it out to you. Are you sure it is not what you think they said?'

He read out my statement and there was no abuse in it, merely a simple 'Get out of the way'. I looked incredulously at the lieutenant, who looked back at me blankly. The major ended the enquiry soon after that and asked me to return the next morning. He was alone when I walked in. He asked me to sit down and offered me a cigarette.

'I wonder if I could ask you what exactly happened; what the boys said to you. I have also heard that there were others besides you in the fight. There were three of you, not you alone as you have stated so far.'

I explained. We were three. I had not told the truth because I had not even consulted the others about reporting the incident. I took the responsibility on myself. I thought I should risk being able to satisfy the camp authorities alone.

'Major, conditions are sensitive today and little things can be magnified and get out of hand. I thought it worth taking the chance.'

He looked understandingly and asked me to return the next day for the rest of the enquiry. As I was leaving he asked:

'Did the boys abuse you.'

'Yes.'

He looked away. He finished the enquiry and told the soldiers that they must have drunk enough to see me multiplied. He did not mind their drinking, but they must mind their language; words and even a tone that seemed innocuous to them sounded different to people in other countries. He was satisfied that it was a minor incident, but it required strengthening the military police patrolling, especially on Saturday nights.

After the others left his room I stayed on to thank him and asked if he would drop in for a drink that evening. He said he was so weary of the mess that he would be glad to visit a home. He was pleasant company and reminisced about his service, but something I could not explain to him was the Indian attitude to the war. He looked at it as a soldier, uncomplicated by any political overtones. Hitler to him was no more than a menace that must be dealt with. He did not approve of the Russians, but he did not disapprove of Hitler and Nazism itself. He liked India, but he disliked the Congressmen. With such simple beliefs it was difficult to argue, and he did not force his point. Before leaving he asked Gärd if her excellent hospitality could encourage him to inflict some soldiers on her. She said, of course, yes, send them over.

Next evening, as I walked up the steps, I saw two soldiers sitting with Gärd, one of them with a bandaged head. She introduced me to them and said they had come to offer some kind of apology.

CHAPTER ELEVEN

ETTIT WAS OUR Chairman for thirteen years, and when he retired in 1953 he left an organization so different that one barely recognized it, and all one saw was the change and growth that he had so masterfully induced. At his farewell his successor, Hoskyns-Abrahall, summed up his achievement well when he said 'There is not one among us here who does not owe something, if not all, to you for the furtherance of his career.' An ellipsis in it was that many Indian and European managers had failed to keep pace with him or just refused to accept him and had gone away, among them some of the ablest.

Pettit came from one of the British families settled in Argentina and was married into a similar family. Such families sent their children to England for education but many of them returned to settle. Pettit went on from preparatory school to Rugby and finished at Cambridge, after which he returned to Argentina to join the British American Tobacco Company, and later Unilever. He bore the mark of a man who has grown up away from home, uprooted at a tender age and consigned to the monastic life of boarding schools and college halls. A charming host, an entertaining companion on tours, a permissive boss, yet he had no friends and he never relaxed at work. I think his only outlet was his hay-fever, which through his early driving years was the escape valve nature provided him. As he built up relentless pressures he used to reach a stage when the fever suddenly laid him low. He came back looking refreshed and ready for a long bout of energy, when he would sometimes travel from Bombay to Delhi and back, a journey by rail of 900 miles and twenty-six hours each way, twice in the same week. At this pace he often wore out others.

I worked with him and watched the Company grow through those building years till he had reorganized it to his satisfaction; and then he did not seem to need his hay-fever any longer. Though a confident man, I think he needed concrete success to reassure him, not just the satisfaction of effort. I rather thought he lost something more than his hay-fever. I detected a growing tenseness, a little harshness, a weakening of his coping mechanisms, the denial of a catharsis. I don't know what happened to him, but I liked him less at the end, in his very successful days, than at the beginning in his unsureness.

Pettit's unsureness stemmed from a deep strength and not from fear;

the winding up to meet the challenge and a tensing up to ensure success. There was in it a capacity for withdrawal, and as long as he retained this capacity he was flexible in his strength; when he dropped it he became brittle. It was then we had some conflicts after ten years of working together, and it disappointed us both. I was the loser, and yet I believe the last three years under him were a kind of detransference that I needed for my next phase of growth. Being unsure I needed the testing situation to learn by myself. Sometimes I wonder whether he did not drop me deliberately as he dropped his hay-fever; whether he had not realized that the transference had gone too far and begun to sap me; whether his plan for my future did not need a return to myself and my ambivalent basic strength with its own sureness and unsureness, trust and mistrust.

There were three of us in the company that Pettit apparently picked for growing and three more disparate characters one could not imagine, myself, Harvey Duncan and James Wheeler, and in us he put a lot of trust and effort. Duncan was a talented beachcomber who had earned an interesting living in many ports east of Suez and been through scrapes of every kind, a hedonist who never shunned any pleasure that came his way. But under his brash exterior he had an original marketing mind and great advertising talent. In fact he brought the word marketing to us; where in the past we sold and advertised, he marketed, and he made us feel very old-fashioned. Without much education or formal training he had rolled from one country and one job to another, and somewhere in China he had joined the firm. In dealing with the Chinese compradors he had learned a great deal and probably taught them as much, and shocked them with his capacity to match their ruthlessness, and he soon commanded the respect of the old-fashioned Indian traders. What fascinated me was where he could have acquired his sophisticated advertising and marketing skills, working in countries where marketing must have been a simple cadge as cadge can.

Duncan came to Bombay early in 1939, as an account executive in the advertising agency that was formed out of the old advertising department under Rist. The news came to me when I was on one of my long marketing research tours, in a letter that was characteristic of him. If I had heard that I had been fired by the firm, it only meant that my services were transferred to the new agency; we had never met each other, but he was glad to be my boss and our mutual ignorance would be an added advantage; one of these days he hoped to meet me, but till then I could keep my problems to myself because he was too busy sorting out his own. I heard no more from him till I walked into his room three months later. He was small, dapper, handsome, with brisk staccato speech and manner, and put me to work straight away, explaining his plan.

He had been consigned to the new advertising account of Dalda, a vegetable cooking fat, an unknown brand name chosen from among a whole list of brands because it sounded like a slogan. It was to be our only domestic small pack vanaspati, and he was going to make it the leading household brand in India. It was going to be the Sunlight of cooking fats. Modesty or caution were conspicuously absent from his plans, yet some years later when I succeeded him his forecasts of sales read like past history, so accurate were they. The same evening he showed his first experiment in demonstrating cooking with Dalda.

Outside the Novelty Cinema in Bombay he had constructed a small wooden stall and hired three men to run it; one cooked, the other talked, the third walked about inviting the passers-by and distributing leaflets. The cook stood behind the counter rolling out some dough which he cut up into small squares. By his side he had a paraffin stove with a deep frying-pan. He scooped out large spoonfuls of Dalda, melted them in the pan and floated the squares till they fried golden brown. The demonstrator talked about the virtues of Dalda and invited people to try it out for themselves. He asked them to take some Dalda, which they put on the back of their left hand and with their right index finger carefully rubbed into the skin to feel the grain and how it melted, and then they smelt it. He would then offer them another small lump, which they put on their tongue and again felt the grain and the way it melted. Meanwhile he kept up an encouraging patter, and when he saw a look of satisfaction on their faces he would ask them to try for themselves the sweets fried in Dalda. By now a crowd had gathered and he quickly engaged them in the sampling act. At the end he tried to sell them small tins, which many did buy and proudly took away wrapped in a coloured leaflet.

Duncan asked me to explain this curious method of testing the fat by rubbing it on the skin, smelling it and then putting it on the tongue. I explained that this was how they always tested ghee made from milk, which Dalda simulated in appearance, texture and flavour. They would find out whether the grain of the ghee was hard or soft, whether it melted easily at body temperature, how it released its aroma when melting, and only when they were satisfied with these tests did they put it on the tongue, again to test the grain and its flavour. Ghee to an average Indian has to be treated with great ritual; it is an integral part of food and religious practice; it is ambrosia, the food of the gods, and the cow from whose milk it is made is sacred. The Dalda he was trying to sell was competing with a prototype that was more than just a cooking fat. But ghee was becoming scarce and expensive and was therefore often adulterated. Dalda, at half the price, looked like ghee, felt like ghee, smelt like ghee and tasted like ghee.

Duncan's eyes lit with a new marketing comprehension as he looked at the crowd and the wrapt attention with which they went through this ritual. He had never seen anything like it. On the way back he was thoughtful; he said he perhaps needed a different marketing strategy altogether. He had not realized what a formidable competitor ghee was, and yet if the emotional attachment to it was so strong it made the task even more worthwhile. He loved the spectacular and saw his task thus. Between us began a working partnership from which I had all to gain. Pettit encouraged it.

Wheeler was the third. A simple English boy, a junior in the accounts department in London, he was sent to Bombay for six months while one of the accountants went home on leave. He stayed on for 22 years. When I first saw him waiting for the lift, the week after I joined, I thought of the favourite line of George Robey, the English comedian, 'Does your mother know you are out?' Wheeler looked barely out of school, thin, lanky, with hair down his forehead, his fists deep in his trouser pockets. Twenty-two years later when he left the Company as financial director, he looked the same except that his hair was grey. He and his wife Betty were the first English couple we became friends with and in time deeply attached to.

Pettit tried him in various places, in sales, in administration, in personnel and in accounts, and was constantly inducing growth in him; but while he prodded me and stretched Duncan, sometimes remorselessly, he was always gentle with Wheeler. He cultivated him and his wife socially and helped them in every way. I think he realized their emotional needs with a sensitivity that few otherwise credited him with. When I got to know them I discovered an aspect of the problem of an English wife. Betty was a simple girl, very English, of an environment that could never be reproduced abroad. Most others got used to the comfort of life in India, the servants, the leisure and the higher standard of living that came from the bigger jobs their husbands held, well-appointed entertainment with grace and ritual. Betty disliked it all.

She longed for her little house in London, the chores she had enjoyed doing, cooking, cleaning, shopping and looking after the baby. She resented the way of life imposed upon her with no choice, not even the right to rebel. The older wives were tolerant because she was so young, so straightforward, and they made such a handsome pair. They hoped she would settle down and see it all in terms of her husband's career. Betty gradually did settle down, and paid the price. She kept on paying it in instalments till long after it had ceased to matter.

With us Betty relaxed and spoke freely. I loved watching her face, dark with chestnut hair thick and parted in the middle, the high cheekbones, the sculptured lips and the hazel eyes that could look sullen and rebellious, yet gay when she was happy.

As I saw it, Betty paid the price in the way she acquiesced. She did not give in, she just gave up; and like a hibiscus flower, which she so reminded me of, she wilted as soon as she had bloomed. I wondered whether it would not have been a more sensitive way of helping to have sent them back home instead of building him up here; but those days the young English were sent abroad for a lifetime, and once abroad there was no choice but to make a career of it. Return before normal retirement was only considered on medical grounds, or for failure in the job. Only rarely did someone exceptionally bright or well connected, more often the latter, return for promotion.

There was a logic to the system of exile. It dated back to the days of the sailing ships, when the East India Company employees rarely returned home for leave because the journey was long and hazardous, and only men looking for a career out of England came abroad. After they had worked here a few years, the level of responsibility and the income they enjoyed could no more be matched at home. They were therefore committed to a career and a way of life from which they found it difficult to extricate themselves until they had saved enough and earned their retirement benefits. Faster communications, steamships and cables, made little difference to the basic system. They went home more frequently, but it was still a long exile.

A community in exile forms for itself a different kind of island from the one that has settled, however uneasily; and this was a community of the rulers. Uprooted from home, they denied themselves new roots for fear of becoming of the country, like the so-called domiciled Europeans, also pure in blood, but unacknowledged by the non-settled, the so-called 'pukka'.

Living thus in the artificial atmosphere of an environment within an environment, not likely to return home for at least another quarter century, they nevertheless felt the need for some kind of roots. Their brothers in the Indian army dedicated themselves to their regiments, their men and their sports; those in the civil service became committed to the peasant and, in their own light, to his welfare; but those in commerce had only their work. In the earlier years they at least had to travel a lot in the bazaars and markets, where they came close to a part of India, but as times changed most of their work could be done from the head offices and branch offices, through correspondence and agents, with diminishing contact with the world outside. They worked long hours and invariably returned to office on Saturday afternoons, even on Sunday mornings, and always on Indian holidays; not really because the pressure of work demanded it but as a safe commitment to something. There were those who amused me, like my first chief, who used to go into the rooms of his colleagues before lunch on Saturday, tell them that he proposed to return in the afternoon and how much he envied them for not having to. This meant that they also had to come back unless they found some valid excuse.

Their women similarly created their own islands, combining some mild social work with entertainment. They drank coffee and played mahjong, and took the children to the swimming pool. Some played golf, most also did some work at the European hospital, the Y.W.C.A. or a home for old indigent women of European descent. A few were really devoted to social service for which the scope was of course endless. Few did any professional work. In the evenings and on weekends the couples adjourned to the community's own islands, each 'entire of itself' but not 'part of the maine': clubs, beaches, swimming pool, golf, homes, all carefully fenced off.

Betty wondered why she had to be part of it all. It might be good for James to work here, but he would have got on at home too, and they could have had the life that was theirs.

The three of us came very close to each other in work. Duncan suggested to Pettit that with the war, marketing research was restricted, and the work I had been doing for Rist checking newspaper circulations could well rest for a while; he wondered therefore whether I could not join him as an assistant. Pettit had recently invited Duncan to move over from the advertising agency to the Company to run its marketing department. Duncan liked the idea in itself but not the prospect of working directly under Pettit. The agency atmosphere, free and easy, suited his temperament, while the discipline of a company would irk him. Besides, he and Pettit were temperamentally so different and socially worlds apart. Pettit belonged to the Royal Bombay Yacht Club, lived in a spacious duplex flat and entertained gracefully. His was a life of hard work and urbane pleasure. Duncan, a bachelor, lived in a hotel and did not care whom he cultivated so long as he enjoyed himself. He took malicious pleasure in not conforming to the image the executive of a large British firm was supposed to create. He thought over Pettit's offer for quite some time before saying yes and spoke to me about it because he wanted a sympathetic sounding board.

'You know, this is going to be the end of my career. I had hoped that I would stay long enough in this job and in India, which I like, to save something. I am tired of rolling; I not only gather no moss, but get rubbed smaller and smaller. I like doing things my way, and if Pettit had any sense he would leave me where I am. But I am afraid I have little choice; it is too early to look for another job or move to another country, so let me submit; who knows, I might even end up as a staid burra sahib, married and rearing a family. Hell,' he added, 'what will I do with all my fancy shirts and ties with my initials embroidered all over.'

His words proved prophetic. Less than five years later he left India, and soon thereafter the Company, broken in health and spirit, condemned, with all but his cynicism gone. His luck had run out. He had even for the first time in his life fallen in love, been accepted and then rejected. In those short-lived days of his love I saw in him a tenderness that was a miracle in a man so cynical. She was considerably younger than he, innocent, gold and pink, and he could not believe his fortune. But it did not last long, and the last blow was his oncoming deafness.

Years later I heard that he landed back in England and started a restaurant that prospered until he ran into competition with a nightclub across the road. This was more than Harvey could swallow. He dashed across to discover that it was run by a woman, cool, able and attractive. Soon there was a flash back to the old Harvey Gale Duncan, who had beaten fate and circumstance for twenty years from Bombay to Brisbane and Sydney to Shanghai. He put into his last marketing campaign all that he had ever possessed, and it worked. He ended up owning both Harvey's Bar and the Bamboo Club, and married its proprietress. She gave him a daughter about whom people said he never stopped talking. I never saw Duncan again; I did not want to. Some things in life are best left unrevived. Years later, someone from Singapore walked into my office. He had heard that Duncan had worked with me and wanted to know if I knew his whereabouts. The card he sent in said, 'A friend of Harvey Flash Duncan'. He genuinely believed that Duncan had been christened Flash; for that was how they had always known him.

In this year 1941, in an airconditioned office in a new building, Harvey felt ill at ease and insisted that I keep him company in this sanitary outfit, as he called it; and soon he persuaded Pettit to get me over. Rist told me one day that Pettit would like to see me. I went across, puzzled, as until then nothing had brought us together. In his large hexagonal office overlooking the harbour, I walked into carpeted luxuriance of polished teak furniture and a large glass-topped desk. Pettit himself was a large man, handsome, with iron-grey hair, immaculately dressed, with a well-intoned, well-accented voice. He walked to the door to receive me and we talked about what I did, my wife, our five months old baby, my home, my years in England and Sweden. When he had put me at ease he began:

'I hear you started some new work that has not been done before, making a survey of some several hundred newspapers in India. Do you feel that you have finished what you began? I know work is never finished, but do you feel you have taken it far enough to try something else, something new again, marketing for instance?'

I have never felt any good at interviews, so I mumbled something about not knowing how well one was doing; besides, I did not know marketing, apart from what Mr. Duncan kept talking about. He laughed.

'Well, that is just what I had in mind. Would you consider coming over to us, as his assistant? With your background, I believe you will have a contribution to make. The knowledge of the country that you have acquired through marketing research and so much travelling will be very valuable, as also your knowledge of us, our ways and methods which I think is equally of importance.'

I accepted his offer and thanked him, much impressed by his simple graciousness.

'Thank you. I am so glad. I hope you go far. In anticipation of your acceptance I have prepared a letter offering you the job at an interestingly higher salary. I believe you should receive the increment now rather than after you have shown your work.'

He got up and stretched himself to his full size, walked around the desk and held out his hand. I shook it. He walked up to the door, opened it for me and wished me well. I looked around the room again and left. Twenty years later I walked into that room early one morning, before anyone had come into the office, sat down in Pettit's leather chair and stared at the chair in front, where I had once sat as tense as today. The harbour was busier, the ships' masts flew the Indian tricolour, on the wall there was a picture of Queen Elizabeth; nothing had changed, only the times. I could hear Harvey's rasping voice, 'So you made it!'

From Pettit's room I walked straight to Harvey and said, 'Well, I see you did not want to sink alone.' Harvey insisted I share his room; he hated being alone and besides, he added, 'I always return late from lunch and Pettit has already begun to check on that. Now you can take the telephone instead of the poor peon, who always gets it wrong and says 'Duncan Sahib still eating lunch'.

Duncan was nothing if not consistent in his unpredictableness. On the first morning when I joined he announced blandly that he had been waiting for me to start and now he could go on his local leave, which he proposed to spend in South India selling Dalda, and he was off at the end of the week. My protests only made him laugh. He thought 'head first' was the best way of learning.

'But have you asked the Chief? I am sure he won't think much of your idea of leaving him alone with a novice.'

'The Chief thinks it is a great idea; needed no selling at all.'

'Then it is Pettit who thought of it.'

Duncan just laughed. I don't think I have ever been through a more exhilarating fortnight. Pettit saw to it that I was stretched and, through no coincidence I suspected, Duncan had left behind as much as he could undisposed. Years later I read in Philip Woodruff's *The Guardians* about a district officer who said to his assistant:

'This is your sub-division or your job. These are the lines on which I want it to be run. Now go and run it. If you make a really serious mistake I shall have to overrule you; otherwise I shall not interfere. If you want advice I am here to give it. If you want a definite order you are free to ask for it. But if you make a habit of wanting either, you will be of very little use to me.'

The Guardians certainly knew how to delegate.

This was my first experience of Pettit. It was also my first taste of power. I had the whole office to run the way I wanted to; utterly in-experienced, but with someone behind me who understood. If I used my commonsense and dropped in for an occasional run-through, he felt sure I would keep afloat till I learned to swim. He patiently re-ceived me each time I went to see him, but I soon sensed that he waited to hear what I proposed to do rather than provide an answer. Any mistakes I made he would be prepared to pay the price for.

My being the first Indian brought the inevitable problem of acceptance by the Indian staff. Overstretched myself and unwilling to admit it, I loaded the clerks with rather more work than they had been used to or, as I suspected, were prepared to accept from me. Perhaps anxious to prove myself I wanted quick answers to provide quick replies to anything that I was asked. Soon one of the clerks protested and said that Mr. Duncan never loaded them like that.

'But do you find the work too much? I know I have passed down a lot, but I am sure it is not more than I am doing myself. Knowing Mr. Duncan I should think he works at twice my speed.'

'Well, we are "overdead" with work since you took over.'

I felt I had to assert myself. 'If there is anything you cannot finish, I will. Please bring all the arrears to me; in fact I will also take over all the mail as it comes in.' Half an hour later the clerk walked in with two peons and placed file upon file on my desk. Some files I felt had nothing to do with me, and he must have emptied the whole office on my desk. I asked him if there was any more, and he said 'no' and walked out. I knew I was being tested.

For the next two days papers kept pouring in, and I worked long hours trying to cope. On the third day the clerk put his head in.

'Did you send for me?'

'No.'

'Oh. I thought the peon said you wanted me.'

'No, thank you. I am doing fine.'

The following day the peon came to take away some of the files. I told him to leave them where they were. That afternoon the matter came to a head. The clerk came in and asked me how long I was going to keep the files. I told him I was managing quite well and was nearly up to date.

'What are we going to do then? Every time the Chief passes by he wonders whether we have any work to do because we have neither files nor papers on our desks.'

'Well, that should suit you. You were "overdead", now you can live long, and I will do all the work myself.'

At first he frowned, and then he saw the humour of it. I laughed and told him to take all the files back, and we said no more about it.

Duncan came back from tour more full of ideas than ever. If rivers of milk and ghee once flowed in India they were now going to flow with Dalda. The population was rising fast and there was not going to be enough ghee; vegetable oils would have to take its place. But as people preferred ghee, the next best thing was to sell them Dalda, untouched by hand, sold in sealed tins, containing vitamin D. . . . and so Duncan ran on and on. I found his enthusiasm very infectious. Here was an opportunity that would not come his way again; the chance of creating a new habit and spreading it across a sub-continent, the first branded, packaged food in a country where everything else was sold loose, weighed and taken away in one's own container. But his bold targets needed bold planning, and so he plunged himself into a five year plan that would dot every marketing i and cross every t. It was an experience to watch him at work, with his collar unbuttoned, tie loose, hair over his forehead and a cigarette drooping from his lips. He looked so different from the cool, immaculate Pettit sucking his pipe.

Duncan began to evolve what must have been the first complete marketing plan in India, divided neatly into selling, advertising and consumer promotion. He started by redesigning the pack, which was tin, and he reintroduced it in different sizes, the square 10 lb., the round 5 lb., 2 lb. and 1 lb, and a special $\frac{1}{4}$ lb. tin for sampling. He cleaned the label design and brought out boldly its main feature, a palm tree, which over the years was to become a familiar symbol, and the brand name Dalda; a household term that became generic for vanaspati. This green and yellow tin was to spread so widely in the country that you were never far from an empty one. When twenty million tins are sold in a year, among a people who never throw away anything, and much less empty tins, but put them to the most ingenious uses and make each tin last for years, a hundred million empty tins over a few years become a ubiquitous sight. This gave me later the idea of making an advertising film whose theme was the empty Dalda tin. Upon the Persian wheel in the country, rows of Dalda tins scoop the water out of the well and deliver it into the wooden channel; on the shelf of the village grocer rows of neatly stacked tins store herbs and spices; on the window sill of a small town flat the holy tulsi plant grows in a Dalda tin, providing every morning a few leaves for oblation; a group of women at the communal well washing clothes and pouring water over themselves with an empty Dalda tin; villagers walking across the fields in the evening on their way home from the market, carrying tins fitted with lids and spouts to contain the oil for their lamps. In any tinsmith's shop you can see the ingenious modifications he carries out to fit the Dalda tins for a hundred uses.

Duncan's new advertising took his discovery of the smell-feel-taste test as its theme, repeating itself through every medium he used, demonstration stalls, newspapers, leaflets, films, girls visiting homes. He built gay little stalls on pneumatic wheels with colourful canopies. The cook stood inside with a table in front of him displaying the tins, and made simple sweets while the demonstrator talked to the crowd. After a while they folded up and pushed the stall to the next prominent street corner. He also built motor vans with a large replica of the round tin on the chassis, and a platform at the back with a folding table top, and fittings for relaying speech and music. When the first three vans were ready, first of their kind in India, proud Duncan in his cream coloured convertible led the cavalcade through Ballard Estate with the loudspeaker pitched high to 'Marching through Georgia'. Outside the office the vans stopped, and out stepped smartly uniformed drivers, cooks and demonstrators, with Duncan in his safari outfit in front, ready to lead them into the jungles of India. As Pettit came out to inspect this guard of honour, they all stood to attention. Some of the sahibs looked out of their windows and shook their heads, but Pettit, as much a sahib, looked ahead.

Duncan then produced a Dalda film and his first cinema van. The film had all the ingredients of an Indian picture: song, dance, pathos, humour, social uplift, march of time, and coincidence. In 1200 feet it depicted the story of a father who had got his daughter satisfactorily engaged, but could not afford to cook the wedding feast in pure ghee, so he was naturally worried. As the wedding day drew nearer the budget mounted, and he wondered what was going to be the answer, because as important as the dowry was the feast, and whoever thought of cooking it in anything but pure ghee? A young relation brought the answer: Dalda; but it was to be kept a secret till after the feast. Anxiously the father looked at the guests from behind a curtain and, lo, they were eating so heartily that a new worry arose: would the food run out! After the metal plates and cups were swept clean and the feast was over the father revealed his secret, the green and yellow tin of Dalda with the palm tree. The story ended on a happy note: the young man explained that he had picked up the idea from a demonstration stall in the street and had actually tasted Dalda and food cooked in it before he recommended it. The film had a catchy theme song, which for years afterwards wherever I went to sell Dalda would be sung and whistled by the little boys who followed me. In the placid life of a village or small town the excitement aroused by the introduction of Dalda was not easily forgotten, nor the product, at least not its name. We sometimes rented an empty shop for a few days, plastered it with buntings and colourful advertising material and set up a temporary demonstration centre. The little boys would cluster around at the sound of the theme song. The news would spread and people flocked to see what had upset the monotonous tempo of their life. Children were our great asset.

It was a stiff task building a sales organization, with a network of salesmen, supervisors and sales managers all over the country. India has a long tradition of trade, of selling and distributing. Over two thousand years ago, Indian traders of the west coast, from Malabar to Cambay, traded with the Mediterranean, sending their spices and silks, textiles and timber, to a Europe bereft of luxuries. Their trading chains stretched deep inland to collect the goods, transport them to the coast and ship them for delivery in Europe by the overland route from the Red Sea. Their hundis, the bills of exchange, were honoured all over the then known world. Many amassed wealth, with which some built temples, among them the famous cave temples in Maharashtra. On a wooden beam in one of the cathedral-like temples there is carved the name of the donor, a prosperous merchant of the second century.

Trade became a caste in India accepted by the system as a hereditary right, not to be poached by outsiders. The wisdom and experience of generations was concentrated in one channel of activity, and training through childhood and youth had but one aim, to produce a trader. Even in my young days the traders had their own schools in the Punjab, where their children were taught a special script, perhaps to keep their books safe from the prying eyes of the revenue collector. The only other thing they were taught was arithmetic, largely mental, doing abstruse calculations in the head. They learned to memorize their multiplication tables from one to twenty, not only whole numbers, but by quarters, halves and three-quarters, so that a trader boy of eight could snap back the price of seventeen and three-quarter yards of cloth at thirteen and a quarter annas per yard before other children could multiply seventeen by thirteen on paper. They only went to school till the age of ten or so, and after that they sat below their father's seat at the shop, and by the age of fifteen they could confidently run the business.

While business was in their blood and opportunity for quick profit never missed, its very hereditariness was a disadvantage in the new age. Many expanded into large trading businesses and some also went into production, but with the control always firmly retained in the joint family, which alone produced the management, their capacity to adapt themselves to the new western ways of doing business was limited. It was not always easy to make them forego quick profit for a slow but long term gain. Their tradition was the pure market law, to push the price up to what the market could bear in a shortage, or down to where it would buy when there was abundance. To sell at steady prices deprived them of the pleasures of playing the market up and down. Many made quick fortunes that way, and as quickly lost them.

We had major distributors in port towns and a network of wholesalers in the country, several thousand of them. All were private family businesses with a proprietor, brothers, sons and nephews and, if the business grew large, minor relatives and members of their caste and community. Often partners came together as young men, and as they prospered were joined by their respective families, often again to break up when it came to the turn of their young sons, whom succession and not choice had brought together, as had been the case with their fathers. The fathers often saw the writing on the wall and amicably divided the business in their lifetime rather than leave it to break up afterwards. Sometimes the fathers cemented it by marriage, or brought a mature son-in-law into the firm. The older generation regarded a partnership as a sacred brotherhood that seldom broke, but with the new generation it was different.

There were many variations on the theme of family control, but seldom the acceptance of an outsider, however able and trusted, into control. It was surprising how, upon the death of a husband, the widow could step into his shoes and run the business with a firm hand. One of our big distributors died childless, leaving an aged and ailing partner and an inexperienced nephew only recently brought into the business. He had, however, a bright and competent young manager whom he had trusted and treated well; so we in the Company felt that this man could run the business while the nephew matured. To this the widow agreed, but she reacted most violently to his suggestion that he might be given a small share in the business. I went to see her to intercede on the manager's behalf and in the interests of all.

'No,' she snapped back, 'he is a servant in the business; he is not of the family and never can be. He can demand his wage and I will pay him well, but there can be no partnership between a manager and the family. He has to accept his position.'

'But what will you do if he leaves you?' I asked.

'I will come in and run the business myself.'

And she did, because the manager had his ambitions and left. She asked me not to underrate her; she would run the business with her nephew to our satisfaction, if only we gave her time. Impressed with her courage, I had no choice but to accept her. I did, however, ask out of curiosity, 'Do you know anything about our business?'

'Yes, quite a lot. I never went out, but when my husband came home he talked to me. He unburdened himself and I listened. I have no feel of running it, but I know enough about it to feel that it will not be difficult.'

She ran it for some years and ran it well. The nephew gradually took over and we did not see her again, but I am sure she never gave up interest.

Although one considered the fathers old-fashioned and became impatient with their resistance to quick change, the sons who became modern were usually a greater problem. They somehow fell between two worlds, with the advantages of neither and disadvantages of both. They lost an innate and haphazard shrewdness without gaining a systematic and informed approach. When they sat in a chair like us, instead of cross-legged on a divan like their fathers, they made themselves different from their customers, who called upon them no longer, nor did the young men take the trouble to call at their customers' shops as we and their fathers did. It was an uncertain world of transition that belonged neither to the bazaar nor to Ballard Estate. And sadly enough, while these boys tried to cultivate us socially, both the English and we much preferred to meet their fathers. I always enjoyed Lala Ramchand's parties more than his son's.

Here was, I discovered, a world within a world. Rather, there were three concentric cultures in one world, mine, Lala Ramchand's sons', and Lala Ramchand's own, with the last as the core culture. As I saw the son's problems of adjustment to a world new to him, mine dissolved; but somehow I was impatient with him though never with old Lalaji. Ultimately the day came when Lalaji retired and the business was run by the son, when we had to terminate our fifty year old relationship. It was difficult to convey to the son, while Lalaji understood, that our real problem was that the business could either be run in his own personal old-fashioned way with such modifications as we felt desirable; or entirely our way with an efficient professional impersonalness of defined systems, delegation and structure. In fact I discovered, as I learned more about the two systems, theirs and ours, that their usefulness to us lay in precisely what they stood for— Lalaji's personal credit, his knowledge of each customer's social and financial position, his inexpensive old warehouse behind the shop, the loyalty of the younger members of the family and community.

We once considered having our own distribution system, with our own chain of one hundred and fifty warehouses with staff and delivery vehicles. It was argued that we would improve the service to the retailers, and save money. The plan was all drawn up; in fact Pettit had even selected me to organize the service and run it. The idea stemmed from a visitor from London, but the story went that when he outlined it to his colleagues back in London, a wise old man who had spent his early years in business in India listened carefully, and at the end of an enthusiastic presentation made one remark:

'Do you really feel we should ever be able to do it cheaper than the man in the bazaar, or even as well? My answer is, never. There are few in the world who can beat an Indian wholesaler for cost or service.'

The scheme was dropped, and just as well. In time we improved their systems and built in refinements to suit our growing needs, but basically today the bazaar wholesalers serve as well as they have done for nearly a hundred years since Sunlight soap first landed in Bombay. After my first enthusiasm was over I began to respect their old-fashioned ways and learned to tinker with them as gingerly as possible. Old Lalaji used to say:

'Tandon sahib, tell us what to do and leave us to do it in our own way.'

In each succeeding generation of sales managers I heard the same question put: 'Would we not do it better ourselves?' and the answer was always the same: 'No, wait till you have understood the system; you will learn to respect it and not want to drop it.'

But the problem arose when Lalaji's son wanted to change it. While there was a wholeness to theirs and a wholeness to ours, and gradual change according to need was always taking place, any change that did not contain a meaning or was only part of a compromise gave a bad fit.

Lalaji was to blame for much about his son. The only boy among a number of sisters in an Indian home can be brought up with such solicitude and anxiety to fulfil his every whim that petulance is usually its only reward. I once offered Lalaji to train this young man, when he left college because his mother thirty-five miles away could not bear the separation and the thought that he was not receiving his home comforts, and her constant care. The boy felt the same way and was glad to go home. I suggested he should come to Bombay and work with us for a year, first as a salesman in the field, and gradually rise to management, on the condition however that we should pay his salary and expenses like with other trainees. Lalaji rashly agreed, but when the news reached home the mother was adamant. She could not bear another separation, and that a thousand miles away in foreign lands so far from the Punjab. Lalaji tried to persuade her in the best interests of the son, although in his heart he was not absolutely convinced either.

Ultimately the mother agreed on condition that she could accompany the boy with suitable staff. I was worried at the prospect of a young Dalda salesman travelling about with mother and servants, possibly a younger sister who could not be left behind, and I soon backed out of it, to everyone's relief, not least the young man's.

A remarkable feature of the old generation of traders was their deep sense of financial integrity. With never anything committed to paper, they trusted each other for unlimited amounts; their word was a guarantee. They seldom chose bankruptcy as the easy way out; and if they were forced to accept it, sons and grandsons have been known to honour the debts. How could anyone perform his father's or father's father's death anniversary each year if an unpaid debt remained behind? Till it was paid, how could the departed soul rest and accept oblation with any sense of satisfaction at duty performed?

The first time I went on tour with one of Lalaji's salesmen we went from town to town booking orders from the local wholesalers, and all the record he kept was a pencil entry in a little notebook. In one town we met the salesman of an old British distribution firm. He carried elaborate printed forms on which he filled in details of the order booked in three copies, each signed jointly by him and the customer. I asked Lalaji's man how he managed to transact business with no records. His answer was simple: 'On trust'. But, he added, the wholesalers of the chaps with the elaborate forms might cancel their orders or refuse to accept the goods if the market in the meantime went against them. 'My wholesalers,' he said proudly, 'never!'. And indeed he was right. You can question a document, but not your own word. You have to live in a town, known to all and related to many. How could you live if your word was no longer trusted? Who would give your daughter his son in marriage? You might break your word about the dowry!

I loved working with Lalaji and his kind. Their warmth, kindness, and above all their trust, once they felt you would not mislead them, their sense of quick profit combined with genuine piety, made one cautious about the responsibility they placed in one's hands.

A harder task in a way was the building of a sales force of the new kind. For some years the Company had employed a few salesmen who travelled in a leisurely way, mostly to big towns, and booked orders on behalf of the port town distributors. Their task was simple; it usually meant accompanying the European sales managers on tour as guides and interpreters, to sell imported articles whose brand names and wide distribution had been fostered over many years by the pioneering efforts of earlier generations of cold-weather visiting sales managers. Those that still remained formed a piece of British social and commercial history. Derisively known as boxwallahs by their compatriots in the administration and the army, because they carried their samples in boxes, they used to arrive in Bombay at the end of the monsoon, and settle at the Taj Mahal Hotel.

Their daily routine was strenuous. A large egg and bacon breakfast was followed by a visit to the bazaar, which imposed a strain of hospitality in numerous cups of sweet tea or fizzy drinks. Here they worked for three hours or more, starting with the distributors and visiting in turn all the main customers. At midday they gathered at the Harbour Bar of the Taj with their counterparts from other companies for a couple of hours of steady beer drinking, followed by large pink gins before lunch. In the afternoon they slept off the strain of the morning. In the evening, a short walk along the sea, a bath and change into white shirt and trousers and black tie, and they again settled at the bar for whisky sodas, pink gins, then brandies after dinner, and ended with cold beer at midnight.

Their work in Bombay completed, they did the standard chukker to Clarke's at Karachi, Faletti's at Lahore, Great Eastern at Calcutta and Spencer's at Madras. When the heat set in, in April, they returned to Bombay to take the boat home, with the customary joke that the best view of Bombay was from the aft of a boat. It was a hard life that killed some while young; but the consistent superior quality of their products and their orderly, planned selling methods made what they sold into household names. As their business grew their firms set up branch offices in India, and then they came for two and a half years' duty and six months' home leave. They now brought their wives with them, and the pattern of life became less hectic.

Our Indian salesmen were trained under these free and easy itinerant managers and followed in their footsteps with corresponding success. They too were usually a hard-living lot, and like their English managers posed a problem when men like Pettit introduced new marketing methods, imposing new disciplines to which neither were used. They now had to submit to a thoroughly regulated system of travelling and work. Fixed itineraries were drawn up for each salesman taking him around his territory in a planned way. For every tour, arrivals and departures, number of days in each town, order in which the dealers were to be called upon each day, sales targets and display material were planned in advance, and the progress had to be recorded, day by day and town by town. The managers were asked to make random checks, which left little scope for doing things your own way. I ran into my very first problems with one of these rugged salesmen.

Gopi, a favourite of the trade and the Company, was an individualist to the core. He liked to be left to get the best sales out of his area. The new form-filling and working to schedule irked him, and he accepted it with transparent hostility. To me, inexperienced and raw, fell the task of training him, and Pettit set it in his usual way. On a visit to Gopi in Poona he took me along. In his presence Gopi was at his best. He went from shop to shop introducing his burra sahib, drawing an effusive reception from each shopkeeper, selling as much as he wanted, each dealer playing up to the occasion by showing just the right amount of resistance but eventually accepting what Gopi thought in his sales wisdom would be best for him to buy. Pettit was most impressed, but in the middle of the morning he suddenly decided to leave me to continue the selling and took Gopi away to another part of the bazaar.

I had never sold anything in my life. Left with a handcart full of Dalda tins, some advertising material for display and a quiet little man from our wholesalers, I set to my task with more resignation than courage. In the first shop I entered I thought of Gopi, how he virtually took over the shop, conveying a complete sense of assurance about what was good for the dealer and generously waving aside his protests. To some he would say, 'No, you try and sell this first and next time I will give you more'; and to others he would equally blandly sell more than they wanted with the assurance. 'I know what you can sell; all this Dalda will go in no time and you will be running out of stock before my next visit. What sort of a salesman will you call me if you have to disappoint your customers?' I tried to remember Gopi's ploys but my tongue was tied when I approached the shopkeepers. After some inconclusive sales, hot and sweaty as the morning advanced I took off my jacket and tie and at least tried to look like a salesman. Just as I was arranging some Dalda tins on a shelf and dusting them to make their labels shine, Pettit returned. I think the sight of me moved him. He told Duncan afterwards that he was impressed by my literally having rolled up my sleeves. I had not sold badly, but more important my daily sales report was neatly filled in and the advertising material properly affixed in prominent positions at the proverbial eye level. Gopi looked displeased at this display of a gentleman salesman in shirtsleeves, which he considered affectation.

A few months' later I came over one hot June midday to meet him on tour. At the wholesaler's I was told that Gopi had left the previous evening, contrary to his new itinerary. So I took the next train to a town seventy miles away, drove straight up to our wholesaler's shop, and was informed that Gopi was resting at the hotel. In some temper I reached the hotel and woke up Gopi. He blandly told me that he did not feel like working and wanted to rest. To my protest that he could not play about with his itineraries, he replied that he could always finish his job in half the time that these new-fangled disciplines demanded. He added archly, 'But would you like to go selling, Sir, as you did in Poona?' I said I would and told him to go back to his rest.

Rarely had I felt more nettled. I went back to the wholesaler determined to get even with Gopi, who had added a calculated piece of insult by suggesting that he might accompany me after all as I had no experience of bazaar selling. With the salesman's daily report folded under my arm, I set out from the wholesaler's godown with a handcart full of Dalda, determined to sell it all. I worked till late in the evening, selling for dear life. At nine o'clock, as I trudged back to the godown, I had exhausted the handcart stocks and made a record sale of over two hundred and fifty rupees of Dalda. As I reached the hotel I saw Gopi sitting cool and fresh on the lawn sipping his beer. All my meanness came out as he enquired how I had fared and said he was feeling fine now and would go back in the morning to finish the day's work.

'Well, Gopi,' I said, 'I have sold all the bazaar could buy for weeks to come; but you can try your luck.'

'What did you sell?' he asked.

'Over two hundred and fifty rupees worth, but maybe you would like to teach me what a lot more you could sell.'

He raised his eyebrows. That was a lot of vanaspati for those days. He realised that I had been as mean as he had been to me, and in fact saturated the market.

I tried hard and in different ways, but I never succeeded with Gopi. There was a watershed between us; between the old, leisurely though hard-selling days, and Pettit's new methods, where the whole operation depended upon a system. A journey cycle, as it was called, put on a schedule a whole month's work for a salesman. This Gopi found irksome, like some of his sales managers. It deprived them of the freedom they were used to, but there was no doubt that it produced better results.

The clash came soon. I had sent Gopi to the north to develop some new markets. Working so far from home did not suit him, but even more he disliked having to introduce himself to the new disagreeable system. When few days later I met him he said he was returning to Bombay for a short rest.

'With whose permission?' I asked.

'Oh, in the usual way. I have worked for several weeks at a stretch and I think I will go home for a while, but if you like I will wait till you have finished your tour.'

I thought I might as well grasp the nettle now as later. Gopi was undoubtedly pushing the point further each time.

'I suggest you return to Bombay tonight. I will finish the tour alone, and please report at the office next Monday. I will have a word with the Chief about it, but so far as I am concerned you can consider yourself through with us; at least with me.'

He was taken aback and protested that it was no insubordination, he merely wanted to go home for a few days. This was the way he had always worked and he saw no harm. I felt some remorse, but I had had enough of Gopi. His influence on the younger men who were being broken into the new ways was disruptive. On my return to Bombay I reported the matter to Pettit who had been expecting some such thing. He realized that I could not manage Gopi and it was best to give me my head through my first crisis. He listened with his usual patience and left me to decide. Duncan was more positive. In the office there was much talk and open hostility, but eventually Gopi left. He tried to make up but I felt I must decide now, once and for all.

Many years later, a large chauffeur-driven car sped past me and signalled me to stop. Out of it jumped Gopi. Balding, portly, suave and effusive as ever, he greeted me like a long lost friend and thanked me for what had turned out to be the beginning of a prosperous career.

Among the new and younger types, too, there were problems, largely cultural. The new ways clashed with our inherited ideas, which though rating the craftsman high, did not value labour. Pettit insisted that the salesman's job was a whole from the moment he entered the shop. Most of the young men, to begin with, disapproved of the very idea of walking beside a handcart or carrying the handbag that contained the report forms, samples, a pot of glue and a stapling machine, a duster and a wet sponge to clean the fly-blown unsold tins; but when it came to the chores of putting tins on the shelves and cleaning them, or stapling and pasting the advertising pieces, they positively rebelled.

One of them, whom I was training in the bazaar on his first day with us, remarked to one of the older sales managers that he would rather work as a coolie than be our salesman. The old manager looked pleased as he secretly agreed, while to me there was no argument about it.

'Don't you like working like a coolie or do you find yourself not up to it?' I asked.

'Well, just to show you, I will work for a month, if only to prove that I can do it, and then I quit.'

He went back to work and stayed with us for twenty-three years. He rose to head our best branch and took great pride in showing the young salesmen the dignity of labour.

CHAPTER TWELVE

WITH THE TURN of the tide of war, as the Japanese were at first halted and then gradually began to be pushed back in the Far East, and the Germans in North Africa, the conclusion became obvious and a matter of time. In India there was a kind of stalemate between the Government and Congress. All our leaders were in jail; the top leaders were all put in the same prison, the fortress of Ahmednagar, except Gandhiji, who was lodged in an extraordinarily ugly palace of the Aga Khan, outside Poona. Either the Government was facetiously generous in allowing them to live together like one of the many evacuee governments of the time, perhaps naively believing that with nothing to do they might break the impasse, or it might have been to facilitate negotiations when the moment came.

So the leaders sat in idleness, planning and dreaming of the future, of an India free and ruled by them. They would undo the trends of a thousand years of history, of domination and exploitation, when the interests of the masses were excluded by the needs of dominion. They made a post-war, post-independence plan that would quickly and dramatically get India out of the morass and put her on the road to industrialized affluence, welfare, and international equality and influence. They would build a socialist society, with the state in control of key functions. They would write a constitution combining the best of all political systems. While they veered towards the system of the Western democracies, their economic thinking leaned towards the socialism of Russia, in which they saw fulfilled their aspirations for a non-exploiting, progressive society of heavy industry and cooperatives.

I used to get into arguments over this. Everyone agreed that all that was wrong with the society and the economy was the British. In subtle ways, sometimes openly and sometimes covertly, they thwarted all progress. Openly, they were not interested in the effective spread of education, in improving communication, in industrializing; subtly, they kept choked the mainsprings of progress: the social change so necessary to encourage economic growth. All our ills, social and economic, were either of their making or encouraged by them. If the Brahmin did not accept the untouchable, it was because he was not made to; if the trader profiteered during the war, it was because, as Nehru said, he was not strung from the first lamp-post; if the Hindu women did not enjoy all the rights of man and more, it was because there was no legal statute to permit it.

To an extent this was so. As rulers they were not particularly interested in waking up dogs that had slept for so long, but what one doubted was the calm assumption that the moment they went and we came in, the society would suddenly wake up and dramatically set about to undo all evil, and usher in good with an unerring instinct. It was difficult and sad to argue with this naive optimism, such arguments always left the impression that those who did not share this optimism almost did not want it to happen; as if there were in them an underlying opposition to the coming change; something which did actually exist in the minority communities.

Among the Christians and Parsis of Bombay and elsewhere, who had accepted the British as their special protectors and acquired cultural affinities with them, there was open fear of change. With exceptions, they were unhappy at the possibility, now increasingly a likelihood, of the British going. It was argued that they were afraid of being deprived of their privileged position, which I think the British had given them out of a genuine desire to encourage the underdog, though also of course to ensure their loyalties, to create small islands of agreement that could always be relied upon. It was understandable that the minorities did not want their islands to be swamped when once the support of the British was withdrawn.

The minorities misunderstood their position. All they would actually lose were the excrescences, the relatively unimportant trappings of their British connection, but these they seemed to value because they set them apart from the rest, which was just what the rest resented. They had nothing to be afraid of as minorities, even with the alien qualities that distinguished them. A group remained a minority only as long as it resisted assimilation and retained its distinction. In the case of the Christians, they were all Indian, mostly of relatively recent conversion, only set apart by their faith and their names, and the distinctiveness of a closed endogamous group which imitated the British. The Parsis were ethnically different, though over the 1300 years of their domicile in Western India they had married and intermingled. While adopting Gujerati language, food, dress, and customs, they had sufficiently altered these to give them a Parsi touch.

It was in the end a plain fear of the dominant Hindu community not giving them a fair deal just because they had been the favourites of the British. In identifying themselves with the rulers they had to an extent to disidentify themselves from the rest of the people. Their attitude had acquired some of the aloofness of the British, and some visible mannerisms deliberately cultivated struck us as somewhat ludicrous. Personally I found them a little pathetic and felt sad that they should have so isolated themselves as to become afraid of the mainstream. I was equally sad at the attitude of the mainstream, which did not have the bigness to let the little streams run their own course until they felt comfortable about returning to its bosom.

I felt sad too at the abundant complacency which claimed that everything was wrong with everyone else, with the British and the minorities, with those Indians who saw anything good in them or anything but good in us; that as soon as the dark curtains of British rule lifted there would be a bright vista of a long straight road to progress. I had once got into an unhappy argument a few years earlier about the British and the Germans. Nothing was right with the British; everything was understandable about Nazi Germany.

In the Company we began to plan for the time when progress could again be resumed, unhampered by all the restrictions that the war had piled up. I had the feeling that, necessary as it had been to restrict during the war, there was something inherent in the character of the British administrator, who was essentially unsympathetic, often hostile, to trade and industry, and had always regarded business with distaste. His model was the English county gentleman, and in the earlier days he often came from a county family, a second or third son coming to India in search of a career that combined adventure with sport, power and profit. To this kind, business was an unattractive profession with which you did not soil your hands.

On the other hand, the Indian trader, usually also a money-lender, had ways that endeared him to no one; but whereas in the days of the East India Company the factors, and later the administrators, had shared his exploitation, and therefore tolerated and encouraged him, the new civil service was not dependent upon him for trade or revenue, and was openly contemptuous of him. I think the neglect of India's trade and industry through these valuable fifty years was largely due to this attitude.

The administrator was basically a law and order man, and his efforts were mainly addressed to the interests of the villager, as he saw it, in maintaining peace, land records, title deeds—things the peasant had not known for centuries, with some attempt at development in irrigation and communications. There was a list we were made to learn by heart at school: Blessings of the British Raj—peace, post, telegraph, roads, schools, hospitals, canals, and I think one or two more like that; all of them useful innovations by themselves, but most of them hardly touching the villager. He had no one to correspond with; normally no place to go, except the nearest small town market; he was illiterate; and the nearest hospital was in the district town, twenty, thirty or fifty miles away, with no means of getting there. With the exception of the Punjab and some relatively prosperous irrigated districts here and there, this was still the picture of most of rural India a hundred years after the Queen assumed power and the insignia of Empress of India. The villages stood still. There was no attempt at giving them communications or a voice. No roads led to the village, except the tracks made by bullock carts, nor was there a post office, school or dispensary. The villager was left in an idolized splendour of isolation, at the combined mercy of the past, the monsoon and the moneylender. The monsoon was often fickle and sometimes failed, and with it his slender livelihood; but the past never failed him in the comfort it gave through familiar ritual and ceremonial, though its demands at births, weddings and deaths could be exacting and onerous. And this is where the money-lender came in 'to help balance the budget' – a money-lender's advertisement I saw in Boston many years later.

The administrator genuinely loved the peasant, but I do not think he understood his real needs. These were simple – the felt need for credit, constantly needed to maintain life, honour and death, even the memory of death; and the unfelt, but more urgent need for education, though on the surface he seemed content with the learning contained in his cumulative racial memory and his ritual. The administrator helped him with neither. He tried later to do something about credit by discouraging the moneylender and opening some cooperative credit institutions, but these were so hemmed in by his love for rules and regulations that the illiterate peasant preferred the money-lender's high rate of interest on loans given at the moment and on word of mouth to the irksome form-filling of the cooperatives. The new regulations meant to curb the money-lender only managed to increase the cost of the load, and so the administrator neither provided the answer nor an alternative to the peasant's need for credit.

When later the trader and the money-lender became industrialists, the old mistrust continued, augmented by the fact that he often openly allied himself with nationalism and supplied the Congress Party with funds. The rising voice of the legislatures and the press achieved a few gains for the nascent industry in the way of tariff protection, but the administrator did little to encourage it either directly or indirectly by providing even the elementary infrastructure. Right up to 1947 two of the most industrialized cities, Bombay and Ahmedabad, were not even connected by road.

The trader, never loved, began to be thoroughly disliked during the war when he exploited the law of supply and demand to the fullest. Where there were shortages he charged whatever he wished, and where the supply was adequate he waited to sell till the prices went up. He became almost whimsical towards the consumer, and many times one walked out of a shop feeling sick at his cynicism, as when he would raise the already extortionate price just because one protested.

'But only a few days ago you charged me less, and the price has not gone up since.'

'No', he agreed triumphantly, 'but the price goes up right now. I asked you two rupees; and if you still want it, it will be two rupees and a quarter. If you don't, it will be more when you next come for it.'

Complacent in the assurance that he would always get more and more for his stock, he felt reluctant to part with it. It was bad business to sell to-day unless he charged the premium that he would get to-morrow.

The administrator passed laws and made rules, and made them yet more stringent when they did not work, till a maze of regulations spread across everything. There were prosecutions for refusal to sell, and I was flooded with telegrams from wholesalers in the lock-up, praying me to get them released, because they had refused to sell in retail and under our instructions sold Dalda only to selected retailers on a planned quota. Pettit rushed to New Delhi and persuaded the Department of Civil Supplies to issue a special exemption to our wholesalers so that we could continue orderly distribution, but I found my problem was how to get the administrator to accept it in his district.

One realized the immense power the administration gave to its men on the spot. This had been its tradition, and the secret of its success. If the man out on the limb chose to go his own way he could go pretty far before he was pulled up. When he proved right he was regarded as an eccentric, and if he was wrong he was only moved. One of our wholesalers in Ferozepur was locked up for a few days for refusal to sell, and in spite of the letter from the Company he produced quoting Central Government's exemption, the English Deputy Commissioner refused to withdraw the prosecution. To save the poor wholesaler I travelled all the way up to Ferozepur to call on him. This was my first experience of dealing with a British administrator.

Whether he behaved as expected of him or was like that by nature, his curtness was disconcerting. He spoke of the traders and their untrustworthiness and how, if he had his own way, he would put them all behind bars, for nothing would teach them to drop their anti-social ways but the plain fear of being treated as common criminals. He sounded very frustrated and this I could understand. The war had placed upon him burdens of a new kind, to which was further added the general political sensitiveness and the rising communal tension in the district. He now had to deal with an unfamiliar set of problems arising from the new civil supplies department, which mostly meant keeping a lot of dishonest traders in check; a new function he least relished.

I explained to the Commissioner how our system was designed to ensure as equitable a distribution as was possible under conditions of acute short supply. Compelling a wholesaler to sell to all and sundry would only mean that stocks would immediately be cornered upon their arrival, whereas we tried to distribute them to a selected list of retailers on a pre-determined quota with a fair chance of their being sold to genuine customers. Prosecuting the wholesalers for refusal to sell under the Act would produce no more Dalda nor channel it to the right people. That was why we had obtained a special sanction from the Central Government exempting our wholesalers from section 9 of the Anti-Hoarding and Profiteering Ordnance under which this man had been prosecuted. We had convinced Government of the need for the exemption. To my passionate arguments his reply was simple and curt.

'That may be so in New Delhi, but here you have to convince me.'

'I don't know how to convince you then.'

I was up against power, delegated to the end of its limits. His action would be supported all the way, but it would as surely be defeated by the Court; though only after a protracted and costly case. The system had a strange ambivalence; it gave the executive naked and arbitrary power, but also provided a check through the judiciary which was independent and often suspicious of the executive. Both sides had equal freedom. The exercise of power could always be turned back at the boundaries of justice, but until then it would be a law unto itself, sometimes lawless in the law it tried to enforce. I remember a story my father told me—how a man who felt aggrieved said to a minor village official:

'But surely there is the Sirkar!'

'Sirkar, who is the Sirkar? Here I am the Sirkar.'

The Deputy Commissioner had told me just that. The chain of

arbitrary action had continued down the ages from the Moghuls, the Marathas, the Sikhs, to the British, and we did not then realize that one day we might be adding our own links.

The administrator sat in his chair in his airy brick-built office, dealing with just another situation; he was always preventing people from doing wrong or punishing them for doing it. There was nowadays nothing constructive left; the interest of the pioneering days had gone, the excitement of breaking new ground, opening up new areas to peace and order and to development. Now he was desk-bound, attending to stacks of files, coping with an ever-growing multiplicity of new departments and legislation, mostly of a negative kind, controlling transport, food and supplies, prices and procurement of food, controlling nationalism.

He looked at me wearily. I could understand his distaste for the business he came across, but I felt hurt to be included in this distaste; that my attempts at developing a modern idea of integrity in trading mattered so little to him that instead of praise I was met with suspicion. Back in Bombay I heard the wholesaler had been released, and there was a touching telegram of thanks from him.

Some years later, travelling in the Punjab with Maurice Zinkin, who had been in the I.C.S. and had joined Unilever after 1947 and returned to India, I related this story to him. His reaction was sharp and unequivocal.

'Of course he was right! The exemption New Delhi gave you neither altered the rule nor directed him in any way. It was given for you to produce before a local authority for their consideration, but as long as the rule remained it was up to them to decide in their own right. The letter was not a directive to the Deputy Commissioner and did not bind him in any way. Right or wrong, in the exercise of his judgement, the power and discretion of the man on the spot always remained his. His decision could be examined by the authorities, and he could be criticized for a wrong judgement, but not stopped from exercising his discretion.'

Maurice went on to add, with his characteristic verve, that the day the power of discretion of the man on the spot was interfered with would be a sad one for the administration. I confess I did not see it that way then, and few did. Later, years after the administrator had lost power and a political system had taken over, I realized the significance of what Maurice meant. The politician naturally preferred the discretion to be his.

Later another case came up that had its lighter side. An English district magistrate in the U.P. was trying one of our wholesalers for a similar offence. As usual I wrote him a letter explaining our distribution system and enclosed a copy of the exemption letter from the Central Government. It had worked in most cases, but this magistrate regarded my letter as contempt of court and ordered that I be produced before him under an arrest warrant. I was saved by a technicality. Recently one of the U.P. High Courts had decreed that a stormy petrel of Indian journalism, an Irishman, B. G. Horniman, be produced for contempt for writing a prejudicial article. He was the editor of the *Bombay Chronicle*, and the virulence of his pen matched a fellow country man of his from another age, William Hickey of Calcutta. Both usually had the English as their targets. Horniman had settled in India, was violently anti-administration and lost no chance to advocate Indian nationalism and flay the Government. In this case an amusing situation arose. The British Chief Justice of the Bombay High Court, though he no doubt had his own views on Horniman, refused to let the summons be served on the grounds that the Chief Justice of the U.P. had no jurisdiction over a citizen of Bombay. The British judiciary had often refused to uphold the British administration, but this was a rare instance in India of a British judge protecting a British citizen against another, equally senior British judge. This case came to my rescue, as the Government advocate reminded the magistrate that under this judgement in Bombay he had no jurisdiction over me. But the magistrate was not to be thwarted. He passed another order that I should be produced before him the next time I entered his district.

The war was nearing its end, and Unilever decided to send a rather remarkable man to India, Roger Heyworth, youngest of three brothers in Unilever, all of whom rose to its board, the eldest becoming its Chairman. Roger, as he was known to all, had spent some time in a Japanese camp in Hongkong, where he had landed from Singapore on the day the Japanese occupied it, and had only recently been released on exchange. I think they sent him to India to get a feel and a measure of the Company and the country, as it seemed obvious that the end of the war would mean a transfer of power and a considerable growth in the country. For this task he was well suited, as he combined a sharp intellect with an intuitive and sensitive understanding of people. He appeared more at home in Bombay in a week than I had found some Englishmen do after a life time.

He sent for me one day and said he wanted a general chat. This in itself was something new, as indeed was everything else about him.

Although the office was air-conditioned he had taken his coat off, loosened his tie and unbuttoned the collar. He sat in his chair with one leg over its arm, with the shoe laces untied and the shoe dangling off his foot. He half got up and waved me to another chair and we sat away from his desk, near a window, from where he could look out at the Bombay harbour. He was strongly built, of medium height, but the thing you noticed immediately about him was his large head, with thinning hair neatly parted, big round eyes behind glasses, and a friendly, high-pitched laughter that was very infectious and disarming.

'Talk to me,' he began unexpectedly.

I began to talk about Dalda and the general situation in the Company and the country.

He interrupted me, 'I know all about that, I want to hear you talk,' and his face burst into laughter. I discovered how he mixed encouragement with crispness. Slowly I began to describe how we had worked on Dalda, the early problems of introducing a substitute fat in homes that had always used, almost with reverence, ghee; how Dalda's strong and logical appeal cut into a tradition for which we would not be forgiven for a long time to come; for the more logical and successful our advertising, offering the purity and economy of our vegetable fat in place of the often adulterated but always expensive ghee, the less they forgave us their own acceptance of this logic. It was our most interesting social industrial phenomenon of the century, and while I was glad to be associated with it, there was occasional embarrassment.

'Do you mind it?'

I said yes and no. I found the work exciting and satisfying because the field was so open to new marketing in India that any effort brought quick, almost disproportionate, returns. I enjoyed the travelling that took me to all parts of the country. On the other hand, people still wondered why I sold Dalda instead of being in Government or politics, because particularly Dalda was not regarded a respectable product. My friends, and even people I barely knew, asked me to put them on our Dalda quota list, but always with a patronizing air – 'You know, we have to use Dalda nowadays; you can't get pure ghee any longer and it is so expensive.' To them from ghee to Dalda was a come down, but even the Dalda had to be sought as a favour.

'Would you rather have been working for Government?'

'I don't think so.'

'Because it is British and not your own?'

'Yes, perhaps.'

'You would rather not have been working for a British firm?'

'I don't know.'

The conversation changed facets fast, and was full of surprises. He seemed to be doing a quick reconnaissance and wanted an approximate idea of the heights and hollows. He was utterly candid about what he wanted to know and spared neither my feelings nor his own. Surprisingly I found my customary reticences dissolve before his ruthless curiosity. I cannot say that I enjoyed it; nor did I find it irritating. Instead, I learned something new, that purposeful curiosity combined with sincerity, such as he conveyed, did not hurt but brought candid answers. His questions went like the probing hands of a surgeon which passed over the body lightly, but pressed whenever he wanted to know more, making a mental note to leave anything that needed a deeper enquiry for a further session; and it was clear that there would be more sessions like this. I did not mind the prospect and perhaps even relished it.

On the next occasion he went straight into an after-Indian-freedom-what session. He agreed with me that the stage was past for Dominion Status, and that the question whether we would leave the British Empire would be a matter of our choice and not Whitehall's.

Anything less than complete freedom made no sense to him, even from Britain's point of view. India's economic problems were too great for Britain to meet without India's support. We should tackle them ourselves with any help that Britain could give and India might ask.

He laughed and went on:

'Not only can't we do it, but I don't see why we should take any responsibility for your problems, and all the blame that will go with all the mistakes that are bound to be made. I think it will be in Britain's interest to give you the kind of freedom you want. Once having decided, we should not hold back but meet your wishes all the way.'

That struck me as a curious attitude, for everyone else advocated hastening gradually, in slow deliberate steps, to make sure that the country was ready at each stage—the sort of thing that made one very impatient; and here Roger showed impatience in the reverse direction. He went on to say that he saw it in practical business terms. British interest was no longer imperial. Right now they had to concentrate on the war, with Indian help or without it, but once they had finished, their interest in India was going to be purely commercial and industrial; a frank return to the original trading connection of the Company's days. Britain would gain more that way than by hanging on by the worn out strap of power. What did I think would happen to British business in India after independence?

I expected that that would depend upon the safeguards built into the instrument of transfer of power. British business had already been expressing concern that the transfer might lead to discrimination and interference with their freedom to operate, and had suggested a commercial treaty of safeguards with sanctions.

This Heyworth pronounced to be nonsense. A commercial treaty whose only purpose was to safeguard the interests of one side after its imperial connection had gone was worthless with or without safeguards. A foreign community could only continue to conduct its business with the goodwill of the host country, and there was a better chance of such goodwill if no pre-conditions were laid down. If British business had a contribution to make, it was sure to be welcome. He laughed, 'Of course, no matter how well we behave and whatever is our contribution, there is no certainty that you will always know your best interests.'

I saw why his brother had chosen to send him to India, a country soon to be free to mould itself its own way. Roger Heyworth could convey the right picture. He started from the simple assumption that India had to be free and would be free—what would she want to do once she was free; who would be the new administrators and managers, what is their mettle, their fears and aspirations? He would take a close look at the business and its environment, and what might be done to attune it to the future.

He explained to me another day that he saw the business with Indians in charge of it; but not Indianized merely to satisfy Indian sentiment. It would be a pity to be dictated by a Government about what was in the best interests of the business. Governments are often poor judges of industrial problems, and in their enthusiasm to industrialize rapidly they can think of costly but unprofitable ventures. The firms would have to insist on their right to decide; otherwise they had no place, no value.

India, he thought, would be right in expecting them to help in her growth and to enter new fields that required skill and investment and involved a measure of risk, but assuredly a delayed return. For this they should try to create areas of understanding with Government and it was imperative to develop men in the business who would be understood and trusted by the future Indian leadership.

He spent a lot of his time in New Delhi meeting government secretaries at all levels. He was fortunate in getting to know Maurice

Zinkin, whose brilliant and effervescent mind was just what he needed to sharpen his ideas on. Maurice brought him into contact, especially socially, with the circle of British and Indian government servants into which businessmen, British or Indian, were rarely admitted. Quite different personalities, they had yet much in common, especially their ideas on India, her development and the place of the new professionalized business in the society after the war. Not long afterwards, when Independence came and Maurice Zinkin left the Civil Service, Roger Heyworth persuaded him to join Unilever in London and return to India two years later.

The process Heyworth began with me, Zinkin continued. I find it difficult to describe it. I think they were both trying to persuade me to accept the responsibility that circumstance had brought my way. Roger sensed my reservations and my holding back, despite my complete commitment on the surface. He sensed that underneath I was trying to evade the logical consequences of the process I had accepted implicitly, and that unless I accepted wholly it would not work. He was right in the way he visualized the future of the business and the scene around, and also in his insistence that my commitment had to be complete. He sensed too that emotionally I was not ready yet to give such a commitment to the business.

I had sensed it too and it had worried me. I did not know with whom to discuss it. Inside the Company I felt alone because my Indian colleagues were all junior to me and they had their own doubts and anxieties, and discussing my problems with them would have made them even more uncertain about themselves. They looked to me for strength, and had they sensed that I had my own hesitations they would have felt let down. The first wave of Indianization had suffered a setback, when nearly twenty Indian managers had left, some because the war offered better opportunities and others because they did not fit in and the Company let them go. But the effect was a generally lowered morale, which I would have accentuated had I displayed my own lack of commitment.

Now I could no longer avoid facing up to my problem. With Independence things began to move fast, and I drifted into deeper commitment and a greater unhappiness. Roger Heyworth must have watched me like a doctor a patient moving towards the crisis of an illness, about which he can do very little except watch and hope. I did eventually pull through after a long struggle, on occasions very painful, over the next ten years, but Roger Heyworth died, and though he set me on my path he was not there at the end.

CHAPTER THIRTEEN

THE WAR CAME to an end. I was in Calcutta at the time, staying at the Grand Hotel, which was full of American officers on leave from their outlying units. I had seen few Americans before the war brought them in large numbers. Apart from the Ludlow jute factory in Calcutta, Firestone, American Express, Union Carbide with just a small Ever Ready torch battery plant, Dodge & Seymour, an early import house, and the assembly plants of Fords and General Motors, there was hardly any American business in India, though there had been early trading with America back at the time when ships from New Orleans used to bring ice as ballast to Calcutta, to take back tea, jute, indigo and other commodities. The arrival of ice was an event in those days that involved much social activity among the parched British community of Calcutta.

There were of course a number of American missions, one running the well known Forman Christian College at Lahore, another the Woodstock School at Mussoorie, and a number of small schools and hospitals all over the country, of which the one at Vellore was famous for its surgery. The total American connection was small, both in size and impact, but from a distance we admired them, if only because they had no empire and wanted those who had one to liquidate it. Of course, they had also fought the British and beaten them, but one did not really think of America as a former colony, nor their war as a war of liberation; it had been their own government after all, though in time they found that the King behaved like an absentee landlord. Today, while Hitler was trying to win an empire, Mussolini and Hirohito striving to expand theirs, and Churchill trying to save one, Roosevelt, it was common knowledge, would have liked to see the whole iniquitous institution dissolved and freedom given all round.

The first American soldiers began to arrive in India late in 1941, and our first impression of them was their informality which made them so unlike the British. As I saw them around the country, in trains and hotels, I wondered what they would be like as rulers. We could only judge by what we saw; their informal ease, their shock at what they saw in India and impatience with her rulers for leaving it at that, and their own thoroughness in organizing and getting things done. Judging by all this, one concluded that they would at least be more efficient in their exploitation.

Their officers and men went about similarly dressed, to us indistinguishable in language and demeanour, while British officers and men patently belonged to different worlds. Their crumpled beige uniforms, unpolished shoes and forage caps placed anyhow upon the head, their loose build and easy gait, left epaulets the only distinction. But the greatest surprise which finally brought to an end a British sartorial custom of two hundred years, was the sight of them going about under the blazing sun of their first summer in New Delhi in light cloth caps instead of solar topees or pith helmets. At one time the British used to wear spine pads, huge helmets with a thick khaki cloth hanging from the back to protect the neck, and still soldiers and civilians alike wore their topees which the town Indians copied. When the Americans appeared with virtually no protection everyone predicted that they would die in their thousands long before facing the enemy. But they survived their first summer, and the topee did not; others began to shed this ugly headgear and soon it was a part of British history.

Strange was also their early generosity. They did not understand the value of the rupees which when translated into cents made everything it bought seem ludicrously cheap. This often made them look more foolish than generous. Coins less than a rupee they usually gave away, as they could not be bothered to count parts of a cent. Many stories went round. A tongawalla protested at the fare an American soldier had paid him. After some bargaining the American gave him more and walked away, but the man ran after him and shouted: 'Amreekan Sahib, why aren't you taking your horse and tonga away; you have paid for them, though it was less than I asked.'

The British generally disapproved and thought them brash and ignorant while the Americans did not conceal that they thought the British had done a poor job in India. They criticized them openly for the poverty, illiteracy, poor communications and general inefficiency—presently more blame than the British deserved was laid at their doorstep. The British were on the defensive when they talked about the problems they were up against instead of frankly admitting that they had come here to trade, and ended up with an empire at their feet. The day was yet far off when the Americans would acquire their own burdens abroad and carry them with great earnestness.

We still saw America only in the image of Roosevelt, who stood out as the shining knight in the cause of freedom for all, who disagreed with Churchill and included India in the Atlantic Charter of four freedoms. Our admiration for the Americans was genuine and deep. Roosevelt held his own against Churchill and sent one of his roving ambassadors to India, the first of his kind to visit us. He came to study the general situation, but unfortunately then all the Congress leaders were in jail, and he could only meet British civil servants and a few Indians to assess feelings. The British felt that this move added insult to injury.

At the same time there was a good deal of sympathy among Americans in India for the British, because of our leadership's call for complete non-cooperation with the war effort. They could appreciate that we might not want to fight the war for the British, but they could not understand why we were fighting the British themselves, when war was being fought against two ruthless enemies who, if they won, would give us no quarter. The Americans themselves had kept out of the war through its crucial early period, and only joined because the Japanese drew them in, but at all times it had been obvious where their sympathies lay. I do not think they understood the accumulated strength of our feelings.

As individuals they were friendly and informal, anxious to start conversations and to be invited to Indian homes. But they were up against a barrier when it came to their custom of dating. At that time it was unthinkable for Indian girls, even in the cities, to be familiar with men and go out alone with them. For dating, the only girls available were the Anglo-Indians and a few westernized Indian Christian girls. In Calcutta, which was their base, the Anglo-Indian girls had a wonderful time. They forgot their traditional loyalties and dropped the British officers and men in favour of the Americans, who had more money and better goods in their canteens and, what counted more, were genuinely warm and generous and showed no trace of embarrassment when taking them out. The British officers felt and could not help showing a certain discomfiture when seen in public with an Anglo-Indian girl. The girls sensed this, though maybe they did not mind, but with the Americans they could now feel at ease.

Yet it is surprising how few marriages it led to, considering the many that took place later in Japan. The girls in Calcutta came of partly European stock, always spoke English and dressed in western clothes, which made for ready familiarity. Yet the relationship seemed to remain at the simple level of having a good time. The girls were used to this from the British with whom affairs had seldom matured into marriage. There must naturally have been some to whom Luckies, Mars bars, black bras and bourbon were not enough, in whom deeper feelings were evoked than a leave weekend's excitement. Maybe it was the very veneer of western manners that kept the men off marriage, while Indian girls, had the opportunity been there, like the Japanese might have compelled in them a more lasting desire. There must have been many sad instances though of genuine disappointment, like a pathetic letter by an Anglo-Indian girl I once read in a Calcutta newspaper.

The American soldiers certainly livened it up wherever they went, and made the Chowringhee of Calcutta a more cheerful place than it used to be. The shopkeepers loved it; the rikshawallas loved it; the waiters and hotel servants loved it; and so did the families who received them. The shopkeepers displayed their goods to catch the eyes of this new type of customer to whom buying was habit rather than a need; the rikshawallas held long conversations with them, each side eagerly expressing their own views without understanding a word of the other, and in their happy moments a couple of soldiers might install the riksha pullers in the cabs, get between the shafts and race each other. The waiters loved serving them because there was always a laugh, a friendly word, an incomprehensible crack and a generous tip. As visitors to a home they made friends with the children and treated the older people sentimentally like their parents back home.

There was a sergeant called Solomon, Solly for short, whose visits to a family I knew were the event of the week. The drawl of his language and his sunny disposition made him welcome. One evening Solly looked slightly morose and explained that he had had an argument with one of his officers. My friend, who was a reservist major, was mildly shocked, and Solly added that he too was shocked with his captain.

'All I said to my captain was "Gee, captain, I don't like your attitude".'

'You don't like my attitude, why?' asked the captain.

'I didn't like the way you spoke to my mate there, just because he asked for leave when he was not due any.'

At this, Solly went on, the captain got mad and bawled at him to mind his own business.

'You see, captain, that's why I don't like your attitude.'

And having registered his protest, Solly walked away with disgust written all over his face. He had so wanted to bring his friend along that evening.

I was in Calcutta when the news of the bomb came, and the word atom acquired a new meaning. The reports of the havoc that challenged creation itself held such surprise and shock that one could not take in its enormity. Before the Japanese could even separate the dead from the living and find out from the living what had happened, down came another bolt from the sky, this time mainly to satisfy the scientists' curiosity about the device's behaviour in its capacity for destruction when it was exploded in mid air. At last the scientist gained an upper hand over the military man who had so far consulted him, used him, but kept him at a distance.

I used to stay in the Grand Hotel where most of the rooms were reserved for American officers. With the news of the bomb, my friends asked if I would like to move out and stay with them. I said I didn't think it necessary. Next evening the news of the surrender came and the hotel all but went up in flames. Men fifteen thousand miles from home, some since three or four years, burst into an orgy of drink and noise to express their pent-up tension. As I lay in my bed that night with the door bolted, it terrified me. They leapt in the air and banged on all the doors, they yelled and hurled imprecations, they beat a tattoo on cans and buckets with pieces of broken furniture as they ran down the corridors. The next morning I moved out.

The end came with unexpected swiftness. The Japanese war machine was after all intact, and we had expected a long bitter war of attrition with the Japanese pride yielding ground literally by inches in a long struggle from Assam to the Solomon Islands, over hundreds of scattered islands to the heartland. But in less than two days it was all over. One wondered if the thing would ever have been dropped, not once but twice, over the enemy in the west, over a white populace; whether there is not a kind of impersonality where people of colour and creed different to one's own are concerned.

Our own problems were not long in starting. A relatively small but testing situation arose with the trial of a group of officers from the so-called Indian National Army. They had defected during the war and joined Japan. They could not be called traitors to their own country because, although the Viceroy had declared war on behalf of India, Indians had never really agreed to it. On the other hand, they were volunteers who had taken an oath of allegiance to a distant king who was their supreme chief, and under military law they were traitors. Out of over one hundred thousand officers and men, the British Government decided to try three leaders, all Punjabis: a Sikh, a Hindu and a Moslem!

When the empire fell like ninepins in Burma, Malaya and Hong Kong, large numbers of Indian troops, who had borne the brunt of the attack, were captured by the Japanese. There were in these lands also large numbers of Indian settlers, and stories came of the often un-ashamed preoccupation of the British civil and army authorities with saving their own civilian and military units and letting the devil take the hindmost—in this case the Indians. Two roads led out of Burma to India, the more comfortable one was reserved for the British, who were well provided and cared for as they retreated, while the Indians were left to fend for themselves on a trek that later became known as the Burma Road and stirred the conscience of the world.

Among the Indian soldiers there was great bitterness and this the Japanese exploited, helped by Subhas Chandra Bose, a former President of the Congress, who had made a dashing escape from British sur-veillance in his house in Calcutta, through the whole of North India, Afghanistan and Persia, till he reached Germany. From there Netaji, the leader, as he became known, had been taken by submarine to Japan, where he announced the formation of an Indian National Army, with himself as Commander-in-Chief. He travelled to Singapore, which had the largest concentration of Indian prisoners of war, and persuaded some of the officers to join him, soon followed by other ranks in large numbers till a sizeable army was formed, which should one day march into India with the Japanese to free the Motherland. The part it eventually played was insignificant, but it acted as a boost to India's morale, and when the British decided to conduct the famous I.N.A. trial popular feelings rose to a high pitch.

Of the irony of this strange drama which they played with such sad perfection, the British surely cannot have been unconscious. It was as if some intuitive sense of history led them to 'beat retreat' before lowering the flag a year hence. The Empire's Consul, the Viceroy, himself a famed soldier, cannot have been unaware in the hour of victory that the sunset was coming with tropical speed, when he decided to hold the trial at the very Red Fort of Delhi from where the last Moghul Emperor, Bahadur Shah, was led out a captive in 1857. It became a test case, Nehru put on his barrister's black robes after many years, but the man who ably fought the case was Bhulabhai Desai, the leading advocate of Bombay and a member of the Congress. He held that under international law, if a country had undertaken the respon-sibility of defending the citizens of another country and failed to dis-charge this duty, the loyalty of these citizens lapsed and they had the right to defend themselves as best they could. The British, he averred, had failed in Burma. He was successful in his argument and the three accused were released on discharge from the Army.

The British seemed to indicate through this acquittal that they were passing on the ultimate and the larger decision in this case to Indians. They showed a rare intuition; for a year later when independent India was fighting its first own war in Kashmir, the Indian Army flatly refused to take back one single I.N.A. officer, despite all the covert pressures from the Congress leaders. The men whom Nehru and Desai had defended as heroes; men who had broken their sworn allegiance to answer a call to higher duty, to serve their own motherland rather than the country that held her in bondage: all the rhetoric of the trial failed to move the Indian Army General Staff, many of whom had personally known and served with these men. Nehru and his colleagues having won the trial had to accept defeat in the implication of its result; and it was to their credit that they did not make the issue public, or press it beyond a seemly point. The feelings of the men responsible for the new army had to be respected, and their feelings apparently were very strong.

Once when I was travelling to Bombay from Madras, a young Maratha captain got into my compartment. He looked strained and nervous. We had a night's journey ahead; he began to talk, and we talked till late into the night. He had been to Sandhurst and joined a cavalry regiment before the war. His regiment was sent to Malaya, and when the Japanese invaded from the north they were one of the first to take the shock. There was really very little fighting, he told me; they mostly retreated, lost their units and rejoined them till they reached the sea and could be pushed no further, and there they all fell prisoners to the Japanese at Singapore. He spent the rest of the war in a prisoner-of-war camp in Singapore and shared a cell with a Punjabi officer about whom a legend had grown.

Life in the camp, he said, was hard and one's main consideration was how to spend the least energy to be able to survive on the meagre diet. However, they were more fortunate than the many who were sent to the Siam Railway or to the Solomon Islands, especially the latter from where few returned. He described life in the camp, the interminable hours of waiting for nothing, lying in their bunks staring into space, punctuated with incomprehensibly brutal treatment by their captors, so senseless that it could only be explained, he thought, by the scant value the Japanese attached to the life of anyone who chose to be taken prisoner.

But there were lighter moments. His cell-mate, on a morning of particular boredom, wrote a skit in verse on the Japanese officers. A few days later, when the Maratha was alone in his cell, a Japanese lieutenant and some soldiers entered without knocking. The captain got up to attention, but the lieutenant pushed him aside and without a word they proceeded to turn the cell inside out, searching their few possessions, their clothes, and tearing open the partitions. After a half hour they walked out. Apparently the camp authorities had got to hear about the poem and were determined to get hold of it. When his mate heard of it he was most amused, but the Maratha was relieved to hear that the poem had been lent to an Indian medical officer the same morning.

Some days later the cell mate called out that he had a new idea for a verse. The Maratha jumped out of his bunk, put his hands around the throat of the verse-writer and threatened to choke the idea out of him, for if the Japanese heard of another poem they would raze the camp to the ground.

His anecdotes, though amusing, gave glimpses of the suffering he must have gone through. There was no trace of bitterness in him and he regarded the Japanese with amused contempt. They had given his cell-mate a really bad time, seeming to pick on him with unusual hatred; maybe it was his appearance that irritated them. He had a tall, robust Punjabi build, a large cavalry moustache and an overbearing manner, all of which seemed to make the small Japanese want to slap him. They often did, and things worse than that, but nothing broke his cheerful arrogance.

After the surrender the Japanese guards went round to the same Indian officers asking for testimonials certifying how well they had been treated:

I asked the captain where he was going, and his answer was short and clear.

'On a very painful mission to New Delhi, to testify against some old friends—the I.N.A. undertrials.'

'Really. Poor chaps. I suppose you can understand their position,' I said.

'No. Unfortunate they no doubt are but there can be no sympathy for them.'

'But I thought they displayed great courage in resolving their conflict.'

'No. There could be no conflict. I am afraid I can only see it in my own simple light. They were men who had joined voluntarily, and as officers no circumstances could absolve them from their oath. Even if we assume that they were mercenary soldiers, they still owed allegiance to whomever they agreed to serve.'

'You wouldn't consider taking them back?'

He replied quickly, 'There is no room in the Indian Army for them and us.'

Things that were simmering now reached the boiling point with the Indian Navy mutiny in Bombay. Communal tension also soon broke its banks. The whole country was restless, and the British realized that freedom could not long be postponed. The mutiny was an ugly signal which they were quick to recognize. Everyone looked to Nehru as the man of the hour.

I was on my way back to Bombay from Bihar, where I had visited my elder brother. My younger brother had recently married my sister-in-law's cousin and the bride had been on a visit to them. She was now returning with me to Bombay where they both lived with us. We were in an airconditioned coach, which had a series of compartments connected by a corridor. At Allahabad there was more than the usual commotion of an Indian railway station. A crowd converged on our coach, and when the excitement died down I discovered that Nehru had boarded it. After the train started moving I walked up the corridor and found him sitting in a four seat compartment. I had never seen him before and felt an urge to talk to him. Back in my own compartment I wrote a short message on the back of a visiting card.

'Panditji,

'You don't know me, but I have a great desire to meet you. Unfortunately your compartment is full and I am wondering if you would consider it impertinent on my part to suggest that you might walk over to our compartment at the end of the coach. We would feel honoured.'

I rang for the attendant and asked him to take it to Panditji.

'Who?' asked the Goan attendant.

'Pandit Nehru.'

'Who is he?', he asked innocently.

'Haven't you heard of the great leader, Pandit Jawaharlal Nehru?'

'No. I know there is some big Indian, not a sahib though, travelling in the end compartment, because there were many people at Allahabad to see him off, but I don't know who he is.'

'Never mind, take this card and give it to him.'

Afterwards I felt foolish and regretted my impulse, but soon there was a knock on the door and Nehru put his head in and said simply, 'Did you send for me?'

I got up in great confusion and said, 'Well Sir, that is putting it very graciously; do come in.'

He came in and sat down, and talked in a shy, hesitating manner.

He asked me about my family and my work. I reminded him of the somewhat caustic remarks of his book, *Unity of India*, about the luxurious airconditioned coaches, with the privileged few sitting in cool comfort behind blue glass windows. He blushed at this and said that he did not like travelling in such style, but the train was full and there was no accommodation anywhere else. He did not like air-conditioning anyway.

'You see, I had a message only this morning from Sardar Vallabbhai Patel asking me to go to Bombay immediately in connection with the naval mutiny, so I took the first train.'

After a short while he got up and said that he must go back and do some work; he was trying to finish a book. As he was leaving, my young sister-in-law asked him if he would sign her autograph book. I felt embarrassed and apologized, hoping that he did not think we had asked him to come over merely for this. He laughed and said, 'No I understand. Children are like this,' signed and went out.

Soon afterwards the press published correspondence between Jinnah and Gandhiji, who had invited Jinnah to meet him, suggesting that as Jinnah was travelling from Calcutta to Bombay, he might consider breaking journey at Wardha, which was on the way. Gandhiji added that he would normally have travelled to Bombay or Calcutta himself, but he was not keeping good health and would like to avoid the journey. Jinnah replied curtly that he would be pleased to see him, and his address was Mount Pleasant Road, Bombay. I thought of Nehru walking up to my compartment on the train.

Independence came sooner than we expected. Mountbatten, from the moment he landed, showed that he was in a hurry to give India freedom without any qualification about membership of the Common-wealth or a commercial or political treaty. If Indians could get together and work out a formula, they could have independence any time and on any terms, but the formula should be acceptable to all parties. The Muslim League flatly rejected joint independence and pressed for a separate state of Pakistan. Feelings ran high; there were riots in Bengal, then in Bihar, followed by West Punjab, and as the flames rose higher Mountbatten suggested dividing India into two independent states of India and Pakistan. Reluctantly Congress accepted it, and naturally Jinnah. One felt there was no alternative to the division.

After months of rioting, the news came as a relief. Mountbatten and the Indian leaders were going to speak on the radio, and on my way back from the office I stopped at a shop to listen. Mountbatten was crisp and clear. He would have preferred a united India, but there was no choice, and, the job done, there must not be any regrets; one had to look forward. Jinnah was never in any doubt about the outcome, the only just solution, and he was glad the others now saw the sense of what he had been advocating all along. Nehru, emotional, stirred to the depths, decided to look ahead.

As the fifteenth of August drew near, despite the rumblings in the Punjab, our spirits lightened. We Punjabis accepted partition fatalistically. After centuries of change, this was just another turn of the wheel of fate. For nearly a thousand years we had lived under Muslim rule and we would do it again, this time in the shadow of India, whose secular strength would ensure justice to us in the Muslim state. Thus reasoning, the members of our families left across the border looked to the birth of the new state neither with joyous anticipation nor with craven fear, but with sober realism tinged with sadness. We and they would in future belong to different nations, for there was no doubt that the Muslims, having won Pakistan, would make the new state a strong independent reality, as distinctive in personality as possible, in a conscious effort to break all visible links with India. I kept thinking of an Urdu poem we read in school about the long-necked birds, the koonj, that each winter fly high all the way from Siberia, seeking the sun of India. Once when the flock was flying eagerly towards home, a hunter took an idle shot and wounded one of them, and left it wounded where it fell. The bird bid its companions fly on and leave him, hoping one day to rejoin them, though he knew in his heart that there would be no reunion.

About the only cheerful day that year was the fifteenth of August. Bombay was happy and festive, as I had never seen it before. The new tricolour in saffron, white and green with the blue Ashoka wheel fluttered in millions, from every window, lamp post, tree, tram, bus and car. Everyone was out in the streets, gay, happy, confident. The price of freedom, those left behind in a foreign land, were forgotten for the day. There were meetings, long speeches, pledges and confident predictions by the political leaders, who promised Rama Rajya, accepted by the masses with thunderous cheers. Nehru stood above the main gate of the Red Fort of Delhi and spoke to a multitude stretching as far as the eye could see. The next day, Mountbatten drove from the Santa Cruz Airport into the city, the first and last Englishman to receive a hero's welcome in Bombay.

On the third day the monsoon that had long withdrawn returned in cool and nourishing torrents, and on the fourth day, as the colour ran out of the paper flags, all cheer vanished as news from the Punjab began to pour in. First in West Bengal, then in East Punjab, next in Rajasthan, then in the U.P., an upheaval began that uprooted nearly fifteen million people. In a few weeks took place the largest migration history has ever known. How many of those who left their old homes never reached the new will never be known. Who was there to count the dead? Not the law for there was none left; nor the relations, for they were fleeing. Like a string of Divali crackers, where one bursts after the other, this fire raged on till it enveloped the whole North, from Peshawar to Dacca.

There was no end. As the religious frenzy slackened, war broke out in Kashmir, where even before the two armies had sorted themselves out of the one force they were engaged in fratricidal combat. But as the snow on the mountains paralysed the two armies, and the people in the plains wearied of hatred and slaughter, a man walked up, bowed with joined hands and extinguished the life from lips that barely had the time to call on God. Even hate recoiled at what it had done and averted its face. Peace descended.

A month or so earlier a man had sent his card in to my office. He was the editor of a newspaper in Poona. I supposed he had come to persuade me to advertise Dalda in his paper, but he seemed too proud to sell. He said he ran this paper to advocate a cause and not for a living and the cause was a Hindu India. He asked me if I was a Punjabi or a U.P. Tandon, and when I told him where I came from be became very eloquent. He talked at length and with feeling about the injustice to the Punjabis, for whom, along with the Marathas, he had great respect. They were the fighters of India, who had taken the shock of every invasion and were the last to be overcome by the British. Right through history the Punjabis had kept their entity, faith and customs, but to-day for the first time they lay broken. The land that had been theirs since the dawn of history, the flat fertile soil between the rivers, was no longer theirs, and no one, except some abducted women, remained behind.

Words poured from him like a torrent. He was a small man, muscular and trim, with short cropped hair and intense dark eyes that shone with sad anger.

'It is strange,' I said to him, 'that I as a Punjabi should feel less strongly, and less express my feelings, than you from so far away.'

'Yes, I do feel very strongly.' And he walked out.

On the evening of the thirtieth January, as I walked up the sweep of steps to our veranda, Gärd told me she had just heard on the radio that Gandhiji has been assassinated. My immediate reaction was a silent

157

prayer that it may not be a Muslim. When the name was announced of a Brahmin from Poona, I remembered it. It was the newspaper editor who had been to see me.

Two months before Partition, we three brothers had managed with some difficulty to persuade our father to leave Lahore where he had lived alone since our mother's death. Each of us and our families used to visit him and keep him company in turn, and he was loath to leave his home. But when his close friend, a Pathan neighbour, told him with tears in his eyes that it was safe no longer, even for a lone old man like him, he moved across, and with him our last link with the Punjab broke. Seventeen years later I visited Lahore for three days, but alive though it was, it was dead to me. In its reincarnation I did not recognize it.

I tried to forget by sorting out the debris left by this overwhelming tide. There were salesmen and staff, the Dalda wholesalers and their men, all of whom had moved to this side. Daily I received pathetic letters from their friends and relations, wondering if I knew what had happened to them. I spread the word as well as I could that on crossing over they should contact us, and we would do all we could to help; they should rest assured that they would be provided with jobs as soon as they had recovered enough. I made the same offer to our Muslim wholesalers who had moved or were hesitating. I would help with the exchange of their business, the premises, their houses and furniture, and even their Dalda delivery trucks, the horse carts and hand carts. In the end it worked out well, and each man and his family was as comfortably settled as times permitted.

One day, dictating the answer to an anxious letter from the parents of a young salesman who was by now overdue, I told my faithful secretary Ramachari to vary the end of the letter to express a fervent hope that the boy was now safe and well. Something in the hunch of his shoulders as he left my room made me call him back to read the last sentence again. 'Sir, the last sentence read, I fervently hope the boy is now safe in hell!'

I had not realized the bond we had built with our Dalda wholesalers till a tragi-comic incident occurred. Our wholesaler in Sialkot wrote to me that all was going up in flames and they must leave. He had sent his family to this side for safety, but a letter had just arrived that a Dalda consignment was on its way. He would remain behind to honour the documents, pay in the needed amount into the bank, and then leave, but would I in the meantime try to stop the railway wagon with the Dalda at Amritsar before it crossed the border. He was anxious for the documents not to be dishonoured, and equally that a good twenty tons of Dalda should not reach the other side. I managed to stop the wagon at Amritsar, where the wholesaler reached a few days later. Contrary to all practice, I told him that he could receive delivery and sell the Dalda in Amritsar itself, which was not his territory, in any way he liked. I heard subsequently that, homeless and penniless, he had sold the Dalda tin by tin in the bazaar at Amritsar at whatever price he could get and begun life again with several thousand rupees in hand. Years later when I met him at Meerut, where we had settled him, he embraced me in the Punjabi fashion of greeting a long lost friend, with his arms around my shoulders, and said:

'That was the only time we both disobeyed the "system". I literally auctioned every tin while telling the people openly what had happened, and, as there had been no Dalda in Amritsar for weeks, they cheerfully paid me whatever I wanted. They really gave me a new start in life. And,' he added softly so that the others did not hear, 'I took your name with each tin.'

My English colleagues in charge of the other marketing divisions, maybe partly because British sympathy at this time seemed to lie more with the other side, thought I was going to unnecessary lengths.

The Company was fast taking new shape, and the effects of Independence were soon to be felt. I had already been asked to take on additional responsibility, and an Englishman had been put under me, the first in the Company to work under an Indian. The Chief followed up with an invitation to dinner at his home, and this set me a problem. I thanked him and said I would let him know. The next day I conveyed our regret on account of a previous engagement. A month or so later he invited us again. This time I thought it over for some days and eventually wrote him a short note explaining that, while I deeply thanked him for his invitation, I must be honest enough to say that we could not accept it—I hoped he would understand. He never referred to the matter or showed any reaction; he discreetly ignored it.

All kinds of testing situations arose. Another English colleague had invited a visiting Indian scientist to lunch and asked me to join them, but forgot to tell me where the lunch was. I waited in my room, and at about a half past one he rang up wondering what had happened.

'Aren't you coming to lunch?'

'I have been waiting here because you never told me where.'

'I am sorry, it is at the Yacht Club.'

I froze at this. Recently the Club had relaxed its rules and Indians could now enter as guests, but this I could not bring myself to do. He guessed the reason for my hesitation and added.

'It is now open to Indians, so be quick and join us here.'

'I am sorry, most sorry, but I cannot come.'

'You mean you don't want to come.'

'Yes.'

He rang off, and never referred to it again. I felt doubly upset at this irony, upset because in the past there had been places in India that were closed to me only because I belonged to India; and perhaps more upset that they were now open; upset that the Chief should for years not have felt that he ought to invite me either to his business lunches or to his home, and when he did I should feel that I must say 'no'.

As I was the senior Indian in the firm, overtures came from all directions. Would I consider joining the Gymkhana Club? Would I join the European Hospital Benefit Scheme? This was a scheme started by the European residents of Bombay since Government's St. George's Hospital had lost its European semi-exclusiveness after Independence. Pettit explained the scheme to me, saying that it was common for expatriate communities to start their own hospitals to provide the standard of medical services to which they were accustomed at home, and to satisfy their desire to be tended in an illness by a compatriot doctor. On the other hand, they did not want to make their hospital exclusive, though naturally it could not cope with accepting all and any Indians. They would therefore like to evolve a scheme under which the European firms would become subscribing members and receive a special rate for their European and Indian managers and their families. It would of course be open to other Indians of suitable kind. The firms that became founding members would each have a representative on the Board of Trustees, who had to be of European birth. He was anxious to invite Indian managers in the Company to join the scheme subsidized by the Company. So far, those of us who so chose had in the past carried our own medical insurance, but he now proposed to start a medical benefit scheme within the firm.

I reacted with what was now becoming my expected style: a 'no'. I agreed that since St. George's was opened to the public it was necessary to start a new hospital for the European community with standards that the private and Government hospitals of Bombay did not have or could not afford. I also appreciated the desire to be treated by one's own; in fact in England I had usually myself turned to an Indian doctor. Medical care in Bombay was no doubt expensive and any assistance the Company could offer would be welcome. But while I approved of the idea of providing the Europeans in the Company with their own hospital, I could not see the relevance of sharing this facility even with select Indians. I would personally prefer to choose where to go, and even use their hospital if my doctor so suggested, but would not accept a medical scheme that tied one down and left no choice. In fact I wondered why they needed to ask any Indians to join the scheme. A European medical welfare plan, to be run by Europeans for Europeans, was quite justified, like their right to have a school for their children, or their own recreation ground. Generous though the offer was, I was sorry I could not accept it.

In the other case I was not sounded directly. There was now some-one else in the firm who was more amenable. Though the Yacht Club only admitted Indians as guests, the Bombay Gymkhana had opened its doors for membership to some Indians working in European firms, because with their own numbers diminishing they needed sup-port and they probably also wanted some mild Indianization. It was suggested that our managers might be given the facility of joining a club, preferably one offering sports facilities, like the Bombay Gymk-hana. I kept away. I still remembered how a friend of mine who was invited to play in a tennis tournament at the Gymkhana had found his clothes removed from the dressing room on the Secretary's orders. Even as a guest player he could not use the Club's amenities.

I felt I was becoming negative and was far from happy. Although I searched deeply into my motives, I found there was no rancour or desire to get even; but that there was hurt involved was as clear to me as to them. Any attempts I had made years ago at socially integrating myself were long forgotten by either side, and the balance we had reached over the years was now being upset with indelicate haste. Things could have been left to slide into a new harmony; there was no need to Indianize social relations so hastily.

Independence had certainly changed overnight the equation that had been progressively moving in the same direction for a hundred years; in fact, from its inception it had carried within it the momentum of change. The tempo had varied; some times it dawdled and at others it rushed, but always inexorably forward. There were always the same things said by each generation: it is going too fast, 'they' are not ready for this yet; while we said, it is not fast enough; but all the same the movement continued in the direction envisaged by Macaulay. When Gandhiji appeared on the scene he disclaimed the idea of change in measured doses, to which the liberals of the early Congress had agreed; he asked for change, complete and without commitments; without preparation. If you wait to prepare to hand over, there will always be good enough reasons never to hand over.

But that was change in terms of political and power relationship; interestingly, no one referred to social relationships; the sensitive ones did not ask for it. Why then this sudden desire for throwing social bridges – where was the need? The Europeans in business had inherited from the British in the services a pattern of relationship that was aloof and self-contained; in fact they had followed it even more meticulously; possibly because Indianization had begun the last in business. A balance had been reached that I saw no immediate need to upset. The administration had gone; did the removal of support imply to European business a vulnerability and need for protection through cultivation of social relationships? Did this sudden discovery of the need for social contacts imply a fear, a mistrust? Was the onus put upon us to respond and to reassure? I believed this was so, and in my negativeness I was evading this onus.

There was a senior director in the firm of great character and lovableness, which stemmed from an indeterminate past that stretched from Poland and Germany to Holland, Britain and India. From Poland he had as a child moved to Germany; as a youth he had worked for a Dutch family of margarine manufacturers, and he had come to India in the early twenties to represent them. Vanaspati, vegetable ghee, had then begun to be imported from Holland and Belgium, and it was he who first organized the sales all over India. He travelled extensively, building the network of distribution that I had inherited. He had never really belonged anywhere, and each of the many languages he spoke had the accent of another, but he was essentially Jewish, with the deep sense of humanity that only someone like him could possess, who had been uprooted so often and never known a permanent home. Before and during the war he had helped an endless number of refugees from Europe; some he had helped settle in India; others after a time went away to England, Australia, Canada or the United States. He was simple and humble, and looked at you with deepset eyes that reflected a history of suffering.

He sometimes took me home to lunch, and maybe aware of my possible future, he would drop in at my office and talk discursively about the past of the business, how he had set it up and the problems he had faced. In me he sensed an understanding and love of the past, and he talked to me about his own life and work like a kind of folk-

lore. From him I acquired a feel about the vanaspati business. Where
Pettit gave me the order and system of a modern business, and Duncan
its marketing flair, Leser taught me the core of humanity that a business
ought to have, making each one a person to it. In my youthfulness I
often defied him and wished to deal with someone harshly when I
thought this was just. He would walk into my room with a knowing
smile on his face, and begin by saying. 'I have heard about it; I know
how right you are, but . . .' I often gave in. He never made me feel
in the wrong, only made me understand that where there was justice
there could be compassion too; my own upbringing, my father's
austereness, had contained little compassion, only justice.

Leser had watched my growing restlessness in the new circumstances,
but had wisely refrained from discussing it. I now felt the need to talk
to him and he put me at ease; he said he had been waiting, hoping I
would come and talk. I did not have to say much. As I began to explain
my feelings I looked out at the harbour, and watched the ships that
now flew the new tricolour from their masts; it was strange to see this
rebel of not so long ago fluttering alongside some of the oldest flags of
the world: Swedish, Dutch and British. I looked at Leser, to whom no
flag meant more than its nationality.

'What should I do?'

'Forget the past.'

'But I am not trying to remember it. I am doing nothing about it.'

'No, but you are holding it against the future. And that distorts the
present.'

'What should I do?'

'Just what you are doing now. Bring your hurts into the open;
they will heal. If you keep them hidden in the dark they will remain
tender and suppurate.'

'But why can't I be left alone; I am not letting anything interfere
with my work; I am friendly, courteous; I don't demand any new
privileges; I don't want any updated equality; I am content with the
gulf as it has existed in the past; in fact, I want it to continue as it is,
I don't want any bridges. Mr. Leser,' I said with my voice slightly
raised, 'all I ask for is to be left alone.'

Leser looked at me and said patiently: 'You cannot be left alone.
How can you be left alone? You may be called upon to run this business one day, and it will be a much bigger business than it is today, and
part of a world mainstream. It will be far more complex, and many of
its complexities will be the makings of your own people. So you can't
escape the future, though you must escape the past.'

He got up to go and put his hand over my head as if to bless, and walked away with infinite sadness in his form, saying very softly, as if to himself 'What have we not gone through and what have we ever held against anyone; and there is no end in sight yet—perhaps there never will be.'

I walked into Chief's room that afternoon and asked him if he and his wife would come to our new house to dine with us. We had just completed the house and they along with the Lesers would be our first guests, which would be most fitting.

Things went well for a while. There was a lot to do in those early years of Independence when there was optimism abroad and a will on all sides to achieve. It was a period of new adjustments in the business, in industry, in the country and in the world. Roger Heyworth, it appeared, had carried his sensitive understanding back to London, for a new pattern seemed to be emerging. Its special feature was the appointment of an Englishman of a type unusual for India. His appearance and name alone distinguished him from the rest. He was tall, lean, with an ascetic look and gentle, almost clerical manner. He spoke to everyone with grace and diffident dignity, and treated even the sepoy outside his room with a self-effacing courtesy. A.J.C. Hoskyns-Abrahall, in both name and manners, left people puzzled, but I soon sensed the purpose behind his appointment. His total oppositeness to any Englishman we had ever had in the Company seemed justification in itself in the new context of things. He not only had no commitments to the past but a marked unconcern with it; nor did he display any particular interest in the country and his environment. His aloofness interested me as perhaps part of the new pattern of the uncommitted executive type coming to India for a few years to do a specific job of work, and then return to his career and life at home, unless he was wanted elsewhere for another job. His ability marked this assignment as an interlude and a step in the progress of his career, so different from those in exile in the past, sent to serve a lifetime in a foreign country, where most of them could only run down in the skills they once brought, and eventually fall back on a form of proprietary rights, waiting for an early retirement.

Watching Abrahall I wondered whether the thesis that the growing speed of communications between India and England hastened the end of the British Empire did not acquire a revised truth. The soldiers and clerks of the East India Company had had to be tempted to settle in this country, marry and learn the language, to make their exile bearable, but when ships became faster and did the journey of months in days, the expatriates began to regard themselves as belonging in England—not in Anglo-India—visiting India on short assignments, doing jobs that Indians were being trained to do and acting as leavening as long as the connection was to continue. Abrahall seemed to me an example of yet a new thinking, part of a process that was to become known in Unilever as 'isation'. The true significance of this process came to me many years later when I taught International Management at an American University. Whether he himself realized it or not, Abrahall was the first catalyst of the new kind, a role he filled with an attractive weariness, for whatever its historical importance the whole process appeared boring to him—yet, or perhaps because of this, he seemed the man most fitted to play the role. As a true catalyst he did not himself seem involved in the process. Having been torn away from England, after spending the war years in Canada, he could not have cared whether he was made a part of the process in India, Malaya or the Philippines, and this very unconcern made him in my eyes the most suitable as a catalyst. His modest but unmistakably able ways conveyed to me a sense of the new order, a new kind of assurance.

I do not know in what terms I was stated to him as a problem, but he seemed fully conscious of it and made no attempt to hide it. His attitude was healthy and seemed to convey that while he would be glad to provide me with a new kind of background, he would have to leave the rest to my good sense; and if he was not going to rush me or upset me in the process, he was not going to particularly upset himself in the process either. All this I sensed and was at the same time deeply impressed with the simple sincerity behind it. I began to respond, and occasionally even gave him a glimpse of my problems as I saw them. He sensitively refrained from taking any more interest than I permitted him and seemed content to let me handle things my way, well or badly. We were indeed soon to run into a problem where he left me to test my own feelings.

As part of the new form of training Unilever sent us two young Englishmen. One of them, John Defrates, had done his spell of national service in the Navy, then read literature at Oxford and brought to business a very sensitive but cynical mind which in no time created a poor impression upon his somewhat teutonic boss. Dubious from the start about young Defrates' business acumen, matters came to head when he found him quoting Shakespeare in an official letter to a merchant. Though the subject of the letter was the purchase of groundnut seed and oil, John's reference was amusingly relevant. What upset his boss was that John was neither bored at his work nor facetious or flippant, but perfectly natural in quoting what he thought was an apt reference at that point in the letter. The boss was clear that John would never make a good businessman, at least not a serious buyer of commodities. Pettit on the other hand felt a responsibility towards his charge, and while he agreed with John's boss he felt that he ought to be given another chance. He got the idea that it might be a good test for us both if he attached John to me. He would be my first expatriate trainee, and a problem at that. So he called me in and explained his feelings that though young and wayward John was able material that he would like to see developed, and he felt that I could do it. He knew that I would try it with an open mind because, if anything, I would be amused rather than appalled by John's informal approach to business. I said I would be glad, in fact, welcome the chance of taking over the rest of John's training.

I think John too was amused by this challenge to us both and displayed much keenness in dealing with it. He turned to his sales training in Dalda with an earnestness that I did little to disturb for fear of encouraging a 'relapse'. He travelled assiduously through the hottest months and the monsoons, sharing the life of the salesmen, scrupulously consuming all the sweets and coloured drinks that the Dalda wholesalers placed before him. They also took to this fresh-faced young English sahib because there had never been an English trainee before. Pettit was pleased with the change. And then the blow fell on poor John. He was dismissed and paid his fare back to London.

I had felt that I was fighting a losing battle, but the more I realized it and the harder I argued his case, the less chance John had of success. I later wondered whether, left to fight it himself, he might not have served his interest better.

John was very interested in the country and soon made many friends among the younger Indians, and informal by nature, he fell in with the Bombay film crowd where he met Maria, a beautiful girl from Goa. She worked in the films in supporting roles and could with equal ease play the vamp or a simple country girl singing and dancing to Goan folk tunes. Maria was quite the opposite of John—he was serious and scholarly, she was full of laughter and fun, with only a Goan convent school education. She was essentially simple and very affectionate, and this must have fascinated John's sophisticated mind. A few years earlier Maria had married an English pilot who flew Dakotas for an Indian airline, but they had not been married long before he crashed and was killed. Maria who had just had a baby was thrown back to work to support herself. John fell in love with her. Maria tried to discourage him but with doglike devotion he followed her everywhere. Gradually she thawed and eventually agreed to marry him.

John immediately went up to the Chief and told him of his intention to marry, and if this was not enough surprise, he added that the girl was Indian and worked in the films. It was pointed out to him that he was still under training and ought to wait till he was confirmed. This John considered irrelevant and said so, which did little to assuage feelings. He did not see what difference a few months' waiting would make. If the idea was to give him time to change his mind, it made him only more determined. He explained to me later that he thought he was being dissuaded not so much from marriage as from a marriage that was disapproved of. Had he sensed approval he might have waited, but now he saw no reason why he should wait at all. He went ahead and got married. The Chief never acted emotionally or hastily. He casually broached the subject with me once or twice, and my reaction was equally casual. If Defrates wanted to marry this was his business. One day I was called to a meeting to discuss the Defrates' affair. I was asked how I rated his performance and I said it was good.

'How would you regard him in comparison with his Indian colleagues?'

I thought the questions were leading up to Defrates' confirmation and said simply that while John was excellent and better than most Indians, there were nonetheless some whom I would rate higher.

'In that case is it right to confirm him?'

'Why not?' I said astonished.

'You know it is our policy to Indianize, so that a European we employ must be equal to, if not better than the best among the Indians. It would otherwise not be fair to them, nor do we want less than the best Europeans if they have any justification to be here. You yourself, surely, would agree with that!' I did not.

'If we accept that, few Europeans in the Company would have the justification to remain in India.'

He asked me what I thought of the marriage, and I repeated my views that it did not concern me nor the Company. She was a nice enough girl, and I did not think John's marriage would make any difference to anyone.

'But do you think she will be acceptable to Indian society?'

'Yes.'

'Don't you think there may be a prejudice among his Indian colleagues against a girl who works in the films?'

'No, I don't think so; in fact they have a lot of Indian friends both in the company and outside.'

At this stage he rang up the amenable soundingboard. This was an Indian whom I had introduced to the firm, impressed by his apparent qualities till I discovered to my chagrin that he was utterly self-centred. Worse, to further his interests he had developed a complex style of feigned independence which somehow always let itself be persuaded the way the right wind blew. With Pettit he practised this with consummate skill. I never knew whether Pettit saw through it, but he certainly used it to his advantage.

While we waited the meeting broke up for a few minutes. Abrahall and I walked up to the toilet. He had kept out of the discussion and left the argument to me. He now said somewhat warily:

'I did not realize you felt so strongly on the subject.'

'Yes, I do. You are right, I do feel strongly about it. We have talked about injustice to Indians, and I would not like to see the first English-man working under me treated unjustly.'

We went back to the meeting. The amenable soundingboard was asked the question how Defrates' marriage would affect his relations with his Indian colleagues.

'Well, Sir,' and I guessed the tactfully chosen words that were to follow, 'Mr. Defrates' marriage is naturally his personal affair but it would be understandable to think that his Indian colleagues are likely not to approve of this marriage. After all . . .' and he continued carefully to suggest the prejudices that I knew did not exist but were calculated to suit the situation.

'How would you compare him with his Indian colleagues?'

'I believe, Sir, that he is an able man but there are a number of Indians who are as able and abler. I would say that good though he is he is not among the best, though I must admit I have not had much contact with him at work.'

'I agree,' I interjected. 'I don't think you know anything about the quality of his work. I do and I think he is very good.'

The meeting was closed at this point. It was decided that we think it over, though there was the point about the problems the marriage might create for Defrates with his Indian colleagues!

I knew Defrates would go, and a few days later he went. He did not seem to mind very much and thought the whole episode unnecessary; at his age he could surely decide when to get married and to whom!

CHAPTER FOURTEEN

THERE CAME A crisis, my first in business, and a kind that the new life was not to lack later. Some rats had been fed in a research laboratory on a diet containing vanaspati but deficient in vitamin A. It was said that their third generation lost hair and went blind, and this was attributed to the vanaspati. A question was asked in Parliament, and the minister confirmed that the laboratory had found this to be the case. There was immediately an uproar and a demand to ban vanaspati and permit only the sale of liquid oil. Government averred that in some shape, as margarine or shortening, oils were hydrogenated all over the world, and nowhere had scientific opinion suggested banning hydrogenation as a health hazard. The Government instead referred the matter to a committee of scientists, who in turn sent the brief to a number of laboratories to conduct prolonged experiments on animals, children and adults to test the comparative nutritive value of ghee, vanaspati and groundnut oil in diets equal in all other respects. An anxious year and a half followed, in which the many who opposed vanaspati kept up the attack. Ban it now, they urged—why wait; at best it will never be proved the equal of ghee.

In all my years with vanaspati there were always problems, and I often wondered why. Here was a product, wholesome, economical and fulfilling a need; yet always under attack, in which the public that wanted it and the Government that should have provided it both joined. I sometimes wondered whether it did not suffer from the fundamental ambivalence of being wanted, and hated just because it was wanted in place of something else. If, perhaps, as in Europe with margarine and butter, there had been an open choice between ghee and vanaspati—ghee in abundant supply, cheap and of good quality—vanaspati would have been treated on its own merits, accepted or rejected. As it was it was the other way round; the ghee they wanted was scarce and bad, and the vanaspati they did not want was abundant and pure. The problem of vanaspati was therefore created by the very solution it provided. It was not the problem of a suspect food, for it had been pronounced wholesome by science all over the world, but a deeper problem of a society unable to face the hard choices before it, and settling for the soft options. Instead of ensuring good ghee, a formidable task since it was part of the yet more formidable problem of an inefficient agriculture, or accepting and encouraging vanaspati, since it at least provided a working alternative, the course suggested was the softer option of banning vanaspati on the ground that its absence in itself would solve all the problems of ghee. The vacuum of demand alone would provide the needed stimulus for ghee to become pure and abundant.

It was the soft option solution suggested by the protagonists of many causes. Ban the manufacture of mill cloth and the dying handloom industry will automatically revive, and so will the decaying rural economy. Let us go back to the legendary days of peace and plenty by just walking out of the present and setting our face against anything that symbolizes modernity; discard machines, industry, science, medicine, urbanization, and all the complexities that they characterize today, and revert to handicrafts, handloom, ayurveda, and the simple past. Another aspect of the soft options was the naive faith that legislation alone could solve a problem. The more intractable the problem, the more sweeping needed to be the legislation, the higher the penalties, and the stronger its enforcement. To smother the cause that needed to be tackled was evading the hard choice; that the problem remained was the fault of someone else.

Because the problems remained unsolved, compromises had to follow. Panditji, when pressed by the cow protectionists to ban vanaspati now, stood his ground and said that it was for the scientists to declare the results, and if they found vanaspati harmful he would not hesitate to ban it, but if they found it harmless no action would be called for. The scientists experimented for nearly two years and ultimately rediscovered what scientists had discovered elsewhere fifty years ago, that vanaspati was harmless; that it was as assimilable and digestible as ghee and the raw oil it was made from; that like its source, groundnut oil, it lacked vitamin A, but when the diet was reinforced with this vitamin the growth rate of children and animals was comparable with those fed on milk fat. The Indian scientists recommended however that vanaspati should be made to a melting point corresponding to body temperature, 37 degrees centigrade, so that it would have the maximum digestibility, and that it should have vitamins A and D added to it.

This verdict did not satisfy the opponents, and innuendoes were made about vested interests influencing the scientists, and the interests of the cow, dairying, agriculture, and the whole rural economy of India sacrificed to keep this nefarious product going. The attack came with renewed fury, this time on a moral plane supported by religious arguments; and now support came from a new quarter.

Gandhiji had once written an article in his weekly, *Harijan*, saying that some friends had drawn his attention to the harm vanaspati did to dairying and the cow, that it was an imitation product at best, and made no contribution in the process of converting oil. He thought there was a point in it and left it at that, a thought to be examined objectively and fairly. But the inheritors of his tradition saw it in emotion alone. To them no examination, no proof was necessary; vanaspati should just be banned, for they were convinced that this was the key to the whole rural problem of India. They fervently believed that unless vanaspati went no start could ever be made to solve it. The decks had to be cleared of the excrescences of industrialization; in the place of the loom, the charkha; for the modern oil press, the kolhu; for alcohol, nira; for vanaspati, pure ghee.

Mashruwala, one of Gandhiji's closest followers, had remained at Wardha, Gandhiji's last ashram, and continued to run the *Harijan* after the teacher's assassination. He picked up the controversy and gave it a new angle. Gandhiji had believed in always distinguishing between truth and falsehood, non-violence and violence, reality and imitation. Mashruwala concluded that vanaspati not only did harm to the cow, but was a spurious coin that drove out the good currency, ghee, and in imitating ghee it contained a falsehood. It must therefore be banned.

Coming from Wardha, in Gandhiji's own paper that had for years been his means of thinking aloud and conducting a dialogue with the world, this pronouncement on vanaspati was *ex cathedra*. Government felt embarrassed at the charges levelled at them of trying to please the industrialists at the expense of the poor millions. Their embarrassment was indeed acute because not so long ago Panditji had assured Parliament that this was a matter for the scientists to decide. Having got their verdict he was now being pressed to ignore it and take a contradictory stand. Government eventually gave in and decided to refer the whole issue to Public Opinion.

This was the first time such action had ever been taken, nor has it ever been done again. Parliament referred the issue, to ban or not to ban vanaspati, to all the States' governments, leading municipalities, chambers of commerce, institutions of national and local importance, political and religious associations, and to members of the public at large, to express their opinion. It was an extraordinary spectacle. Anyone could express an opinion and send it to the Parliament Secretariat, with or without giving any reasons in support. The Cow Protection Society—Go Seva Sangh—exhorted people to save Go-Mata, the

Mother Cow, and called upon the country to raise its voice against vanaspati.

Never before had a product, a plain cooking fat at that, acquired the prominence of a widely debated national issue. There had been doubts in other countries about the effect of margarine upon butter, and where an agricultural lobby was strong, as in U.S.A. and Australia, some restrictive legislation had been passed; but these were countries with abundance of butter and an affluence that could afford it. But here was a case of emotions stirred in a society that was short of everything and could ill afford to spurn even an ersatz product.

As Pettit was the chairman of the Vanaspati Manufacturers' Association and had to lead the defence of the industry, I was drawn in, and I threw myself in with unusual zeal. My duty apart, I felt I was fighting a modern cause against the old and outdated. It was a crusade against the fantasies of those who wanted to merge in the timelessness of India and resurrect a past which could never be made to live again. They talked from the highest level about traditions, heritage, glory, the kingdom that was Rama's, the Vedic Age of milk and honey: all this would return if only we pressed the button of bans — ban vanaspati, ban sugar, ban longcloth, ban tea, ban alcohol and restore the pristine and viceless past. I felt moved too by the ease with which we slid into a compromise. Our scientists knew all about the work done abroad, but they were told to satisfy themselves. Despite the pledge to abide by their findings, the matter was now turned over to the most amorphous of all judgements, public opinion, for how could it be gauged or quantified on a national scale, short of a referendum? And so a most confused public argument began.

The Cow Protection Society, with the tacit support of the party in power, began its campaign in right earnest and held an Anti-Vanaspati Day with meetings all over the country protesting against hydrogenation and demanding the ban. Whatever an average individual's previous views, the moment vanaspati was termed the enemy of the cow it became anathema. It was no use arguing that ghee was ghee, it came from the cow, but as there was not enough of it why should vanaspati be blamed for trying to look like ghee, if people wanted it. Nevertheless, fight we must and we did against such archaic sentiments.

I travelled everywhere organizing our salesmen to approach the trade and their associations, prominent citizens, especially doctors and university teachers, and canvass members of the public for signatures; but no matter what we did, each editorial in the *Harijan* undid things. Danger to the cow, when spelled out by Wardha, made the case for vanaspati quite hopeless. A thought came to me in the last resort. I suggested to Pettit that I would like to go to Wardha and meet Mashruwala himself for a heart to heart talk. He was taken aback by this suggestion, and characteristically wanted to examine it appreciatively but critically.

'What do you hope to achieve?' he asked.

'Well, Sir, I realize the strength of his convictions and the depth of his emotions. Let me analyse them. His opposition to vanaspati is an article of a whole faith whose fabric cannot lightly be tampered with, nor can he let go a single strand. He believes in a return to the village as the focus of economic and social growth; to him the towns are unnecessary and evil excrescences. The villager cannot be left in splendid isolation and it is the responsibility of Government to help him, but in the process he must be saved from the contagion of modern economic and industrial beliefs, large scale production, mechanization and corporate effort. His old tools may be improved in a limited way, like the old charkha has been changed to the amber charkha, and his old hand and bullock press to the more efficient kolhu. He should also be given certain simple amenities: his village should be cleaned, his roof repaired, roads built, a new school, a dispensary, but preferably of the old ayurvedic system of medicine, a drinking water well; but no attempts should be made to introduce either machines or the products of machines into his village. I cannot ever hope to change such basic thinking, but I want to try and isolate vanaspati from at least its most rigorous aspects.

'I also realize the risk, the big risk, of my very logical and rational arguments rebounding off his mind and in the process starting something new and far worse. He may conclude that the industrialists are now trying to influence him in the way they had worked on the Government. In fact, he can draw conclusions worse than that and may feel spurred in his crusade to make it an even larger public issue than it is at present.'

Pettit looked at me seriously, but it was like him not to turn down a proposition that showed a promise, however fraught with risk it appeared. Coming from me, in this particular instance, he was intrigued too.

'Do you realize the zeal of the man, the strength of his conviction, the deep honesty behind them, and what your approach may mean to him? It is not just a case of nothing lost if you fail but, as you say, giving an altogether new twist to the controversy. If he is unconvinced and, what is worse, misunderstands your motives, it could blow up into something serious. He is a most honest man, and I deeply respect his motives, but this makes him as an opponent the more serious.'

'Yes, I realise all that, but there is still the chance that I may persuade him that he may do no more than agree to differ and leave it at that, and that alone may bring the controversy to a rational level.'

'Good luck', said Pettit, 'Go and see him.'

I wrote to Mashruwala the next day and asked for an appointment for the following week. He wrote back cordially inviting me. It was the month of heavy rains, and as the old Dakota tossed about in the upper monsoon layer, I sat looking out of the window into the turmoil of clouds. Down below, through occasional openings, I could see the wet green Western Ghats, their deep canyons full of swirling streams. The green was such as I had never seen anywhere; at places I could count eleven shades of it, the greens of the grass, the rice fields at different stages of growth. There were really only two colours, the brown of the water and the green of the growth, but within them the subtle variations turned into a riot of colour. But in all this turbulence there was a soothing restfulness.

In pouring rain I took a taxi from Nagpur to Wardha, some thirty miles away, and as usual on such occasions my mind went into a restful blank in which my thoughts about the meeting moved about like wisps of fog. I arrived in Wardha ahead of time to look around the ashram. In the monsoon green, its neat cottages looked beautiful, with their small gardens well tended. The inmates of the ashram moved about quietly and there was an air of restraint and tasteful calm. Gandhiji's own small cottage was as he had left it, in utterly simple taste. The whole place had the air of an idyll.

At one end of the ashram was a village which I decided to look at. The contrast was striking. Here, after many years of contiguity and close contact, the village lived as it had a thousand years ago. The poverty was understandable, but not the squalor and neglect which a little self-help could have corrected. The roads were dirty with sewage running through their middle, the homes were uncared for, the roofs unrepaired, the garbage unremoved, and there were no fruit or flowering trees; it was like any other village.

For nearly two decades the mainspring of India's rural emancipation and reconstruction had flowed past this village, whose men and women daily visited and worked in the ashram; yet the impact cannot have been much or it had already worn away. The two communities had lived side by side, one deifying the other, preaching its future glory and rightful place; the other seemed to have looked on apathetically. I wondered whether this was significant of the sheer magnitude of the villager's problem or only proved how theoretical was the interest of the ashramite. It could be that the planners had found the resistance to change insuperable; maybe with the passing of Gandhiji, when the villagers no more found themselves in focus, they just lost interest in the effort.

I arrived at Mashruwala's house and was met by a small, thin, gracious man. He thanked me for coming all the way to meet him, and I thanked him for receiving me. I explained that I was not an industrialist or capitalist, just a working manager with a point of view on industrial growth. He sat down on the floor and began to spin. I sat next to him, although he had offered me a chair.

'Mashruwalaji, what have you against vanaspati?' I began by asking.

'Everything', he answered. 'You begin with raw groundnut oil that people have eaten for centuries, but go and refine it, hydrogenate it, take the colour and taste out of it, and then add the colour and taste of ghee. Why don't you leave the oil alone and let people eat it the way they have always done.'

'I would agree with you,' I said, 'if there was any compulsion attached to it. But people still have the choice; they can still buy the groundnut oil, and most do; they don't have to buy vanaspati. There are lakhs of housewives who buy some raw oil, some vanaspati, and some ghee, each for a different purpose, and in exercise of free choice. Each product has its own use, the ghee for flavour, the vanaspati for general cooking and oil for frying. Given ghee at the price of vanaspati they would naturally not buy the latter, but that is out of the question. Why then do you object to this choice before the housewife?'

'Our objections are many. First, and to me very important, vanaspati is the product of machines and I object to machines. Oil and ghee are simple products of nature, processed by hand with the aid of the simplest tools that a villager can make, the press and the churn. They are part of the villager's self-contained life. I do not see the need for taking the oil away to a factory in a town, processing it and bringing it back costlier than it left.'

'Do you know, Sir, I am watching the charkha on which you are spinning and I am reminded of the contraption my mother used to spin on. It weighed over twenty pounds and was a cumbersome thing; it took a lot of effort and produced a meagre amount of yarn. Yours is light, efficient and almost a machine in comparison; in fact, it is a product of modern mechanical thinking. But supposing someone said to you that he could attach a small motor to it so that it could spin twice as fast and produce twice the yarn. When my mother's health began to fail at a young age and she could no more spin enough yarn to clothe us and make sheets and towels for the house, would you then have objected to a charkha that went as much faster than yours as does yours from hers?'

Mashruwala looked thoughtful and I could sense his mind balking at the question.

'No, I don't think I could object, so long as the machine is designed to provide occupation to an individual and improves his productivity.'

'Then I think you have conceded industrialization, because this is exactly how the process began. Iron tyres round wooden wheels, a steel shaft and greased hubs, and one day a small engine in the chassis. From your own loom to the village weaver, to a loom and weaving shed with several men employed in it, to steam and power and the automatic loom. I cannot see how and at what stage you can either stop or reverse the process.'

'Does that mean that industrialization is inevitable and that we have to go through all its evils?'

'Inevitable it is, if you want to live as part of the world society. To print your *Harijan* you need machines, and you need machines to carry it to all parts of India. It is not inevitable though to bring the evils of industrialization with it; we know enough to avoid them; but is the poverty and squalor of the cities really so much worse than that of the village next door? Is it primarily the creation of machines any more than in the villages it is the creation of their handicrafts? No, I think squalor in India has something to do with history and geography. It begins at its worst in the north and changes as we go further south. Villages can be poor but clean, just as I have seen industry in Scandinavia free from its ugliness in Britain.'

We discussed industrialization for a while, and his fears were naive. Like his master he wanted time not to move beyond a point in the past and the problem became serious because many who shared the belief now had the responsibility of running a Government with their minds split. The half-clad needed cloth that only the mills could produce in plenty and cheap, but the expansion of mills had to be banned to encourage the amber charkha which could not possibly cope with the demands of such a multitude. Similarly they wanted to ban the efficient extraction of oil from the seed in favour of the wasteful village presses.

'Sir,' I began again, 'if vanaspati and oil are available side by side, and people have the choice, why should you object to some preferring vanaspati, especially as it serves in place of ghee that they cannot afford?'

'Because vanaspati is a deception and a delusion. The woman who buys it is in fact only buying oil which is made to look like ghee, and she is deluding herself. If she cannot afford ghee, let her accept the truth and buy oil, not deceive herself by buying something spurious.'

'But she knows what she is buying. She knows vanaspati is oil, and not ghee.'

'I would still feel it my duty to prevent her from committing this untruth. Truth is Ahimsa, untruth is violence.'

'Are you not depriving her of a satisfaction?'

'Yes, but only because it is being falsely fulfilled.'

At this stage Mashruwala's wife entered the room with two cups of milk and after serving them quietly withdrew.

'I noticed that your wife wears gold bangles, presumably because they give her some satisfaction.'

He flushed and interrupted me, 'Well, I would rather she didn't. I don't believe in gold and ornaments, but you know what women are.'

'Yes, and I agree with you, though I think she has the right to the satisfaction of wearing jewellery. But supposing her maidservant wanted the same satisfaction but could not afford gold and therefore took brass bangles to the goldsmith and asked him to gild them. Would you object?'

'Yes, I would. I think she should wear brass if brass is all she can afford, and not make brass look like gold. It is self-deception.'

'I think now you are being unreasonable. She knows full well it is brass, and yet you would legislate that no one should be allowed to make brass look like gold, even when it does not deceive anyone and is honestly sold as gilt brass. I think it is you who are being "violent" in imposing your opinion on others. And I think this is just what you are doing with vanaspati. You may like oil, but there are many who don't like the taste of it and therefore prefer vanaspati. For you to ban vanaspati would only deprive them of a choice and force them to use the oil they don't like.'

I continued, 'You are right to demand that the adulteration of ghee should be stopped, with vanaspati or anything else, as much as passing off gilt for gold, but to ban vanaspati is like banning brass itself. Even to insist that vanaspati should not look like ghee, that it should not be given the flavour and colour to make it resemble ghee, to me would be wholly unjustified, but we may have to accept it because rather than accept the ban on vanaspati we would accept a ban on colouring and flavouring it.'

Mashruwala looked nettled by my argument and somewhat taken aback at the accusation of being violent. I was feeling frustrated by his unction and the implied sanction in an attitude that decided what people should eat, wear, adorn themselves with, and was ready, if they persisted in disagreeing, to ban the means of indulging their taste. He would prohibit or restrict liquor, coffee, tea, vanaspati, sugar, textile industries, horse racing, cinema, import of books, export of monkeys, fertilizers, vivisection, vaccination, all modern medicine: the list ran on interminably.

And yet when I looked at him, frail of frame and weighing barely seventy pounds, racked by asthma, there was in him a light of conviction, and a courage cast in the mould of his frail master, who had stood up to the mightiest opponent anyone in the world had ever known.

On the way back in the taxi, through the wet night, a sadness came over me. The task done, the freedom won, masters of our own fate, were our energies now going to be bent to build with tools of yesterday, to preoccupation with the means and unconcern with the end? For years now the controversy was running its arid course about how to revive a dying past and the glory of a mythological Vedic age, while the real problems of the cow, milk and ghee, the village and its agriculture, were barely tackled, in the vague hope that once industry was banned a large enough market would be opened up to revive the countryside and set right its problems.

'Vanaspati may be good or bad for health, but none can deny that it is a corruption of morals. Along with textiles, sugar and other industries it has created vicious economies by making the utilization of food crops and maintenance of milk cattle less profitable than the cultivation of cotton, groundnut, sugarcane, tobacco etc., and thus bringing about deficiencies. The fundamental issue is moral.' (The *Harijan*).

'The cow-centred civilization of India' was what they wanted to revive.

The public opinion poll proved inconclusive, though we managed to get a greater weight than the opponents of vanaspati. But the whole thing was meaningless. The bill was ultimately withdrawn upon the promise of the Prime Minister that a committee would be appointed to suggest suitable methods to stop the adulteration of ghee. The *Harijan* wrote:

'Nehru gave three assurances: that ghee was much adulterated, that Government were anxious to put a stop to it, and that experiments carried out on hydrogenated oils had shown that they were not harmful. He turned down the demand to ban the production of vanaspati because Government were quite clear and convinced of the fact that the use of vanaspati was not harmful to health. By repeated scientific tests and research it had been found that nobody suffered from it, although vanaspati and its like was used by 75% of the people the world over. He continued that Government would instead control the production of vanaspati so that it contained vitamins A and D, sesame oil to make adulteration of ghee easily detectable by a commercial test; and take the colour and flavour of ghee out of it.'

Mashruwala was angry and said that 'such arguments convince none, deceive none. They indicate that both the scientist and the statesman act in collusion with the industrialist and simply create an estrangement between Government and the people.'

On 9th September 1956, three months after the bill was withdrawn, Mashruwala died. An article which appeared posthumously summed up his simple and sincere mind. In reply to a question someone had asked about the so-called soya or groundnut milk, he had replied:

'If the preparation of soya or groundnut milk becomes an industry; if they are manufactured and canned in factories and sold in markets, it will surely be as harmful as vanaspati. But if people prepare and consume them at home, it stands on a different level. Just as there is no competition between groundnut oil and ghee, similarly there need not be any between payas (soya or groundnut milk) and milk.'

For some curious reason he wandered away in a rather different vein about milk.

'It is difficult to determine the precise effect of milk on sex-impulse. All that we can say is that milk and ghee are animal products; also that those engaged in cattle breeding and dairy industry frequently come under the disturbing influence of sex acts of animals at an impressionable age. This cannot be helped. Even otherwise they are not immune from such impressions, because they are frequently around in nature. Efforts have to be made to maintain purity of mind in spite of such influences.'

'One cannot say definitely that those who take vegetable diet exclusively, even abjuring milk and its products, are immune from passion. Sex is a very subtle impulse and to a certain extent assisted with age, and what we consume through our eyes, ears and skin touches also. Diet regulation and discipline in self-control are helpful in overcoming passion. As a Hindi poet has said, "A sadhu living in a forest cave, wearing bark of trees, living on fallen fruit and leaves, and sleeping on bare ground may be harassed by sex passion." But diet is a helpful factor and may not be ignored.'

CHAPTER FIFTEEN

GEOFFREY HEYWORTH WAS an even more remarkable man than his brother Roger. Unilever had steadily grown from a national to a European business, and its overseas units changed it into an international business, but it was under the fourteen years of Heyworth's chairmanship that it strove towards becoming multinational. I watched this process of growth from a junior distance, when its unfolding had only a limited significance for me. I could not become international in the exact sense because the absorption of men from the regions to the centre and their projection to the international scene had not yet begun. To feel international in a country ruled from outside had no meaning, but after independence it was of one's own choosing how close one wanted to feel to the rest of the world; and it is easier to feel close to others when you feel their equal. As the years progressed after independence I could sense this weight of inequality shedding, and curiously the process in my own case was accelerated by the vanaspati crisis, because here was a problem of our own making and our own tackling, for which we could no longer blame the alien.

Heyworth felt that to cope with size and geography, as Unilever sprawled further over the world, you needed delegation to the ends of the limbs, and this could best be done if the overseas units were manned by executives carefully selected, trained and groomed, who must ultimately be nationals of the country. It became imperative as national aspirations required a sensitive understanding of the many new complexities. The process became known as 'ization', a generic simplification of Indianization, Ceylonization etc. The older Lever men shook their heads and doubted if it would ever be possible to train locals to take over complete responsibility. There were natural limitations which no amount of training could overcome, at least not in the foreseeable future. In this there was a certain amount of cynical truth, for limitations one had, but when they were labelled as inherent and irremediable and therefore a kind of genetic bar, frustration and apathy set in and soon the 'limitation' became real; only to prove the point. Heyworth now wanted to hasten the course of 'ization', and in this he was helped by Desmond Bonham-Carter, who on his very first visit to India set a new pace.

Bonham-Carter was a big man, over seven feet in height and proportionately broad. His presence in the Company could not help but be noticed, and he took care to let it be known what he hoped to persuade our Company to achieve. 'Ization', he let it be known, had to be rushed and chances taken to complete it in five years. He seemed to pick up where Roger Heyworth had left. I invited him home one evening and decided to let myself be checked over, which he did without hesitation. His style differed from Roger's, for though equally direct he was sometimes deliberately unreticent and made calculated leakages of plans and information to check your reactions.

We talked about the new Administrative Staff College started at Henley to bring together experienced men from industry and government in Britain to learn from discussion and mutual experience. He felt that its benefit should be spread over the Commonwealth countries and someone from our business in India should be sent. I saw something of the hospital scheme of Pettit in it.

'Why?' I asked. 'You have started the institution to train British executives, and it would be a pity to share such a valuable facility with foreigners. I hope one day we will start a similar college in India to train our own executives.'

I was wary, and in this cold and prickly tone the conversation went on. I think he tried to find out what made me react this way to his overtures, as it certainly was not a lack of interest or commitment in my work.

An invitation to Henley was therefore sent to Chandy, another senior Indian in the company whom I greatly admired and who seemed better integrated than I, at least on the surface. But Bonham-Carter was not easily deflected; there was soon an invitation from him suggesting that I might join a Unilever course called the Executives Management Conference, to be held at their training centre in the country. To his satisfaction, if not surprise, I accepted it readily.

I returned to England after seven years. The last time was in 1949 when I went on a training visit to Unilever for three months and stayed on to spend another three months in Sweden where Gärd joined me with our three children. Sweden, of course, had not been touched by the war, but England was then still very much a country of shortages and damage. In 1956 England was back to normal and on the way to its new life of affluence, but it had changed from the country I knew in the thirties, a different England, better in many ways, though not in all. Bonham-Carter was pleased I had at last decided to come over, and particularly wanted to see me after the course to hear my reactions. I missed Roger Heyworth, who had suddenly died the year before in Ceylon. He had been to India with his new wife, Gerda, whom he had known many years earlier, and married after his Danish wife left him. He looked happier and more relaxed than I had ever seen him before, together at last with a woman he must always have loved; but it was not to be for long.

The course was held in an attractive country house with pleasant grounds. The small group of about fifteen people consisted of directors from various associated companies from America to Australia; men mostly of a high calibre. The leader was an Australian accountant with unorthodox ideas who liked heresy of any kind. He was acid and provocative, and a complete iconoclast, and set a leisurely pace and gave us plenty of time to think and relax. There was a constant exposure to facets of Unilever I had not known. The chairman, vice chairman, the Dutch chairman and members of the board, heads of divisions, scientists, production men and specialists came in a constant stream to talk to us. We questioned them freely, occasionally with unmerciful criticism.

The strand that ran through was delegation, which the chairman had preached and wanted the organization to practise. The rest was new techniques the organization was learning to adopt. I listened a good deal as it was my first experience of living and working in an international group with such breadth of experience, and slowly a realization emerged. Here was an institution, in its own way unique, that had an opportunity to bring together a diversity of cultures and sub-cultures and unite them through a common purpose of commerce into a flexible yet strong framework with a total corporate personality. Similar attempts were being made in the new international agencies to create world departments and international secretariats, but the problems of the two were different. The international corporation usually had to work under constraints, especially in the newly independent nations, and yet make a profit, whereas the international agency, though equally faced with similar environmental problems, was distributing largesse; besides, their organization structure followed more the bureaucratic pattern of governments. The same internationalness made one efficient and lively, and the other inefficient and dull. I was to learn the answer some years later.

After the course I went to attend a Unilever annual conference at Brighton, where one hundred and fifty of the top management in the U.K. and Europe, and those like me who happened to be visiting, assembled on a Thursday evening for a forty hour brainstorming, with the whole board, Dutch and British, as interested spectators. Through the next day, till well past midnight, the discussions went on.

Once the chairman came in, shuffling on his two sticks, modest in a presence assured and felt. In a few minutes the discussion took a new direction, and perhaps because of my presence, but largely because of his own interest, we began to explore the internationalization of the senior talent. He was a man of few words, and these were mostly monosyllabic grunts, but the crystal clarity of his mind and the way it pursued a thought were interesting to watch.

Saturday morning we relaxed while the board went over the reports. I went for a walk by the sea, and remembered coming to Brighton many years ago. The recall brought back a lot of things I wanted to remember and some that I did not. I realized that a recontact with the past was not possible. I had tried it on my last visit in 1949 and failed miserably. I had then attempted a reunion with my old college friends in Manchester, and found that I could not transcend the barrier of the intervening years. The war had changed too many things, and in my ignorance too often I touched spots that hurt. What had happened inside this small circle seemed to mirror what had happened to England herself, once the most stable society in the world. From the patronizing and comfortable Britain of 1929, stern in its confidence and oblivious of the first gathering clouds, to that of 1949, anxious to be left alone while trying to readjust, I perceived the difference.

I was almost afraid of picking up the old threads because of my experience in 1949. A people we had known to be gracious were raw at the edges, and one no longer dared to agree with them, even occasionally, when they indulged in their old habit of self-disparagement. I remembered asking a waiter at tea, on the boat train to Holland, whether the one lump of sugar he had placed between me and a man sitting opposite was his or mine. He flared up and told me that I did not realize there was rationing in the country, that there had been a shortage of sugar and of many other things. However, he added, I could have it. But there had been the lighter side to life too, when in an obscure little restaurant in Soho, to which I had been referred by someone who knew, I was served a steak, my first in London for three months. I had asked for the menu, and an absent-looking Slav girl stared at me uncomprehendingly and said.

'No menu.'

'Then what can I have,' I asked.

'Only steak'.

And when the bill came, I innocently said

'But I did not have one, never mind two, bottles of red wine.'

'No, but you had steak.'

Only too true, I admitted.

Somehow it was not so much the young who were sensitive as the old. The young had lived through it for ten years and it had become a way of life, a hard way but one to which they had become accustomed. If there was a restaurant where you could get a steak on the sly, they did not mind telling one about it. My embarrassment was with the older ones, to whom this was a come-down in life; the common things of the old days were scarce, available only at a price.

By 1956 things had changed vastly, but a mark had been left behind; or perhaps I imagined it. Our connection also had been broken for nearly ten years, and every now and again we made independent little noises about the Commonwealth. On this and on my many following visits I never travelled out of London. My work done I would take the first plane back to Bombay. Strangely I felt ill at ease in an England that no longer ruled us.

From this morning walk by the sea I was nearly late for the plenary session. There was a free discussion on some critical issues, and on international management the chairman drew me in. I said a few words but I was more interested in listening to the heartbeat of one of the world's largest organizations. The general tenor of the debate seemed to be an underlying fear about the organization's capacity to sense the change in time and overcome it.

Around the isolate manager the discussion also revolved at some length. Was there room only for organization men? Who was the isolate and what were his problems? There was general agreement that while his sheer ability put him way beyond his colleagues, what isolated him from the rest was usually his intolerance of the less blessed, as also of organizational formalities and channels of communication. He went ahead and did things, and wanted the rule swept aside if it thwarted him. It was in his nature to experiment, often regardless of cost; he was incautious and tentative, and failure to him was of little concern. And yet all agreed that the organization must encourage him and that there must always be enough of his kind around.

A year earlier I had been on a board in Bombay selecting trainees, with Hoskyns-Abrahall in the chair. Among the group up for the final interview was a conspicuously able young man. At the group discussion he stood out in sheer ability and maturity well above the rest, whom he seemed to irritate. He was impatient with the speed of their reasoning, and would often become apathetic until some argument attracted his attention and he joined in, only to disrupt the group again.

At the individual interview, he was equally brilliant, but he also managed to irritate some of the board.

After the interview we broke into a lively discussion, All were full of praise for the boy, quite the best mind we had come across for a long time, and yet the same question came to all of us: would he fit into the organization? If he managed to irritate some of us, what about his colleagues and subordinates? He was able, highly able, but would he make any effort to tolerate the less able, or accept genuine disagreement? In an organization like ours it was mostly a matter of team-work where the individual's achievement was rarely entirely his own. And yet we all felt we were letting talent go; there should be some way of fitting him in; it was almost a reflection on the organization to turn him down. We decided to ask him back to the board, something we did not often do. The boy returned, cool, almost contemptuous. Abrahall in his mild, scholarly way said:

'You know, we have asked you a lot of questions, but it did not occur to me to ask you if there were any questions you wished to ask.'

'No,' he replied coldly, and looked straight at Abrahall, 'I have nothing to ask though I have something to say. I do not think you will select me, I am not your type.'

'Yes,' said Abrahall simply. 'I think you are right. I am sorry because we are very impressed with your ability.'

'I know, you really want someone else, able, but more likely to conform.'

Shortly afterwards he was offered a Rhodes scholarship to Oxford.

The conference over, I returned to London, to Unilever House for a day, and after a brief visit to Rotterdam, introducing myself to the Dutch side of business, I flew back to India. The whole of Europe was under a blanket of fog, and having just managed to take off at Amsterdam the nearest we could land was at Nice, after trying Rome twice on the way; and from there on to Istanbul, Karachi and Bombay. On the long journey home I tried to take stock.

The Dutch plane, decorated for Christmas, was a last contact with Europe. I felt I was returning to India recharged, though with the core unchanged. I lived in two worlds: the outer shell world of England, Unilever, the western executive; and the inner core world of the Punjabi in me. Looking into the limitless space outside the small square window of the Constellation, I tried to examine my problem. I had perhaps let the two concentric worlds move in contrary directions and created friction. While the outer world was essential to progress, I needed the inner for harmony; if only I could make the two move freely, independently of each other and therefore without friction. But this visit had made a difference. While it had given me a clear understanding of Unilever and brought me closer to a large number of its senior men, it had at the same time sharpened my individuality. Could I be a part of it and yet remain myself?

I watched the Dutch cabin staff trying to create a festive spirit among a planeload of Dutch families returning east, tying bright pinafores on the little Dutch children and setting them to help; I looked down on the sundrenched Middle Eastern landscape below, wondering if a harmony was ever possible. As the valleys below filled with a deepening darkness while the last light of the sun hung around the plane at its height, there were two worlds, the plane flying purpose-fully, disembodied, through space, and the earth, below, moving unconcerned.

A few days after my return Bonham-Carter visited Bombay, and suggested that I talk to our management about my visit to Unilever. I saw a challenge in this and accepted it. I talked about the England I had seen, so different from the one I had known, and the Unilever I had not known before in the new international dimensions it was try-ing to organize. Bonham-Carter listened with interest, and must have sensed a change in me which was really a successful readjustment, with the core still firm. I wondered if he did not prefer it this way to be of any use to them.

About this time the company was reorganized. As the result of a suggestion from the Government an Indian equity company was formed and some shares put on the stock market at the end of 1956.

It was a momentous step by which the three almost independent companies were merged into one. I reminded Abrahall of a breakfast conversation in 1947 at the Cecil Hotel in old Delhi when he had asked our English Delhi branch manager what he thought would happen to our business when Independence came. The manager began a long account of the problem that we would have to face with an Indian government that would be unsympathetic to foreigners in general and to British business in particular. He felt it was but natural that having obtained political independence the country would discriminate and eventually want to get rid of British business altogether. I disagreed and said that all this was unlikely, but what would happen was that 'India' would have to come out of the brackets. This is just what happened nine years later, when Hindustan Vanaspati Manufacturing Company and Lever Brothers (India) Ltd. became Hindustan Lever

Ltd. Abrahall had then laughed and said that that would be no bad thing, much to the disgust of the manager who was not amused.

As chairman of the new company, Abrahall set about the task with meticulousness. The new board had five Englishmen and three Indians, and Abrahall thought that I should give up vanaspati and return to head office to exchange jobs with Maurice Zinkin. After nearly twenty years in marketing I felt awkward at the thought. Maurice had combined marketing research, with which I was of course familiar, with planning, economics and statistics, and the intellectual that he was he had set a standard of advice that being unacademic myself I could never hope to maintain. His new book, *Development in Free Asia*, was perhaps the best contribution to the problems of a developing India, and his observations are even more apposite today than when he made them in the early fifties.

I had no confidence that I would make a success and asked Abrahall the reason for the move. Had I failed at my job? Abrahall of course politely refuted this and said that I had done well in the past and would no doubt do so in the future. It took me some years to learn that in a crisis, if one is diffident one makes all the calculations against oneself, to the extent of giving oneself no quarter. I later saw men much stronger behave in the same way, and the effort it took to convince them that by thus writing themselves off they were being as unfair to themselves as to those who had probably decided it in their interest. I learned too that a little lifting of the fog around such decisions — perhaps some calculated thinking aloud — can help.

Abrahall wanted the board to operate as a team; left to ourselves in our own functional spheres, he wanted us to consult and decide jointly on all company matters. I found his patience and permissiveness helpful in my growth as a board member. My experience at the Unilever course had so enthused me that I suggested he might ask Bonham-Carter if my name could be put up for the Advanced Management Programme of the Graduate School of Business Administration at Harvard University. I felt that my educational and working contacts abroad had been entirely with England, and with the wave of new ideas in management that were now spreading out from America, I would like to visit that country, preferably on a course like this. Unilever usually sent two executives to each of the spring and autumn sessions, senior and handpicked men. Bonham-Carter responded quickly. Yes, he would put up my name for Unilever's approval and Harvard's acceptance; the standards set were very high though.

CHAPTER SIXTEEN

SOON AFTER I succeeded Maurice Zinkin, an institution in Ahmedabad invited me to their annual conference to give his customary talk on market research. My only experience of public speaking had been long ago in the debates at Manchester University, usually more effervescent than serious, but in my fresh enthusiasm I accepted this invitation, the first of its kind.

I found Ahmedabad a strange city. I had been there several times selling Dalda, but this visit after a gap of some years evoked in me an interest in the town that was to last for many years, an interest from which I gained a great deal, but at a price. The first thing I noted was that large sections of the old city wall were being demolished. It was an unplastered wall of unusual beauty, built from brick treated specially to give it a good finish. Sad as it was, it was a sign of the city's improvement plans of the kind that one was becoming reluctantly used to. Civic improvement in India was taking its toll of old beauty; in fact, 'beautification' began to mean replacing a harmony in brick, stone, timber or tile with a disharmony in cement, concrete, steel and incongruous colours.

As I looked at the beautiful main gate facing north, from where the city for many centuries drew its power, I thought of Akbar standing before it with characteristic regal risk. He had heard barely four days ago that the governor of the south western provinces was plotting against him, and decided to teach a quick lesson to him and others who might harbour any ambitions. With a few horsemen he rode day and night from Agra to Ahmedabad and arrived at this gate unannounced. The governor was so shaken by the news that he rushed to the gate and fell at the emperor's feet. Having made his point, Akbar said no more about the suspected treason; merely let the man, as indeed the whole empire, realize his omnipresence.

The town came into prominence when some of its Jain families more than a century ago started a modern textile industry. A plant was imported from England and brought in bullock carts from the coast. The first venture failed, but others succeeded, and by the latter part of the nineteenth century Ahmedabad had a flourishing textile industry, second only to Bombay. The leading Jain entrepreneurs then also spread to Bombay, which because of its port and cosmopolitanism grew rapidly, while Ahmedabad remained just a large textile centre. Undisturbed by the competition that other communities from outside could have offered, these Jain families who controlled the textile wealth intermarried and became an endogamous group, like a large single joint family in which the wealth accumulated and circulated centripetally. Away from the city and the mills, across the river, they built their palatial homes, emulating the style of architecture and living of the neighbouring princely families of Gujarat and Saurashtra.

A new impulse came when Gandhiji built his first ashram on the banks of the river Sabarmati. The mill-owning families began to wear khadi and became discreetly nationalistic. The contact with the new movement benefitted them in many ways. Gandhiji's mediation gave them such peace with their labour as no other town in India ever experienced; swadeshism gave protection against imported cloth. His influence also made their self-interest enlightened, although they did not rise to emulate the philanthrophy of their Parsi neighbours.

After Independence and the death of Gandhi and Sardar Patel, their interest in Congress waned and their influence ceased, which even the formation of their own state of Gujarat did not revive. Perhaps they expected the newly arrived political masters to consult and defer, but these new men did not have Gandhiji's gift of making use of all and making each feel big, as if he had been allotted a special task in his plan of things. The mill owners began to concentrate in a new direction; they tried to make Ahmedabad a centre of culture and education, and with their wealth they opened many new institutions; and to attract attention to their institutions they held conferences to which they invited people from all over India. A real feather in their cap one year was an inauguration by the Duke of Edinburgh.

It was interesting to watch the composition of the people from Ahmedabad at the conference. There were among them three distinct types. The elders of the community, the heads of the mill-owning families, managing agents as they were called, were portly gentlemen dressed in immaculate white khadi caps, long coats and high dhoties; one was the president of the Mill Owners Association, the other the mayor, the third the chairman of the institution which had organized the conference, the fourth, remarkably similar to the others in appearance and ways, was the leader of the local textile labour union. They all made speeches extolling the virtues of modern management, the need for adopting new technologies, and the value of a happy, well cared for worker.

Next, there were their sons and nephews, all dressed in dark American suits, educated at Harvard, Columbia, Michigan, and occasionally in England. They were the top underlayer of the managing agencies, often mere boys in their early twenties, always identifiable by their curious use of the first person possessive whenever they referred to anything to do with their organization—it was always 'my factory' and 'my factory manager'. There was that unmistakable aura of confidence and proprietariness about them as noticeable as the self-effacing air about the third category, their hired professional managers, the technicians and even the research scientists, who invariably came from other parts of India. I wondered why this was so, and could only surmise that the local youth of the controlling families always worked in their family businesses and preferred to start as directors, well above the top rung of the professional ladder, while the middle-class young men of Ahmedabad preferred to start their own small business.

.I was impressed though that these family heads, men of another generation, brought up in different traditions, could so welcome new ideas and encourage their young to adopt them. They patronized education, science, art, architecture and dancing, and endowed well. There were research institutions for textiles, physics and psychology, a design centre, a Tagore theatre, a private dance academy, all in the style of Le Corbusier, whom they had invited to design a number of buildings, including the house of one of the well-to-do young.

The Family homes were what one would have expected. On the first night we were all invited to a party by the doyen of the managing agents' corps. His was a large palace set in virtually a cultivated forest, in which were dotted the homes of sons and daughters. They lived like a brood in separate nests but comfortably close to the parents. The marble entrance hall of the main home had an office with clerks and janitors on duty, and a telephone switchboard. The living rooms were of mixed Western and Indian design, and the whole effect was of well harnessed wealth. On the terrace there were little earthenware oil lamps, a design on the floor of coloured flour in religious symbols, and in the centre an open log fire. Servants went round with sweet and spicy drinks, and after two rounds had been served soup arrived in tea cups, and a vegetarian buffet dinner was displayed in mixed Western and Indian style. On silver trays there were curries, curds and pickles, and on Royal Doulton china salads and stews. Within the hour, by nine o'clock, the party was over. A hundred or more of us all left together. The following night there was a party at the next senior home, that was similar in all ways, but on a reduced scale.

On the last day we all went to lunch to the doyen's son, and here was an interesting evidence of change in one generation. He had built his house outside the parental colony, and though large by all standards, it was modest for the family, but its interior was a wider mixture of America, Britain, Scandinavia, Japan, Gujarat and Moghul, with a touch of South India. The spacious living room was air-conditioned and divided into three styles; one was Indian with large white cushions on the floor and bolsters against the wall, another Scandinavian with low modern chairs, tables and bookshelves; the third was the dining section of American character. Raw silk curtains, abstract paintings, modern European ceramics and glassware, Japanese drawings of lobsters and horses, Indian rural pottery and woodwork, a sitar next to a hi-fi. Bach, Bismillah Khan and West Side Story: with all this it was still a liveable room. There were the same soft drinks, followed by soup, Indian food, a variety of salads and gratins on china with abstract designs, and then an abrupt and early farewell.

As I went from one party to another, eating the same food and meeting the same people, I was puzzled by all this hospitality, showered on strangers with faultless impersonality, part of the pattern of self-imposed duty. Nothing was left uncared for; there was a tea party too on the last evening on the lawns of the Corbusier headquarters of the textile industry, where for the first time the protocol was relaxed and there were some men who looked as if they lived within the city wall.

The conference progressed like all conferences in India I have since seen, except that this one tried all things. There were keynote speeches, votes of thanks, talks, group discussions on the stage, seminars in separate rooms, presentation by the seminar leaders, open discussions, a plenary session, a summing up; but in its rhythm it had a euphonic quality in which the views expressed were all in complete accord. The occasional difference was quickly harmonized, and the whole thing progressed like a melody in which all the right notes were struck. Human relations must always be good, and having accepted this simple truth the conference proceeded to trace variations on the theme. Examples were given of how production increased because Ram, a good manager, understood the problems of his group of workers, after production had declined because Sham, a bad manager, had not bothered to understand his workers. Syndicates of young men, who had worked on such problems since the last conference a year ago, now came forward to corroborate from their experience the goodness of the Rams and the badness of the Shams. Speeches were made with much unction on how the man, worker and manager, should be understood and made to feel wanted, delegated, consulted and promoted. The unction was transparently sincere; but I could not help wondering how much of it was practised; for in such a highly structured and stratified society democratic management could hardly have arrived except in theory.

My own performance was dismal. I had come earnestly prepared about the latest in marketing research, its new directions and likely future trends, but the chairman of the session debunked it all, greatly to the delight of the audience. In his summing up he agreed that the new marketing research theories and practice had a lot to say in their favour, but in real life there was nothing to beat the hardheaded and sound judgement of the experienced man. With much humour he made whatever I had said sound good theory and no more. At first I felt angry, but I soon saw the funny side, for after all he reflected my own reaction to the heavy doses of management goodness that we had received for three whole days. He belonged to an industrial family from Delhi and had a robustness which found the earnestness of the locals heavy going, and when he got the chance he spoke out.

The conference ended aimlessly amidst general euphoria; everybody agreed it had been a great success; we must all meet again; so much had been achieved and the good work must go on. As I looked back it struck me that though it had been a conference perfect in itself it had not been a learning experience, there had been talking for its own sake, an exercise in the statement of the desirable, a search for wisdom and the truth; once the we-all-must-have-good-human-relation-in-indus-try was established as the truth, it had been enunciated repeatedly, like the name of God in its different manifestations, and pursued with the veneration of devotees. There had been no room for disbelief or questioning. But practice—well, that was another matter, a personal affair, like religion outside the temple. The contrast between this and the Unilever Conference was revealing; one was brisk and hard-headed, out to get results, the other got lost in perfectionism.

On the last evening as I was walking across the lawn in front of the auditorium, a woman whom I had seen a good deal around the conference and who was obviously one of its leading lights, walked over to me and asked me what I thought of it. I made some non-committal remarks, and she invited me over for a cup of tea. She lived on campus in one of the faculty bungalows. The interior was a less expensive version of the doyen's son's house, with the same self-conscious taste, a mixture of the many countries visited on conferences and delegations, with Indian art revival thrown in. I wondered if this was not the coming style of the professional Indians' home. But her home had a pleasant understatement, helped no doubt by her smaller means.

We discovered we both came from the same part of the country, the same professional Punjabi background, though her essential Punjabiness must have given way to later influences. We had been to the same college but afterwards our paths had taken different directions. After an early, tragically-ended marriage she returned to studies and set her face against matrimony, taking a professional career instead. She had become attached to one of the Families, to which the group reacted in an interesting way. They closed the ranks around the outsider in an attempt to dissolve the problem, but the outsider seemed not content with the acceptance, she continued to remain both in and out, a constant challenge to the Family's capacity to absorb.

Till late into the night we discussed the subject of the Family, the Institution, the whole culture of Ahmedabad. She explained to me the system of a joint family converted to industrial management, but without losing its essential core. The power centre was very much the head of the family; the sons a board; the mother and the daughters forming a shadow board; the close relations and elders a consultative committee: all forming a tightly-knit in-group in the larger group of the Family that through inter-marriage and inter-investment had become powerful and monolithic. A young man from abroad had once married one of the daughters, but he soon left his wife and a blonde child and went away; and another daring youth from the north also came and went; and both daughters merged back into the family and lived in their separate nests in the wooded estate. This outsider was given the same choice. For a while she also lived on the estate but she would neither go away nor be assimilated.

'But how have you managed to stay so close to the family and yet apart for so long?'

'I think because I have always stayed at the edge. Everybody outside thinks that I am a part of it and yet those inside know that I do not belong.'

'Why did you decide that way?'

'I don't know.'

A withdrawn look came on her face, of someone unwilling, incapable, of facing a problem.

The family reminded one of the Rothschilds: cultured, cohesive, with their heart in money.

I soon found myself becoming compulsively attached to the whole scene: the city, the Family, the institution, her. Here I came across the first ferment of Indian management. Elsewhere, the Marwaris of Calcutta, the Banyas of the north, the Chettiars of the south, wherever industrial wealth had accumulated, the new processes of production had left them untouched personally. They too had endowed institutions, but in an impersonal way, uninvolved, and distant; nowhere as in Ahmedabad was there the same air of an institutional life, rooted and strong.

CHAPTER SEVENTEEN

BONHAM-CARTER CONFIRMED that I had been accepted for Harvard in their spring term of 1958. Would I spend a few days in London on the way, and a week in the United States to get 'acclimatized'? I had never been to the States and had known barely two Americans in my life. I had seen them during the war, but from a distance. One had heard and built up many generalizations about them; and the whole photomontage whirled round as my Constellation winged its way slowly through a heavy February night over the Atlantic to a dawn over hundreds of miles of frozen land, till we landed at New York into the insulated heat of the glass and chromium airport.

New York airport, the drive to the city, the city itself, the Lever office, a quick visit to Chicago and Washington, a snowbound week-end in Connecticut and ultimately a day-long train ride to Boston, ending at the Business School campus, was a week packed with impressions as never a week before. As I lay on a narrow bed in a tiny monastic cubicle, with an adjoining study, shared by someone in another cubicle who called himself my canmate, I felt about as low as on the first night at school. I discovered next morning that I had eight more canmates, and the can was the toilet facilities shared by the ten of us. We were going to live a life together, at work and leisure, for thirteen weeks, and at the end of it stand smiling together and be photographed. We would collect in the evenings, and do our homework together, throw parties to other cans, go to each other's homes for the long week-ends, sometimes a thousand miles away, and of course call each other by first names from the moment we met. This of course created a problem with my name, but they soon solved it by dropping its last three letters. The highlight was the last week, when wives moved in to Boston and each can became a large, happy and more united than ever group, that vied with other groups in who looked happiest.

I found the average American modest and gentle, anxious to be liked and most pleasant to work with. In discussion, he seldom disagreed clearly, and even plain speaking was uncommon, unless it was of the we-are-losing-the-heritage-of-the-founding-father type. The discussions ran at an even tempo, with much humour, but an idea had to be sold carefully, never slammed down, and much less put under the skin. One's appreciation of things American had to be clear, simple, straightforward and not wrapped in humour, at least not of the dry or barbed kind. Sophistry and cynicism had to be carefully avoided, equally any visible manifestation of intellect or philosophy, of which they were highly suspicious. Modesty was a cultivated feature, carefully worn and always becoming, so that one had to take care not to be even humourously immodest. Intellect was well concealed, for the 'egg-head' was suspect, and even the use of an uncommon word, however succinct, was shunned. But one could not help but greatly admire their extreme practicalness. The discussions were always relevant and produced results, avoided generalization and verbalizing, two much feared words. There was thus seldom any attempt at evolving a principle. Philosophy was a word used only for their belief in free enterprise and the American way of life. Anything that transgressed these bounds smacked of heresy.

A stimulating experience I found were the joint classes on labour relations that we held with a similar group of trade union executives, also going through a course in management. Interestingly, it was the union men who first cowed the executives. Their very presence and their belligerence seemed to make the executives lose their breezy confidence. The union men sensed this and pressed their advantage; but soon the executives also swung into action, and every day the two sides were ranged in pre-selected positions in the case studies, the executives always supporting the actions of the managers and the unionists the men.

The professor sometimes used my non-commitment when controversy flagged. I had mentioned to him one day that I would like to ask the union men, particularly the German, their views on co-determination. He agreed, but saved it for an occasion of his choosing. One day when the union men had got the executives on the run he turned to me; and there ensued a revealing discussion.

'Prakash, you wanted to know about co-determination. Let us ask what the class thinks.' And he turned to the executives. Few of them had heard of it or ever imagined such heresy could exist. He turned to the German union man and asked him to explain. It had begun in Germany during the reconstruction, to stimulate the interest of the men by involving them in the operation at the policy determination level. Workers' representatives thus worked with the directors in the process of decision-making and shared responsibility.

'What do you think of it?' the professor asked one of the American executives.

'Nothing,' was the bland reply.

'And you,' he turned to one of the union men.

'Not on your life.'

I had expected this from the executive but not from the union man.

'Well, that is a surprise,' I said to the union men. 'I would have thought you would welcome it. For days now you have been talking about the responsibility of management to produce more in order to give more to the men. You have blamed them for pretty nearly every-thing and under all circumstances, and asked for more and more. Now when it comes to sharing the responsibility to produce that more you chicken out. You disappoint me, but perhaps you don't.'

The executives went into hoots of laughter and the union men into loud protests. The professor smiled as if he had expected it. When the furore died down, the union man began to explain.

'You've got it. We want more and more, but we don't want to have anything to do with how the more is produced. That is the job of the managers. Haven't they been talking about their prerogative to manage? So let them keep it. They have been trained to manage; it is therefore their responsibility to manage. I am not so sure that we would manage well; we wouldn't know how to, but even if we did, once we are inside the board room and share in management we shall have lost our strength to bargain for more. No, theirs is the job to produce more, and ours to demand an increasing share of what is produced; and if it hurts them, we don't care; they must learn to live with it and be more efficient. If in the process of meeting our increasing demands a firm goes to the wall, then it deserves to; someone else more efficient will pick up the assets. It is not our responsibility to keep the inefficient and the outmoded alive; they should give way to the more justifiable.' And as a last fling the union man added, 'And if we ever take over we will take over the entire outfit, and there will be no co-determination.'

My thoughts turned to the Indian scene where many such issues, large and small, were examined through a haze of sentiment. In fact, co-determination like other ideas ahead of our capacity to absorb had already reached India and was picked up by those in power who seemed to feel that they were setting the world an example.

To the other courses, finance and accounts, business policy, and administrative practice, one responded according to one's interests, but a number of us subscribed optionally to one on public speaking and listening. A private individual, who ran it as a business, had evolved some basic rules and practices on clear speaking and good listening. I had noticed that most American executives were poor speakers; they took the merit of short sentences too far, usually punctuating them with ahs and I-means, and found it difficult to speak freely for any length of time, particularly if deprived of the opportunity to lean on humour. This was in marked contrast to most Indians who are facile speakers; perhaps too much to the other side.

Our course aimed at developing consciousness of one's style of speaking, to the point of being able to hear oneself speak. In the playback of our own speeches, we became aware of our shortcomings, especially the difficulty of how to begin a speech and the yet greater problem of how to end it; but the second half of this course, listening, proved even more difficult. I had never given any thought to listening as an art or a discipline; I had just listened and thought no more about it. And yet when we were put through various exercises we dolefully learned that if we were poor speakers we were poorer listeners; we who prided ourselves as executives in attentive and patient listening would have been shocked, had we been told at the beginning how little we heard and, what the course did not directly bring out, how much we interrupted in a discussion.

This course was thought-provoking. If the average American, whom I had found an attentive listener, took in, as we were told, only twenty-five per cent of a speech, how much did an average Indian listen? In our society, as the listener ascended in importance, his degree of listening descended. The young, the subordinate, only listened; the old or important only spoke. Those who believed themselves wise felt it their duty to instruct, and this they performed remorselessly, forcing the less wise to listen dutifully. As soon as someone tried to talk, the wise man would think he recognized what the other was going to say, interrupt him and continue, brushing away any faint attempts by the other, even at trying to convey that that was not his point at all.

In our young days this applied to our elders, who spoke with the fervour of mentors while we listened; and today it goes for our leaders, who regard it their duty to talk, thereby solving all problems. In the British days the press used to report that a delegation received a patient hearing from a Governor or a high official; today it is the delegation that gives the leader a patient hearing. There was a case of an eminent minister who had invited a group of us from industry 'to instruct him' on some issue. He began by modestly referring to his ignorance and how necessary he felt it to learn from us. As one of us started to explain, the minister seemed to feel instructed at once; he cut in and spoke for the next twenty-five minutes, interrupting himself now and again to

say that no doubt we agreed with him. The meeting ended cordially
with the minister thanking us all for a most useful meeting from which
he had learned so much.

It is our tradition to learn by listening. Villagers, and town people,
will sit for hours to hear a discourse by a learned man, never questioning, never questioned, often absorbing very little, but simply lapping it
up. I remembered what Aldous Huxley had once said on this point;
how little Indians listened to even their venerated leaders. He had once
been to a meeting that Gandhiji was addressing, where people had
come from miles, neighbouring towns and distant villages for the
darshan and hearing him. And yet when he spoke, people talked
with each other, walked up and moved about, women suckled
their babies, children ran about chasing each other. Hardly anyone
listened; and yet this was no lack of veneration; they had had his
darshan.

The society has lost its earlier tradition of the guru—chela dialogue,
of discussion, an interplay between the speaker and the listener. Today,
speaking is the prerogative of one and listening the duty of the other.
To me as an Indian here was a new definition of listening; listening
cultivated as much for the benefit of the speaker as of the listener. Here
was something we needed to acquire, a culture of listening unrelated to
age or seniority. It could be the first stage of a truer contact between our
leaders, who have the knowledge, at least the power, and those of us at
the receiving end; between the leaders and the led, a contact today
sadly lacking.

As the course drew towards its end the working morale weakened.
We began to miss the can discussions and sometimes even cut classes.
The week-end parties began earlier in the week and lasted longer into
the nights. I liked the men in their relaxed moods; they were com-
municative; they talked about the country, about their families and
their work, and rarely had I met men more easy to converse with once
they had dropped their executive formality and stopped playing a role.
Life became happier and rowdier as we approached the last week, 'the
week of the brides'. The night before the wives arrived there was one
last fling when the din of empty cans, beer bottles, drain pipes, fire
alarms, banshee howls in the early hours woke up the undergraduates.
Next morning the men woke up to face the brides, and moved into
hotels. The nightly parties were now just cheerful, the husbands
enjoyed themselves soberly.

Early one morning I took the plane to New York, having quietly
warned the Dean that I was going to miss the last day, the graduation

ceremony and the ball. He looked disappointed, but I could not take it; I find it difficult to face farewells, mass farewells at that.

I returned home via San Francisco and Manila. As the plane flew for long hours over the wastes of the Pacific, with a short break at Hawaii, and a little walk to stretch one's legs near the signal hut at Wake Island, I dozed, looked out of the window, drank at the bar below, and tried to wrestle with my impressions. I never thought I would return to the U.S. again, and yet chance and a deep attraction brought me back first with a group of Indian marketing executives; next to discuss with Harvard the new business school at Ahmedabad; and then to teach at Los Angeles. Each return made me want to return again. In Bombay someone asked me if I could have settled there. 'Yes,' I said wistfully, 'if I had been ten years younger.'

Back in India, I looked at things in a new light – of a managerial answer for all problems. The case studies at Harvard, spreading over a wide area of technical and human problems, gave one the feeling that all problems could be solved if only we approached them unemotionally and managerially. I remembered how one of our canmates, when in our first can group discussion we had got bogged down, had brought an inscription and placed it on the table. It said: Are you helping solve a problem or becoming part of it? Our endless discussions in India, always looking for a perfectionist solution and criticizing anything that fell short of the ideal, reminded me now how much we had become a part of the problems we had set out to solve. And yet 1958, when I returned from Harvard, belonged to the years which marked, despite all our complaints and dissatisfaction, much achievement. We were drawing towards the close of the best of the Nehru era. The heavy public sector industry that he had founded was coming to the end of its long gestation. The big dams and multi-purpose projects, at one time over twenty in building at the same time, were nearing completion. There had been a big wave of industrialization in private industry, and things were manufactured that we had not dreamed of a few years ago. The many new universities and national laboratories had taken education and research to all parts of India. Excellent institutions of technical and general teaching were springing up everywhere. Schools, hospitals, roads, communication and air links, the large new townships, and all the new growth, reminded me of the spurt of a hundred years ago in our land of five rivers, for then there too had been sudden growth of a new kind.

Today in the whole of India, growth was at its most spectacular in the new Punjab. Mutilated and truncated only a decade ago to less than a third of its size, it had already rebuilt with unbelievable energy. It looked as if the shock of partition had given it a new vigour. Without moping over its losses, even bothering to think about them, Punjab set to building as never before. Wherever the displaced Punjabis went, whether to settle elsewhere in India or in their new homeland of East Punjab, they became like a new people, regenerated and confident. They set up as small entrepreneurs wherever they went, but the best job they did was cultivating neglected lands wherever they found them in north India. They adopted modern farming, with tractors, trucks and tubewells, and discarded the bullock cart and the Persian wheel. Cut off from the old home in West Punjab, I got a vicarious pleasure from visiting East Punjab every winter when the fields were at their fertile best. I would look again at the green of the wheat, the yellow of mustard, red of the rai, and the blonde plumes of the sugar cane, all waving joyously in the benign and pale winter sun, and return recouped to Bombay. Born and bred on the plains of the Punjab I had to return to them off and on to stand life in the crowded island of Bombay, though its open sea did compensate.

This nostalgia, prodded by Maurice and Taya Zinkin, persuaded me even to try and recapture in writing our family's life over three generations, from the time the British came after their last battle in 1852 outside the city walls of Gujrat, till they left in 1947. It was to be a record of the time since my grand-uncle went to school at Gujrat, later to return there to start as a lawyer, until the time when my uncle, also a lawyer, had to flee from Gujrat in the chaos that followed the Partition. The British had come to a Punjab in a time of chaos, and with the irony of history left it in the same state. I had begun my writing a couple of months before I left for Harvard, and on my return I picked it up. I found it an absorbing occupation to leave the present for the past, to exchange my life in a British firm with my father's in the British administration. It also, I think, helped sharpen my perceptions of the India around me.

After eight years in England and twenty years with an English firm, the break at Harvard, short as it was, seemed to change my direction. In the brief spell of three months I seemed to have given myself to this American experience as if I were looking for a new orientation. This came from two directions. Harvard had unset me from an English, European orientation, in which I had become framed, over to something seemingly much wider and less settled. It was closer to India, with its unrest and state of being than to Europe, especially to England, which seemed "become." On the other hand, writing took me back, far back into the Punjab that had become smothered under subsequent layers. I felt myself stretching forward. I also felt as if I were stretching backward into the past.

CHAPTER EIGHTEEN

ACK IN THE Company, I began to take stock of myself. In its own way the visit to Harvard had been my second moratorium after an interval of twenty-five years. As a student in England, after finishing my degree at Manchester, I gave up work for nearly two years. Apart from a half-hearted attempt at economic research, I did nothing more serious than go to the library and to concerts, walk through the northern countryside, play golf and take an active part in the Union debates. It was a life of idle exploration, in a vague pursuit of excellence, which a woman psychologist at Ahmedabad called by this important-sounding name of moratorium. Having lived through such a one herself, she said it was a kind of flight that sometimes occurred in those who were overstretched and in need of rest or readjustment, though she said that I was otherwise mentally offensively healthy. I had entered university at the age of fourteen and finished a second degree at twenty. Both were of mediocre achievement, but the effort must have drained me out, particularly as the latter had also involved a process of adjustment to a life in England, so utterly different from life in the Punjab. The moratorium was also aided by the arrival of Gärd on the scene. We both left off our studies to do nothing together, visiting Sweden in the summer and at Christmas.

The visit to Harvard, away from responsibility and routine, was the first pause from my work, and I dissolved the problem I had taken with me. A few months earlier I had suffered my first setback in the firm. So far I had been progressing unchecked, and no one junior to me had gone past. Whatever my prospects, I had felt satisfied that I had moved steadily forward, along a line that pointed upwards, but suddenly I came to a halt on level ground. An Englishman, David Orr, eleven years younger than me, of great and visible promise, was made vice-chairman. Under normal expectations, he would remain in front of me as vice-chairman and chairman, for another seven or eight years, by when I would be due to retire at fifty-five. To discover that one had been suddenly written off was quite an experience. I tried to analyse it.

'Ization' had been the policy, declared and pursued. The number of expatriate personnel had been reduced and they no longer formed the management structure, only providing special skills or time till an Indian was ready. It could therefore only be that while retaining the control they did not feel secure with an Indian at the top, or that I had not made it—something I could accept, but not believe. Such a problem is bad enough in itself, but infinitely enlarged by one's inability to check one's own analysis or conclusions. I have never turned to others for advice on matters that concerned me alone, but I felt that in this case I needed to know the answer. I decided to ask the chairman. Knowing me, he was surprised, but glad that I had decided to talk to him. To my question he replied simply, 'Well, it is a "no" this time, but there never is a "no" for ever.' And with this characteristic mixture of humanity and taciturnity, his watery blue eyes conveyed understanding.

A quite remarkable man was Steve Turner, the chairman who had succeeded Hoskyns-Abrahall. No two persons could be so unlike each other. Of humble origin and self-taught, he had joined the firm very young, taking a degree in chemistry at evening classes. Aloof and cold, he went out of his way to be alone, but not really liking the loneliness he punished himself at work, and drank. His formidable character seemed to consist of two layers, the top one, hard and impenetrable; the one underneath, malleable and soft, but, unable to find an outlet, in a constant state of flux. Like a volcano, the hard crust kept the heaving core firmly inside. A generous man and excellent company when he so chose, it was in keeping with his whole make-up of cultivated contradictions to cover his perfectly valid instinct of kindness, for he was essentially a kind man, with a gruff manner and a speech clipped into icy precision that at first used to frighten me and later pushed me away.

He had been manager of the vanaspati plant, where during the war and for years afterwards production of Dalda was never enough to meet the demand, and he was constantly under pressure from me to produce more. With nothing in common between us, either socially or at work, the often uneasy relationship between a marketing and a production man, especially under conditions of stress, was escalated by lack of personal warmth between us. I convinced myself that he disliked me as an ignorant nuisance. It came to a head one day when I rang him up with some usual demand from the marketing side, and probably went about it insensitively. Instead of appreciating his difficulties I made light of them, and when he protested, I was not understanding. His reaction was out of proportion; his sarcasm, of which I had had some taste before, was devastating. Seething with indignation I rang back to tell him that if he was going to behave like that it would be the end of any contact between us, and I put the receiver down, trembling with shame and anger.

My anger I could cope with, but I could not understand my feeling of shame. I began to unravel the tangled skein of my emotions, and a light came on a problem of long ago.

On my arrival at Bombay by a P. & O. ship after an absence of eight years, I had shared the belief of each generation of Indians returning from England that the attitudes of the British had changed; that having lived among them for some years as an equal one had acquired acceptability; that during one's long absence things had moved forward at home to equality between the races. Yet one soon found the same wall, the same gulf. Eight years earlier on my way out, I had heard the legend that on the journey westward the air changed as the P. & O. ships steamed out of Port Said into the cool Mediterranean. The tensions relaxed, the English faces softened, little conversations began, and even the dance floor became hospitable. In reverse, when the eastward bound ship sailed down the Suez, the two groups fell apart, and in the Indian Ocean the gulf widened.

At eighteen, straight out of the simple Punjab, I had not understood what the watershed of Port Said meant. I was just as shy of talking to them before Port Said as after; but on my return it was different. Eight years among them had changed me, and the P. & O. ship did not look frightening any more. I met them unselfconsciously, neither belligerent nor over-compensated. I moved among them as I moved among Indians, but things became strained as we neared Bombay, and broke into splinters at the Bombay harbour. A small incident was enough to unsettle me. In the customs shed, where typical Indian chaos prevailed as passengers and porters rushed in all directions, I stood for a moment not knowing my next move, and in the short moment a voice rasped behind me, 'Come on, get a move on or get out of the way; don't just stand there.' I turned around to see an irate Englishman glowering at me with an impatient contempt I had not seen before. Typically dressed in a cotton jacket, with the collar of the white shirt over the lapels, khaki shorts and long stockings, his pale face under a topee looked peremptorily at me. I moved away mumbling an apology. The whole scene flashed back twenty years later as I heard Steve Turner's voice on the phone, 'Make up your mind, and let me know what you want.'

My mind then strayed back to ten years ago, when Pettit had suggested appointing an Englishman under me; the first experiment of its kind in the firm. This Englishman had come to India before the war and was well ahead of me. During the war he had served with the Indian Army and retired as a captain in a distinguished Gurkha regiment. Upon his return to the Company, Pettit had decided to put him under me, which was an even more trying test for him than me. He rightly regarded me as his junior and, worse, someone who had gained at his expense by staying back while he had served. It made it even more galling to him that he should have been picked for the experiment when there were others, younger and less senior. I do not know how Pettit put it to him, but when I spoke to him he was plainly dissatisfied. I tried to rationalize that it must be a temporary posting to familiarize him with the quite significant advances we had made in marketing, where the whole scene had changed radically during his absence. I was sure he would not hold it against me that he would be learning from me. I was in no doubt of their intention to move him up to higher responsibility as soon as he had caught up with things, and new openings appeared. But he was not a big enough man to realize his long term interest, and working under me worried him considerably. As a first experiment it turned out an unhappy failure for both of us. If I suffered from excessive anxiety to make it easier for him, he suffered excessively from anxiety to make it clear that he thoroughly disapproved of the whole unnatural situation. He felt it the more acutely when I first visited him in his branch. In the head office he could reasonably ignore me but in the branch he had to display me as his chief before his men, and in the bazaar to his wholesalers and retailers, who were traditionally used to seeing an Englishman as the boss. After all, India was not yet independent and, except for a few civil service secretaries, Indians were rarely seen above Englishmen. The whole thing preyed on his mind till he could take it no longer. On this visit to his branch we travelled together from Delhi to Lahore, where before the work was finished he informed me that he was leaving before I was due to take train back to Bombay. With nothing else to do, I asked some of his men to stay on for an informal discussion, men I had known and trained when I was their manager for the branch.

On my return to Bombay I received a curt note from him protesting strongly at my behaviour in talking to his men in his absence, and went on to preach some elementary management principles. It irritated me, but I decided to take it no further. On his next visit to Bombay I told him I was sorry if I had upset him, but his letter had hurt me.

'Good,' he said firmly, 'I am glad because it was meant to.'

Soon he got his chance and was given independent command in a neighbouring country. To this opportunity of building a new company in a new country, with everything in his favour, he brought the same small mind and was a sad failure.

Pettit seemed undaunted and, not content with my first failure, persisted in training me in the art of handling English subordinates. He soon gave me a much bigger problem, where I failed completely. On his visit to England he had selected a young man who had been a salesman before the war. In the Royal Navy he had risen from able-bodied seaman to the rank of lieutenant-commander, and then rejoined the Company as a van salesman. A man of much enthusiasm, Pettit told me, he must have considerable character because he had also done rather well as a boy scout, and risen to a high rank in the movement.

Carried away by Pettit's description, I built him up before my managers, who were frankly disappointed that I had not selected one of them for the job. I explained that on the first occasion we wanted the new job of General Sales Manager, in charge of the entire sales operation, to be defined by someone of experience who would bring new thinking from Unilever. The men accepted this and promised me their cooperation, and in fact began to look forward to his arrival. I arranged a special conference to launch the new man, for I was anxious to succeed this time and retrieve my last failure.

The evening before the conference, on my way to dinner at our local branch manager's house, where all of them were collecting, I called in at the Taj to meet the young man who had just arrived. Excited, I rushed along the corridor and knocked at his door. As I entered and introduced myself, a wave of fear swept over me. I sensed failure again, surer than before.

The men, waiting at the party, asked me to tell them all about him. This was their first English boss, for they had all joined during the war and only served under me. India had been independent for a year, but that year had been an age. The accepted supremacy of the Englishmen had just vanished. The natural order of things until yesterday had ceased to be. Any Englishman from now on was going to be judged only by what he had to offer; and to command respect he had to visibly demonstrate his skills and communicate them to the Indians who worked under him, so that they could learn and take over. He came as a trainer and catalyst and not just to fill a quota percentage; this is what I had conveyed to the men. What was he like, they anxiously asked me. I tried to describe him in the most generous light possible. He was a simple man, essentially practical, self-made and with the confidence and ways that go with it. He would offer drive and competence, and perhaps a contrast to my impatient imagination that more often ran away with things. On the whole they would find him less strain than me and easier to work with. The more confident I grew in describing him the more dubious they looked. Self-contrast and self-deprecation were not natural to me. However, as the party warmed up they cheered up too in a trust that took no time to be shattered when the conference began the next morning.

In his simple cockney he talked to them like men lined up on deck or a troop of boy scouts and gave them a pep talk to get on with the job; he would always be behind them; they could count on him; he did not believe in any highfalutin marketing ideas and big words; he was a simple salesman, out to get results. He got carried away and promised to put the Company right; in this, of course, he expected all cooperation from them and support from the top. Let that be made quite clear, for he was a straightforward man and believed in calling a spade a spade each time. I squirmed as he laid it on thickly. The men fortunately found it difficult to follow his unfamiliar accent and expressions, as well as the directness of his language, but they sensed clearly enough that he was a new kind of Englishman. They had never heard anyone talk like this.

I faced the problem non-plussed. No good at sharing problems, I could not go to Pettit and admit it; and he, blissfully ignorant, did not sense anything; instead he kept emphasizing the virtues he had seen in this man when he interviewed him in London, and his enthusiasm here, and I kept agreeing. As time went, the men chafed under his sergeant-major handling, and he sensed and resented it. He expected me to underline and applaud his approach, which I could not bring myself to do, and I found I was pressed between him and the men. Neither understood the other, but both sides wanted my support against the other. I could honestly not support him any more. I had given him all the support I could before he arrived, and for a while afterwards, and he would still have received it had there been anything to uphold except a tragic and pompous ignorance. The men looked at me resentfully as if to say, what are you asking us to accept?

He was sincere in his own way, and had sensitivity of a kind. He sensed all that was going on around him, the total lack of acceptance, but had no understanding of the cause, and therefore did not know how to cope with it. Almost unlettered, he resorted to his only strength, the determination of a losing boxer who puts his head down and lashes out blindly. He lashed at me, at the managers, the men, at the wholesalers and the dealers. He also found himself isolated from his compatriots who felt let down and ignored him, and the fact that his Indian managers noticed this made it all the worse for him. Six months after his arrival I was due to go to Unilever for a three months' training visit and then on a three months' holiday in Sweden, and during my absence he was going to deputize for me. This, I felt, would give him the opportunity of running things his own way, long enough to work out his own style. It actually proved fatal. He exercised his freedom the only way he knew, in an up-guards-and-at-'em way.

Pettit left him alone, there was little in common between them, and as can happen among the English, they spoke what to an undiscerning Indian seemed two different languages. Pettit's well modulated drawl and this young man's half eaten words, with either the beginning sucked in or the tail bitten off, came from different worlds altogether. In the firm, as was usual those days, after Pettit's Rugby and Cambridge and Abrahall's Charterhouse and Oxford, there were either the grammar school or the secondary school, but here was barely the elementary school. The difference between him and Abrahall was even greater, and yet he seemed to feel more at ease with him than with Pettit, and certainly more than with me. I began to understand this. Pettit had in him more than the characteristic English administrative distance. His aloofness lacked the humanity of Abrahall, whose distance could vary; it shortened when you needed closeness and lengthened when the need was gone; while Pettit's was a permanent distance, the same under all circumstances. I think it was Abrahall who first saw the problem and began to shorten his distance to this young man. But he also saw that it was an untenable situation; the man's capacity was well below the minimum required for the job. On my return Abrahall spoke to me and wondered whether I would confirm his observation; he also wondered why I had not mentioned anything to him. I found it difficult to explain my reticence. I did occasionally go to him with minor personal matters but on all major issues I kept my own counsel and dealt with them as best I could. Used to my ways, Abrahall shrugged his shoulders and left it at that, but decided to talk to Pettit.

Pettit wrote to London that the young man did not fit into the Company and should return home. Their reaction was curious. They said that he had been sent on a considerable promotion, with the attendant risk of a career closing behind him if he failed. From his senior position in India they could not very well take him back to where he was before leaving, and there was no question of giving him a promotion upon an unsuccessful return, so it was best to let him go. In any case he was now an employee of ours. We protested that he was their man, not engaged locally, so as an expatriate he should return to them and then they could do what they liked. Later his old boss in London remarked lightheartedly to Abrahall that his posting to Bombay had been a solution of their problems.

I now had to my credit two failures, leaving me more confused than ever on how to make a success with English subordinates, which apparently I must inevitably learn to do if I were to acquire larger responsibility in the firm. I could not see where I could have done better. Had I discussed the subject with someone, I might have understood it differently, but how could one discuss what was a kind of racial problem with one of the race itself.

My father had mentioned to me how once, at the end of a hot morning's inspection tour, his chief on arrival at a canal rest house after a few moments of courteous conversation took leave of him but asked his subordinate, an Englishman, to stay for a drink. My father, a reticent man, gave me occasional understanding of his relationship at work. I was a little surprised when he related this incident, for he was a man without rancour and never one to show hurt. The incident returned to me over the years, for instance, when I noticed how at the end of his monthly meeting Pettit used to take only the European managers out to lunch, and once when Duncan suggested that he might invite others, he gave an embarrassed, 'No, it would become too many.'

Here was an international firm whose own men abroad were part of its own design but had to remain out of the local pattern. In Ahmedabad I saw the same phenomenon. Despite the introduction of the latest technology and management theory, members of the family were treated as enclaves, subject only to their own laws, rather like the old rule that an Englishman in India would only be tried by an English judge. Similarly, though Indianization had proceeded at a rapid pace, the problem of an Englishman remained theirs; it did not become ours. Long after, when there were very few of their members left, this attitude still persisted. Their own kith and kin were still supra-environment. This lack of mutuality created a constraint quite different from the constraints inherent in work itself.

This was just one of the things I had learned at Harvard: that in any situation a manager is faced with constraints, social and environmental. These are stronger constraints than the operational ones and do not respond to his personal efforts but have to await the slow change in the environment itself.

Harvard wiped away the cobwebs from my mind and filled it with some fresh thinking. I learned to accept limitations, whether they were my own or imposed by the organization or of the environment. I would never achieve what my colleagues from U.S. companies could achieve; I could not even match my English colleague on the Harvard course, who like me worked in an overseas company. I had asked him one day:

'Where do you think you would like to go in the Company; how far do you think you will go?

'The vice-chairman of my Company soon, then its chairman. One day I would like to be on the overseas committee at London—yes, I would like that very much, having been overseas so long. After that the Unilever Board—who knows!'

Yes, I agreed, why not. His ambition more or less began where mine, only by a stretch of imagination, might end. For him it was a matter of calm assumption.

Now, Steve Turner received me back warmly and shortly afterwards offered me finance directorship which I accepted happily. It was, ironically, a return to my original field into which the Chief Accountant twenty years ago had refused to take me. He was right in a way; after so many years my qualification was meaningless. The new job brought me into contact with all sides of the Company.

The fifties were also an interesting period for the start of new management thinking in India. The first waves of this thinking came to us from England because of our closer contacts and the new work that was going on in the Tavistock Institute, but America was soon to swamp it all. India was fertile ground; our enthusiasm to listen to anything new and our ability to turn it into an intelligent discussion gave to the men from American universities and foundations a happy feeling of having come to the right place. Young Indians were now going in large numbers to business schools in the States, as their elders had gone to Cambridge and London to read law or economics; and while the fathers had entered the services or the Bar, the sons were entering industry.

In my first enthusiasm from Harvard, and possibly because the acceptance of my limitations in the Company gave me the need to expend my excessive energy elsewhere, I became quite engrossed in this management movement. The Harvard course in speaking and listening, and the many new ideas the other courses had poured into me made me into an enthusiastic speaker, with some modern managerial experience to offer, which was more than one could say about some others who became professional at management without having managed. The professor at Ahmedabad kept inviting me back, and we began to work as a team. Her academic output was sparse, and she was unable to communicate with more than the smallest group; yet with her forcefulness, which she sedulously kept covered to fit in with the gentler beat around her, she found that I responded to academic stimuli and perhaps provided a vicarious expression of her complex personality and circumstance.

I got carried away by the fascination of this process of change, sparked off by Harvard, by her, and by Maurice Zinkin, a most remarkable man. I think he saw in me the new stage of the British connection with India, the growth of professional management. As a part of this phenomenon I appealed to his deep sense of history. He began to work on me, to bring something dormant out of my mind. I think he sensed the resistance in me too, but he was a determined man. It was as if he wanted to achieve something in me before he left India the second time, having been uprooted suddenly at partition from the civil service to which he had offered his all. From a fine Jewish rabbinical stock, he had a mind of rare speed and versatility, with a projectiveness that wanted always to begin with the answer, a conclusion, a thesis. Let me suggest a conclusion to you and you can demolish it, but in the process we will trim it down to greater relevance till we have reached a conclusion pure of the irrelevant, was his approach. But my Hindu mind seemed to him unconcerned with the conclusion, and after laboriously reaching one, it could, to his astonishment, start all over again because it had seen something new. This frustrated him, and he worked hard to curb and discipline my mind through the year he worked under me; a year of much agony for both of us. But I learned rapidly, and this gave him great delight. I began to project and hypothesize and pay attention to synthesis; at the same time as the professor in Ahmedabad worked on my mind not to be afraid of examining experience and subjecting this to the harsh light of conceptualization.

Maurice Zinkin believed in the mission of the British. Their old role as the welders of India into a modern state was finished voluntarily, but he saw a new role for them. This time British industry, without privilege or power, would offer values and a system of professional management to help create an industrial state. As in the old political state they had developed cadres of administrative and political leadership, so they would help to bring up a class of managerial leaders without whom modern industry would not grow. He put me in the front row of this new generation of managers. We would discuss the subject and its historical background at length.

Three centuries earlier, while many nations competed for the prize of trading with India, as the most determined and disciplined, the British had won. They opened small trading stations and manned them with their soldiers while the traders spread into the hinterland, looking for any opportunity that came their way. Their purposeful base far away was the East India Company, whose only aim was profit. Their masters were hard-headed businessmen, and the men they sent out provided the earliest examples of what management today talks about, delegation, initiative, judgement and quick decisions. A year's distance away from home, these men decided first and consulted afterwards, and any approval or disapproval of their action two years later was only of historical interest. The masters loved a formidable language. 'Tremble ye' was how one company director began his letters — but the men on the spot anything but trembled and did what they thought best, though always taking care to feign humility in their reply.

From this prototype came the administrators, rulers instead of traders, who governed tracts of land and populations sometimes equal to their homeland. Allowing for the times and for their paternalism, which saw their task as of guardians, they did a good job. They were benevolent and interested in the people, and strove to remove the oppression of centuries, but no more. Trimmed of its excesses, time once again stood still. The rapacious officials, the thugs, the roving bands of adventurers went, but the peasant continued to till his land with the wooden plough and scatter his seed and reap his poor harvest. Here and there water was brought in canals and wrought a miracle of lush crops, and a well fed peasantry, but elsewhere the grinding poverty remained. But out of it all came something new that was less noticed than the law and order so lauded by the rulers and the ruled. This was the new class of Indians who were taught to administer, admittedly always under the rulers. But progressively the column above the Indians shortened and they rose higher and higher in the hierarchy of administration.

Maurice Zinkin and I had interminable arguments. As an historian he was a romanticist, lacking in objectivity when it came to the British connection with India. I, on the other hand, was always rejecting, perhaps because he pushed me too far. This rejection I applied to the firm, which also, I argued, found Indians useful. There was no duty or trust about it; it was good self-interest, neither to be decried nor unduly applauded. I did concede however that whether in government or in business, something did distinguish the British from the other Europeans abroad. How often must I have hurt his feelings, never meaning to but always managing to. His belief in the British connection bordered on the religious. The process of Indianization, he believed, was inherent in the Raj and had transmitted itself to its commercial and industrial successors. There was never any expediency about it; it was just that the administrative concept of the British could only work through delegation and trust. This always led to the logical conclusion that the man was built up to a point from which he could not but reach the top. Each next step might be denied him for the time it took the administration to adjust itself, but the final plunge was always inevitable.

But our discussions were not always about the firm or the British; we often talked about the social and economic side of India. The political side he seemed to leave increasingly to his wife, Taya, whom he was grooming as a journalist. Physically and mentally restless, Taya was suited for journalism. She was an indefatigable traveller, persistent, and like her husband she also began with a conclusion, which she however mostly managed to prove. If not, she lost interest and turned to something else. Both were equally and passionately interested in India and always trying to discover what made it go. In me they discovered, to theirs as much as to my surprise, that although I had lived away from the Punjab for so many years my roots were still strong and fresh. I yet maintained a sensitive recall of the Punjab where I was born and brought up as a child, the Punjab since vanished in the debacle of partition. I shared the cumulative racial memory of its lore and custom. It was they who between them made me write a book.

I was very diffident about writing. I could explore and project in conversation but the discipline of writing I found difficult to submit to. Maurice and Taya insisted that I try it because what I remembered about the Punjab, they said, was not commonly remembered and would soon be forgotten. Social history to Maurice was background to history and gave the historian the dimension that contemporary records otherwise lacked. Social history made the past live again in its men and women, their way of life and customs; no serious history is possible without it, he argued. Used only to commercial correspondence and reports, I felt uncertain of writing for print, but under their combined pressure I offered to write one chapter on condition that they sent it to their publishers and obtained their opinion. If the publishers saw a book coming out of it the effort of continuing would be worthwhile.

To my surprise I found I wrote easily, and enjoyed doing it. The past began to live with the clarity of today; its earliest memories were neither vivid nor dim, they were just natural. They came out like old books and toys and clothes discarded long ago and stored in a cupboard. They still lay there neatly stacked and locked away, and it was beautiful to take them out again and examine them with the detachment of intervening decades, without any trace of self-consciousness or attempt at reinterpretation through today's mind. I lived them again, the village, the medieval walled city, the life in its homes, births, marriages and deaths: the memories all had the evocation of when they were and not of a past.

Peter Calvaocoressi, a partner of the publishers, perhaps more encouraging than critical, wrote back that while the style was discursive and he did not want to curb it, he could perhaps suggest that some discipline might be applied to decide upon a format. On second thought, he preferred to leave me alone, but they saw a book in the few pages I had sent.

A book eventually came and was well received, in both its English and American editions.

I suddenly felt freed of the past, the firm, and my anxieties for my future in it. Although the authorship gave me neither prospect nor income, it gave me a feeling of independence. A creativeness appreciated, a creation however small upon which a favourable judgement had been passed by the many reviews it received, made my relationship with the firm appear in a different light, almost irrelevant; their appreciation as important no longer. Withdrawal came easily to me; and with it came a peace of mind and satisfaction, a new calmness in which success in the firm mattered no more.

I had been working hard on the book, on my growing extra-mural interests, and at my new responsibility in finance, determined to give it all the devotion that I had given to Dalda. In a particular fortnight I neglected a cold and a flu, till one day after speaking at a seminar, followed by lunch, as I walked out of the hotel I felt dizzy and unsure of step, with a tight feeling in the chest. I asked a passer-by to hold my arm and walk with me to a nursing home that happened to be only a hundred yards away, and there to the astonishment of the nurse in the reception I gave myself up. I asked her to tell the doctor on duty to look me up when she was free, preferably not before long, and inform the specialist who gave me my annual check-up that I was here.

Through the many checks and consultations that followed, I dozed through an uneasy half-slumber, uninterested in their subdued discussions. Through sedatives, light food, long hours of sleep, and idle gazing through the window at a rusty shield bearer with abundance of yellow flowers, I let the strain of months and years evaporate, leaving me cool and light. I refused to see anyone or receive messages, flowers or books. Gärd came once a day but stayed only for a while because she found me absent and uninterested even in her company. After ten days I went home, and spent another week in a shack on the coast, where I also did nothing but sleep or gaze at the sea through the casuarinas. As I lay down on the warm sand and looked at the blue sea, extending in an eternity to meet the blue of the sky, the problems of twenty years, so alive till yesterday, were no longer part of the present. They became petrified in the past, and where only yesterday they had squirmed and writhed, today they were set and inert. The whole past of twenty years showed softer contours, as if a rare rain had suddenly washed away its harshness; its landscape no longer appeared so inhospitable. But I now realized how much despite this seeming inhospitableness the past had nourished me, what my years in the firm had done for me though really it owed me nothing except perhaps the compulsions of circumstances. Both I and they had given our all, though each side felt the other was holding back. And then it grew on me that I had really received more than I had given; perhaps I was the one who held back. But did it matter any longer, now that I felt freed? The new freedom came out of this past, as a gift for the future that was all mine to determine.

GLOSSARY

Ahimsa	Hindu doctrine of the sacredness of life
Ashram	Centre of community living, usually religious
Ayah	Woman servant
Ayurveda	The Indian system of medicine
Bahawalpur	Muslim State, now in Pakistan
Baluchis	People from Baluchistan, now in Pakistan, bordering on Iran
Bearer	Valet cum butler
Biradari	Caste brotherhood
Biryanis	Rice dishes
Blue, Oxford or Cambridge Blue	University colours awarded for distinction in sports
Charkha	A machine used for removing the seed from cotton
Chela	Disciple
Chowkidar	Watchman
Chukker	Round, circle
Coolie	Unskilled worker, porter
Cummerbund	Broad sash
Dak bungalow	Government rest house open to travellers
Darshan	Sight of somebody or something you venerate
Dhoti	Length of cloth tied round the waist covering the lower part of the body
'Dipity' Commissioner	Deputy Commissioner. Commissioner is head of several districts forming a commission
Divali	The Hindu festival of lights, held in late October
Diwan	Prime Minister
Farmaishes	Types of bread for festive occasions
Gandhi ki jai	Victory to Gandhi
Ghee	Clarified butter, made into pure fat

Guru	Teacher
Gymkhana	Hybrid word from gymnastics and Urdu khana — place for sports
Harijan	Untouchable, literally 'child of God', name given by Gandhiji to the fifth division of Hindu India. The four other divisions, 'castes', are: brahmins, kshatrujas, vaisyas and sudras
Hill station	Holiday resort in the mountains
I.C.S.	Indian Civil Service, founded by the British
Jain	The Jain sect was founded by Mahavir, a contemporary of Buddha. Jains take extreme precautions not to destroy life
John Company	Nickname for the East India Company of London
Kamiz	Tunic, from French 'chemise'
'Karnail'	Colonel
Khadi	Cloth from homespun yarn
Khojas	Muslim sect, followers of the Aga Khan
Kutchis	People from the Kutch peninsula south of Sind, now part of Gujerat State
Lala	Courtesy title for a Hindu, usually with a suffix 'ji' when addressing
Malayalees	The people of the princely States of Cochin and Travancore, now the State of Kerala
Marwaris	Business caste of Marwar (Jodhpur) in Rajasthan
Memsahib	Madam Sahib, mistress
Moghlai	Empire of the Moghuls, hence something of great magnificence
Nans	Types of bread for festive occasions
Nawab	Muslim ruler
Neem	Margosa, a tree with bitter bark which exudes a tenacious gum
Nira	Unfermented sap from the toddy palm
P. & O.	Peninsular & Oriental Steamship Co., the main passenger line between U.K. and India
Peon	Office boy, same as sepoy

Pi-dog	Half-wild, mongrel dog
Pukka	Real, proper
Pullaos,	Rice dishes
Qormas	Meat dishes
Rai	Kind of mustard used as spice. The common Indian mustard is used for oil
Raj	Rule
Ramayana	The great Hindu epic about King Rama, incarnation of the God Vishnu
Rama Rajya	The rule of Rama, the Indian Utopia
Rogan joshes	Meat dishes
Salwar	Baggy trousers tightening at the ankles
Sardar	Headman, courtesy title for Sikhs
Shikar	Hunting
Sirkar	Government
Sunlight of cooking fat	Sunlight washing soap was the product that first made Lever Brothers famous in England, India and elsewhere; in fact the firm was often known in India as the 'Sunlight Company'. Sunlight is still a household name in India
Swadeshi	Indigenous, of the country
Syrian Christians	Early Christian refugees from Syria, who settled in Kerala
Tamils	The people of the State of Madras, now called Tamil Nadu
Tonga	Horse carriage
Tongawalla	The coachman
Topee	Cap, sun topee, sun helmet
Tower of Silence	Structure where the Parsis deposit the dead to be disposed of by the vultures
Tulsi	Holy basil, a plant held sacred to the God Vishnu
U. P. Bhayas	People from the State of Uttar Pradesh, land of the north, are popularly known as Bhayas (brothers) from their way of addressing each other

Vanaspati	(Literally 'king of vegetation') name given to vegetable cooking fat when it was first brought from Holland
White topiwallas	Men who wore the cap of white khadi (homespun cotton cloth), which became the symbol of the freedom fighters, known as Gandhi cap
Zamindars	Big landowners